Impact Investment

The Wiley Finance series contains books written specifically for finance and investment professionals as well as sophisticated individual investors and their financial advisors. Book topics range from portfolio management to e-commerce, risk management, financial engineering, valuation and financial instrument analysis, as well as much more. For a list of available titles, visit our Web site at www.WileyFinance.com.

Founded in 1807, John Wiley & Sons is the oldest independent publishing company in the United States. With offices in North America, Europe, Australia and Asia, Wiley is globally committed to developing and marketing print and electronic products and services for our customers' professional and personal knowledge and understanding.

Impact Investment

*A Practical Guide to Investment
Process and Social Impact Analysis
+ Website*

KEITH ALLMAN
XIMENA ESCOBAR DE NOGALES

WILEY

Published by John Wiley & Sons, Inc., Hoboken, New Jersey.
Published simultaneously in Canada.

ISBN 978-1-118-84864-7 (Paperback)
ISBN 978-1-119-00982-5 (ePDF)
ISBN 978-1-119-00981-8 (ePub)

Printed in the United States of America

10 9 8 7 6 5 4 3 2 1

Contents

Preface   vii

Acknowledgments   xi

CHAPTER 1
Introduction to Impact Investing   1

CHAPTER 2
Sourcing and Screening   11

CHAPTER 3
Investment Analysis and Valuation   61

CHAPTER 4
Due Diligence and Investment Structuring   129

CHAPTER 5
The Term Sheet and Definitive Documentation   167

CHAPTER 6
Post-Investment Monitoring, Management, and Value Building   207

CHAPTER 7
Impact Investing Funds   235

CHAPTER 8
Investment Alternatives, Challenges, and Outlook   255

About the Companion Website   269

About the Authors   273

Index   275

Preface

Lebanon is a beautiful country, with picture-perfect coastlines, lively cities, and, unfortunately, abject poverty in many regions. It was there, in Beirut, that my venture into impact investing began. I was conducting a pro-bono workshop on credit risk, for local microfinance analysts that were supported by the charity Relief International. On the Israeli border towns I took my first onsite visits to clients who received loans and observed how they utilized the funding to operate and expand their businesses. I was truly impressed with the effect the funding had, as I was able to see real businesses in expansion.

At that time in my career, I had just left banking at Citigroup and was still primarily engaged in private-sector finance. I thought critically about that trip, though, and questioned whether I should make impact investing my full-time effort. I hesitated because of prior experience with nonprofit entities that operated very inefficiently. I also struggled with finding clarity on whether my experience and skill set were best utilized in existing impact investing organizations. For years, I maintained my private-sector focus, but furthered my work with Relief International, consulting on microfinance capital market's issuances, and eventually joining its board of directors.

I persisted with traditional finance and combined my prior securitization experience with early-stage company analysis to work on venture debt transactions. As I learned more about venture company drivers and private equity fund operations, I couldn't get the thought of impact investing out of my head. And as fate would have it, right around that time a former Citigroup colleague informed me about a new private equity fund that had spun off of a large commercial microfinance debt investor. The Oasis Fund, managed by Bamboo Finance, was created to invest for profit, in early-stage, private companies that also had significant social impact. When I researched its investment criteria and the impact it sought, I was enthralled.

I decided then that I would give impact investing my full attention and moved to Switzerland to work for the Oasis Fund, where I became an investment manager tasked with sourcing, structuring, and managing for-profit, impact investments. My first year at the fund was mainly getting oriented with the fund's existing investments and simultaneously building my network for new investment opportunities. I also started learning more on topics foreign to me, such as what defines social impact and how to source investments within a social criteria.

By my second year, I had become heavily integrated into the impact investing industry. I was in the field every few weeks, combining trips to work with the Oasis Fund's portfolio companies, meeting with new companies for potential investment, and conducting due diligences for companies that had progressed through the investment process. I regularly attended and sometimes hosted industry events such as general and sector-specific conferences, dinners, and talks. The second year culminated with successfully sourcing and closing two investments for the Oasis Fund and joining the board of directors for two of its existing portfolio companies.

In what would be my final year with the Oasis Fund, I was promoted to senior investment manager and started working on new fund strategy and fundraising. Those tasks and responsibilities provided a more encompassing perspective on the industry. However, over the course of that last year, I encountered undercurrents of problems that I felt were systemic in nature. Difficulty sourcing investments that met most investors' social criteria was a theme that echoed across my peers. This led to very competitive situations where some nontraditional investors took approaches that lacked rigor and led to inflated valuations. With costs of capital near zero for these entities, the problems could be sustained, but ultimately, it was no longer commercial investing at that point, but a charitable intermediary.

There is efficacy in the models in between commercial investing and pure charity, but the scale is restricted by the sources of capital. Unlocking consistent sources of capital from pension funds, insurance companies, and traditional investors requires a meticulously designed investment thesis that is executed professionally, from sourcing to exit, and provides reliable, measurable financial and social returns. I believe that in order to build the desired volumes for a replicable, scalable investment model, there will have to be different social criteria for varying financial return expectations.

Creating investment portfolios that deliver such financial returns and demonstrate that a specific social impact has been generated is what will define entities in impact investing. This is why the brunt of this book and the electronic files accompanying it focus on the investment process and social impact measurement. There are many publications available that have striking images of rural villagers using innovative technologies and compelling stories of impact-oriented companies, but these are largely motivational and show basic causality. It's the day-to-day tasks of impact investors—which involve accounting, corporate finance, valuation, statistical measurement, and social metric analysis—that are the most difficult, but the most important.

Although I left impact investing as a full-time endeavor because of some of these issues, I remain committed through select investments in solar and energy efficiency that my current position allows for and pro-bono work with impact investing entities. I anticipate a full-time return at some point.

In the interim, I can offer this book that tries to address proper investment execution and social impact measurement. As with any of my books, I stand behind the learning process and offer my email directly if you have questions: keith.allman@enstructcorp.com.

Keith A. Allman
New York 2014

I have had the privilege of walking the narrow streets of Mumbai slums and speaking with micro-entrepreneur women whose endurance and creativity merit recognition and respect. I have also heard businesspeople in luxurious offices in Geneva argue that it is not possible to build an ethical gold supply chain. Impact investing builds a bridge between apparently disconnected realities. Impact investing is the promise of channeling private capital to solve intractable social problems while delivering impact, inclusion, and sustainability.

But, is impact investing delivering on its promise? Keith Allman's kind invitation to be a contributing author of this book sparked a desire to share the lessons learned by Bamboo Finance on the importance of adding rigor and accountability in defining, measuring, and assessing impact. Even if we are only at the beginning of the learning journey, we follow from due diligence to exit a responsible investment process aimed at delivering impact.

The impact promise begs for more accountability. Too much money has been deployed with little analysis on effectiveness. Impact investing marries the rigor of the industry of investing with the (nascent) rigor of impact measurement. If impact investing wishes to deserve its name, it needs to be evidence-based investing. Building evidence on what works and what doesn't requires a collective effort. The broader the participation is, the richer the learning will be. The voices of customers at the base of the pyramid, on whose behalf we too often speak, are central to our learning. Also, the entrepreneurs, investors, and academia need to join the conversation. This book seeks to contribute to that learning. I am grateful for the opportunity and excited to read your reactions. ximena.escobardenogales@gmail.com

Ximena Escobar de Nogales
Geneva 2014

A NOTE ABOUT THE WEBSITE

Readers will find professional-level investment material on this book's website: www.wiley.com/go/impactinvestment. See the appendix for more details.

Acknowledgments

While impact investing demands a large body of financial knowledge, it would simply be traditional investing without the social impact analysis. I'm thankful that Ximena joined this project to provide her expertise in social impact and be the counterweight that allows this book to cover the full spectrum of challenges and solutions for impact investment.

Also, while I identify the inception of my work in impact investing many years ago through Relief International, it was my work with Bamboo Finance that accelerated my understanding of direct investments and industry-wide issues. I'm thankful for all of the collaboration, discussion, and engagement with Jean-Philippe de Schrevel, Christian Schattenmann, Eric Berkowitz, Keely Stevenson, Natalia Mouhape, Florian Ulmer, Ana Maria Aristizabal, Marlene Mueller, Elvira Espejo, Anu Valli, and Geetali Kumar.

Finally, it's been three years since I've worked with the team at John Wiley and Sons and I still can't thank them enough for the opportunity to publish on their platform and work with their talented staff. In particular, Bill Falloon has worked with me throughout the years and is a great sounding board for ideas and bringing a concept to reality. I'm also very thankful of the work Meg Freeborn, Helen Cho, Maria Sunny, and the rest of the Wiley team completed.

Keith A. Allman
New York 2014

Many people have contributed to the learnings and insights on impact management shared in this book. I am particularly grateful to the individuals whom this industry seeks to serve. In a quest to better understand their needs, we often intrude in their lives. They generously allow us in, even when our "studies" do not always result in gains for them. Thanks also to our investee companies who help us seek evidence of what products and distribution models deliver the expected impact.

Much of my learnings on impact investing come from over four years at Bamboo Finance, and I am most grateful to Jean Philippe de Schrevel, whose tenacious belief in the power of private capital to solve intractable social problems inspires many of us in this industry. I am also thankful to my colleagues at Bamboo Finance and in particular to Sarah Djari, Ana Maria Aristizabal, and Anu Valli for many hours of engaged discussions on identifying, measuring and expanding impact, and to Tracy Barba, for helping us articulate our achievements and challenges.

I have also benefited from the insights of industry-wide social performance and impact management initiatives, specifically the Global Impact Investing Rating System (GIIRs), the Social Performance Task Force (SPTF), and the European Venture Philanthropy Association (EVPA). Many thanks to Neha Kumar, Olivia Muiru, Flory Wilson, Emmanuelle Javoy, Kelly McCarthy, Laura Foose and Lisa Hehenberger. On a more personal note, I would like to thank my daughter Camille for ongoing stimulation.

My greatest gratitude is to Keith Allman for having invited me to contribute to this book.

Ximena Escobar de Nogales
Geneva 2014

Impact Investment

CHAPTER 1

Introduction to Impact Investing

It is an extremely tempting proposition: Invest money in a business whose product or service offers financial return and at the same time generates positive social impact. All parties seem to win, with an investor making a return and society benefiting. A charity could direct money into an organization that accomplishes the same social mission as one it grants to, but instead is able to receive back and reinvest the granted funds. What could hinder such a paradigm?

This idealistic form of capitalism has surged in the last few years. As of 2014, over USD12.7 billion has been committed to impact investing, representing a growth of 19 percent from the prior year.[1] Numerous investors are active ranging from lone high net worth individuals to a multitude of private equity funds. Even larger-scale financial institutions and investment firms have dedicated funds and resources to impact investing. Ancillary services have emerged to support these investors and further develop the industry including secondary market platforms, capital advisers who specialize in impact investments, and services to validate and rate social performance.

With such fervor, why does it still seem like the impact investing market is constrained? The simple answer is that it is not easy to both create a profitable business that has a significant social impact and also scale that business so that it generates commercial returns for investors and continues to progress its social mission. It comes as no shock, then, that for a number of years in a row, J.P. Morgan's impact investing survey cites "a shortage of high quality investment opportunities with track records" and a "lack of appropriate capital across the risk/return spectrum" as primary hindrances to the growth of impact investing.[2]

---

[1] Yasemin Saltuk. J.P. Morgan, "Spotlight on the Market: The Impact Investor Survey," *Global Social Finance* (May 2, 2014), 5.
[2] Ibid., 6.

Part of the issue is that impact investing appeals to our senses and consciences through innovative solutions to pressing social problems. This thought should not be misinterpreted though, as many of the entities and businesses an investor encounters when reviewing social enterprises legitimately intend to or are actively creating significant positive social value. The problem is that a majority of these businesses are not commercially viable and will not generate the return that many investors require. Our morality wants to support these investments, so the industry has grown considerably to encourage social enterprises, but as investors, we must maintain a fiduciary responsibility and invest at the appropriate risk-return level.

However, as we seek to increase the scope of suitable investments, we run the risk of going over an inflexion point, where social impact has been compromised so much that the investment can no longer be considered an impact investment. This can either occur by investing in businesses that actually do not have significant social impact or by investing in a social enterprise that alters itself to become a traditional company. At that point, we have become traditional investors and the paradigm is lost.

We now find ourselves in a delicate situation, balancing financial viability, monetary return expectations, and social impact. How do we achieve the correct balance? As with most industries, the solution is basically hard work and being equipped with the right resources and knowledge. We must know how to look for the right investments and how to screen out ones that are not financially sustainable or demonstrating the right level of social impact. Once found, we must adhere to a rigorous investment process and vet a company to establish its financial and social value. The investment structures created need to properly balance risk and reward. Documentation needs to be done professionally to accurately reflect the structure created and the intentions of all parties. We have to endure far beyond the investment phase, helping businesses scale and exit positions with financial and social success.

It is easy to discuss the beneficial attributes of impact investing and package it in a way that sells a good story. The hard work is in proper investment execution. To get there, this book addresses the following:

- Knowing how to source deals domestically and internationally, while mitigating foreign exchange and business cycle risk
- Properly mapping out the social impact of a company and the metrics that prove it
- Being able to understand, build, and utilize multi-method valuations
- Drafting a term sheet that takes into consideration commercial and social mission risk
- Monitoring and managing an investment to ensure financial and social returns

■ Understanding the economics and realities of leveraging other people's money in impact investment funds

Although a shortage of quality investments vis-à-vis investors exists and will most likely be commonplace with the high degree of interest in impact investing, excellent investments can be found that marry profitability and social impact. This book and the online resources that accompany it will assist investors in choosing the right investments, help align risk and reward, and contribute toward investors building financial and social value.

WHAT IS AN IMPACT INVESTMENT?

An *impact investment* can take many forms, but all share the idea that capital can be deployed into an entity making a good or providing a service that offers positive social impact, while also generating some level of financial return. The Global Impact Investing Network (GIIN), one of the major impact investing industry organizations, defines impact investments as "investments made into companies, organizations, and funds with the intention to generate social and environmental impact alongside a financial return."[3] Critical to this definition is the intentionality of the investor to deliver on financial and social returns.

The form of investment can be as straightforward as investing money for shares of equity in a company or much more complicated, such as a convertible debt structure. Core investment funds may not even have to be exchanged, as in the case of credit guarantees. The unifying thought, though, is that an investor is committing capital to a commercial business, which aims to compensate the investor for his or her investment.

Geographically, impact investments can be made anywhere. Impact investments exist in emerging or developed markets, as long as the focus remains on coupling social or environmental impacts with financial returns. Although examples in developed markets are less common, programs such as investment funds that target small businesses in East London could be considered impact investments.

With all of these options, the two primary forms of investment into social enterprises are debt and equity, mostly in emerging markets. Much of the recent enthusiasm over impact investing has been targeted at investments in social enterprises. These are companies that are for-profit, but have

---

[3]The Global Impact Investing Network, "What is Impact Investing?" www.thegiin .org/cgi-bin/iowa/resources/about/index.html#1.

created a good or service that provides significant social impact. Given their early stage and venture nature, the more typical form of investment in these companies is equity. Debt does come into play in impact investing, particularly with new debt funds creating specialized products, but equity is still the predominant force in early stage social enterprises.

Debt is also relevant for impact investing when we consider microfinance, which is a specialized sector of impact investing. Microfinance involves lending small amounts of money to individuals or groups of individuals, who then use that money to fund their own businesses. The borrowers agree to pay back the loan, plus interest. Microfinance institutions, which provide the direct borrower funding and collection services, have grown over the years and are recipients of debt and equity investments themselves. All of these would be considered a type of impact investment.

For the most part, what has been described so far are investments. An investor provides capital and expects return. The key differentiator for impact investing is the impact. We will work to define impact later in this chapter, but an impact investment differs from a traditional investment in that the core business product or service provides a positive social impact. A healthcare company that provides high-quality, affordable tiered services for low- to middle-income patients, for profit, would most likely qualify as an impact investment. A healthcare company that builds clinics for wealthy clients and donates 1 percent of profits to charity would most likely not be considered an impact investment. The social impact has to be engrained in the business operations, product, or service.

A specific feature of impact investing is the investor's engagement to measure and report on social and environmental performance and impact. Impact investments should aim to be evidence-based investments. This means the industry needs to build data on the type of interventions that have a positive development impact. Impact investors need to examine and share learnings on the combination of products and services, the type of designs, the pricing and distribution models, and the accompanying services that will result in positive societal impact on the targeted population. Obvious as it is, it may be worth reiterating: Without evidence, we will not make evidence-based investments. In this book, we go through the challenges of defining adequate impact models, identifying appropriate indicators to track, and monitoring and analyzing output, outcome, and impact indicators.

WHO MAKES IMPACT INVESTMENTS?

As we will come to learn later in this book, no other field within finance has a greater disparity of participants than those found to be impact investors. Impact investors differ from traditional investors in a number of ways, but the most important differences relate to return expectations, investment holding periods, and investment motivation. To understand this varied landscape, we should start by looking at some of the oldest impact investors, government institutions.

The International Finance Corporation (IFC), a member of the World Bank Group, is one of the oldest, largest, and best-known impact investors. It invests in a large range of projects, from direct and indirect private equity investments to large-scale infrastructure projects. It would be considered a government institution because it is funded by World Bank member countries. There are a number of other large-scale government funded impact investors, such as IFC, Norway's Norfund, and the UK's CDC Group. The key to these types of investors is that they have a specific mission and seek commercial-style investments, but have a very low cost of capital and longer holding periods than average, which allows them to make investments that strictly traditional investors may not make.

Similar to government-funded investors, in terms of low capital cost and long investment time horizons, are charitable organizations that make impact investments. These organizations can range from nonprofit institutions that use donation money for investment, like Acumen Fund or EnterpriseWorks/VITA, a division of Relief International, to organizations such as Soros Economic Development Fund, which utilize funding from profitable private-sector enterprises to make impact investments.

In the middle of the range of impact investors are high-net-worth individuals who provide their own capital directly into social enterprises. Often they will provide catalytic capital to early-stage ventures or fund business plans that materialize into companies. Similar to the other types of investors already mentioned, these investors have long investment time frames, low costs of capital, and personal motivations for investment that afford them a high degree of flexibility.

Finally, we move up the scale of commerciality to for-profit investors such as GrayGhost Ventures, DBL Investors, and Bamboo Finance. Each of these institutions has a varying commercial approach toward impact investing, where returns and investment horizons are more in line with traditional investors.

HOW THIS BOOK IS DESIGNED

The bulk of this book is designed to guide an investor through every stage of the *investment process*, with a specific look in the last chapter at considerations for an investor who is creating or working for an investment fund.

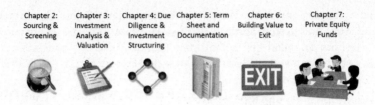

FIGURE 1.1 This book generally follows the investment process that an investor would encounter.

While there are many aspects that work universally for investors, there is a particular focus on equity investments, given that they are the predominant force in impact investing. To help immerse readers in the investment process, a fictitious company is selected amongst three potential investments. This company is then taken through each stage of the investment process. Figure 1.1 provides a graphical overview of the core chapters with a brief discussion of each section following.

Sourcing and Screening

The first phase of the investment process involves identifying potential investments. Most investors have a specific investment thesis that they, or if organized as a fund, their investors believe in. Therefore, it's imperative that the investments the investor sources fit into the investment thesis. For instance, if a healthcare investment fund is funded by high net worth individuals who have an interest in making equity level returns, while trying to address global health problems, the investor must be very careful to find healthcare related investments at good valuations that will lead to strong exits.

While *sourcing* and *screening* investments that fit an investment thesis seems relatively straightforward, time and resources constrain an investor. Time works against an investor since costs constantly accrue. The longer it takes to make investments, the longer it will be before the investment exit returns value. In order to properly place funds, resources are needed, both financially and tangibly. It costs money to undertake onsite due diligences, and to hire consultants, lawyers, or accountants. Often, an investor will hire multiple resources to help with the process. Effective investors place money efficiently and strategically, minimizing costs along the way.

Knowing how to identify regions, economies, and industries that are investable and poised for success is critical to being an effective investor.

Specific to impact investing, the social mission must be fully understood, mapped out, and tested against the investors' social investment thesis. Weighing both financial and social mission viability early on is critical to selecting the right investments for due diligence.

Investment Analysis and Valuation

Sourcing and screening sets an investor on a path with a limited number of investments. The next stop on this path is vetting the company's operations, financial potential, and social mission scope. Usually, due diligence is split into two phases, with the first being a less-committed "desktop" phase, where business plans and financial statements are analyzed. This allows both an investor and investee to be efficient with their time and resources, since deal-breaking issues can sometimes be garnered from such analyses.

For equity investors, valuation discussions start early to make sure there are no significant gaps in perceived value. In order to have such discussions, an initial *investment analysis* is necessary since it lends to the creation of a valuation range. This range is later refined during the due diligence phase. *Valuation* is one area that impact investors must think carefully about. Impact investing is unique in that it brings together a range of investors with very different costs of capital and required returns. In some cases, these return expectations are not commensurate with the risk being assumed.

Due Diligence and Investment Structuring

Eventually, a company will warrant further analysis and full, onsite due diligence is executed. This entails reviewing all operational aspects, management, competitive analyses, finances, and social mission achievement and plan. Another goal of due diligence is for investors to establish their own opinions on the necessary investments structure. Debt investors will want to review all risks and mitigating factors related to cash flow or collateral value. Equity investors will want to check the assumptions made to create the valuation range and determine what investment structure might be necessary.

When a due diligence is complete and an investor is still interested in a company, negotiations around the investment structure ensue. Some investment structures can be very simple and quick to come to agreement, while others can take a considerable amount of time and develop into very complex arrangements. Debt investors will negotiate covenants to protect their priority over cash flow or collateral. Equity investors will agree to a valuation and possibly negotiate preferential rights.

Impact investors have the added requirement of ensuring that the social mission is preserved after investment. This requires properly aligning interests and making sure the structure is able to respond to changes.

Term Sheet and Documentation

Expressing the agreed-on investment structure in documentation is critical to a successful impact investment. The beginning of this phase of the investment process starts with a term sheet that covers the investment structure, preferences, and specific rights. The goal is to have a document that can be converted into a subscription agreement that defines an equity investment or an indenture for a debt investor. Additionally, for equity investors, a shareholder agreement is needed to cover shareholder rights.

Impact investors should also negotiate specialized clauses that protect the social mission and allow the investor flexibility if the social mission is compromised. As an example, a put option, where the equity investor can sell shares back to the company, might be written into the subscription agreement if the social mission deviates too far.

Building Value to Exit

Ultimately, an equity investment realizes value when it is exited. Debt investors technically have their exits through periodic interest and principal amortization. After the investment, but prior to exit, a value-building phase exists. Active investors will take part in board meetings to help shape the company's strategy. Passive investors will be more focused on financial and social metric reporting that is established at the end of the investment and provided periodically. At some point, exits must be completed properly to return funds to the investors at levels that are aligned with their expectations.

Private Equity Funds

Investors frequently establish or work for funds that utilize other entities' money for investment. Leveraging the platform of a fund can greatly increase the amount of money invested, but it brings with it a host of economic, organizational, and impact-related considerations. Most funds operate on management fees that have to be carefully managed vis-à-vis fund expenses. Organizational issues, such as the ratio and size of investments relative to investment managers, need to be carefully thought through. For impact investing private equity funds, a core responsibility is safeguarding the social mission by properly incentivizing investment managers and adhering to strict social criteria for investments.

Impact Investment Evolution

The concluding chapter to this book explores recent developments in the impact investing industry and thoughts on how it may evolve and scale. It's clear that there are problems unique to individual impact investments that stem from investors' disparate sources of capital, sometimes causing irrational risk/return profiles. A brunt of this book seeks to provide solutions to individual impact investment problems through a sound and rigorous investment process. Investment products are also evolving to help mitigate some of these problems and further develop the industry.

However, when looking at a portfolio investment strategy there are contentious issues that divide market participants. Some argue that portfolios can be constructed where there is no trade off between financial and social return. Others believe that for an effective, for-profit commercial strategy to be successful there has to be compromise and capital placed in a gradient of investments, from high impact to traditional. The final chapter in this book explores such topics and takes a position on effective portfolio strategy.

NOTES FROM THE FIELD

Throughout this book, readers will notice excerpts called "Notes from the Field." These are experiences that the authors have had that directly relate to the topic at hand. We hope that these extracts provide context to the topics.

WHAT THIS BOOK IS NOT

There are two important distinctions that should be made from the start regarding the focus of this book: It is not focused on microfinance nor social/green bonds. While we will reference microfinance in a number of sections and provide examples, the focus is not on how to make a loan to an individual nor solely on how to invest funds into a microfinance institution (MFI). There are many good books specifically on this topic. Similarly, social and green bonds have gained popularity, but they are also very specific forms of debt that lend to an entirely different strategy and analytical process.

SETTING FORTH

Impact investing is a unique and demanding field that requires an unusual range of skill sets. This book dives into both social and financial analyses in detail and provides online resources that readers can use professionally.

Those with limited financial backgrounds will gain valuable insight into the investment process and the underlying components required to invest competently. Those with limited social impact backgrounds will learn the topics and methods necessary to evaluate and measure social impact. Most importantly, readers will learn how both the financial and social impact aspects of impact investing intertwine, creating a challenging, but highly rewarding form of investment.

CHAPTER 2

Sourcing and Screening

Investors are in an exceptional position in that they have to do very little beyond saying that they have money to invest in order to get the attention of entrepreneurs. They will receive pitch after pitch for investment opportunities. However, for most investors, resources such as funding and employee's time are limited, and the repercussions of focusing on and choosing too many bad investments are severe. A well-planned *sourcing* and *screening* process can avert time- and resource-draining mistakes. Passive sourcing may work for seasoned investment houses whose reputations attract the best and most desirable entrepreneurs. However, for individual investors, advisers, or new funds, an active sourcing strategy is necessary to find enterprises that excel beyond their peers.

Sourcing strategies generally focus on three critical aspects: geography, industry sector, and impact. Although the first two are common for mainstream investing, the third aspect, impact, is unique to impact investing. Impact investors seek an assurance that the investment fits their criteria and is likely to have a positive societal impact. Active sourcing can be done by trying to connect with local or foreign entrepreneurs; however, time and resources can easily be drained if the country of domicile or business operations is too risky for the investor, if the sector is outside of the investor's expertise, or if the impact is insubstantial. Of these sourcing elements, geographic appropriateness is unique in that it does not require dialogue with a prospective company to properly assess. Top-level analyses can be done to expose problems with investing in certain countries and prevent drained resources from pursuing investments that ultimately are too precarious due to sovereign risk.

Sector appropriateness requires less analysis, but often requires at least some type of information from the prospective company and blends into the screening phase. Usually, an investment teaser or pitch is available and initial dialog is initiated with the target company. Asking the right questions at this time is essential to quickly screen away investments that are inconsistent with an investor's strategy.

An effective screening phase focuses on key components of an investment's sector, stage, business, strategy, finances, and social impact. Deal-breaking issues should be revealed as early as possible, while primary strengths and weaknesses must be weighed carefully before moving the investment along to the next phase of investment process.

SOURCING STRATEGY

Sourcing potential investments is truly the inception of the investment process for any investor, whether impact focused or not. The methods employed and the decisions made at the sourcing stage lead to a variety of paths that often have an influential role for decisions at later stages of the investment process. A robust and effective sourcing strategy can help ensure that the paths with the highest probability of closing a strong investment in an efficient manner are taken, while paths that lead to wasted time, stalled negotiations, or eventual value declines are avoided.

While the concept sounds relatively simple, what does it actually mean to be sourcing? Passive sourcing is a luxury of many well-established venture and private equity funds, where some of the best entrepreneurs deliver well-laid-out business plans with financial projections or early stage businesses with rapid growth that are poised for success. Many early-stage or less-well-known impact investing investors and funds will be inundated with entrepreneurs pitching business ideas, but the average quality of the investment will be lower.

There are numerous reasons why the quality is perceived to be lower:

1. Some of the best entrepreneurs in developed markets take their business ideas to well-known investors and investment incubators, where they compete for funding and, more importantly, mentorship and connections from successful entrepreneurs. While these are typically tech-oriented, it does dilute the pool of high-level entrepreneurs.
2. The social impact element can be implemented with varying degrees of intensity. Although the heart of impact investing suggests that financial return can be achieved with social returns, there is always a point at which the social mission can impede on financial viability. Many social entrepreneurs create business plans that can be viewed as weaker from a business functionality point of view because the social mission is too aggressive.
3. Impact investments often have heightened risk because of their geographic focus being mostly outside of the developed world.

For these reasons, a passive strategy is not ideal for impact investing.

Active sourcing involves targeting investments that are aligned with the investor's focus, risk tolerance and expertise in a region and sector. The easiest place to start is determining if a region or geography is suitable for investment. Local investors clearly will not have to deal with such a macro analysis, but for any individual or fund that has a regional or global scope, country market analysis should be the first step. Country analysis is also particularly important for impact investors since the source of funding and the need for funding are typically in two very different geographies. For this reason, a more intense review and example analysis is provided on this topic.

GEOGRAPHIC ANALYSIS

Geographic appropriateness can be thought of as the first and widest filter to move items to a deeper screening. Such an analysis starts by collecting a robust collection of data sets that capture basic investing requirements and specific investment thesis characteristics. A method of weighting the importance of the data sets should be implemented in order to determine a list of countries of interest and a heat map of their relevant qualities.

Data Sets

There are innumerable data points for each country, but a few key ones that both debt and equity investors should take a deeper look at. A straightforward method to understand the sourcing potential and investment suitability of countries is to create a country ranking system and heat map, based on desired investment-related characteristics. Standard investment characteristics to rank countries could include:

- Ease of starting a business
- Level of investor protection
- Level of contract enforcement
- Ability to mitigate insolvency

Many of these characteristics are implemented in analyses done by the World Bank's Doing Business project.[1] The data here are very understandable and comparable across different topics using the World Bank's country ranking system.

---

[1] The World Bank Group, "Doing Business: Measuring Business Regulations." www.doingbusiness.org.

For impact investing, additional metrics should be considered. One important metric is the Human Development Index (HDI), which ranks countries by submetrics of human development. The lower the HDI, the greater the need for impact investments. General sectors can also be targeted at the country ranking level. For instance, if healthcare is a focus of the impact investor, then an index such as one measuring maternal mortality could be integrated into the analysis. The goal of the analysis is to understand on which countries to focus active sourcing efforts.

To delve deeper into creating such a country ranking method, open the file Country_Ranking.xlsm from the website. This workbook contains multiple country ranking data sets and a method to synthesize the data into usable output. Ultimately, an ordered list of countries that exhibits the qualities an investor is seeking should be discernable from the analysis. To get there, though, the starting point is the underlying data.

In this analysis, there are six independent worksheets that contain data sets relevant to investors and some specifically to impact investors:

1. *Inv protect:* This data set focuses on investor protections. Many countries differ in their attitudes toward investors and the levels of disclosure, board of director liability, and the ability of shareholders to take legal action against companies. Most investors will want transparency, low legal liability for the assigned board director, and the ability to navigate negative situations through legal action. Countries are ranked by the composite level of investor protection for investments in the listed country, with 1 being the best and 189 being the worst.

2. *Start business:* The ease of starting a business can be indicative of how well a government facilitates the needs of entrepreneurs. This data set ranks countries based on four metrics: the number of procedures required to start a business, the time it takes to register a firm, the cost to register based on fees, and also equity required.

3. *Contract enforcement:* For both debt and equity investors, contracts transform conceptual and verbal agreements into a common understanding. More importantly, if one party deviates from that understanding, there should be a strong and efficient legal system to mitigate the situation. This data set ranks countries based on three metrics related to contract enforcement: the time it takes for dispute resolution, the cost of working through such a dispute, and the number of procedures required to achieve resolution.

4. *Insolvency:* Important for debt investors is the ability to lay claim to a company's assets if it becomes insolvent. Debt holders often invest with a priority over the company's assets and accept a lower return proposition

than equity holders for such privilege. However, if the ability to recover value is diminished or difficult the reduced return may not be worth it. The insolvency data set looks at the time it takes to close a business, the cost of closing the business, whether the business is sold off in pieces or as a whole, and, very importantly, how much money a claimant recovers given insolvency.

5. *HDI:* If the prior four categories were the only data sets to include in this sourcing exercise, the top countries would primarily be developed economies that have less widespread need for impact investing.[2] For an impact investor the developmental need is a priority and should be reflected in the analysis. To facilitate this, the Human Development Index (HDI), a statistic created by the United Nations Development Programme (UNDP), is used to rank countries. It scores countries based on life expectancy, education levels, and standard of living.

6. *Maternal mortality:* A sector-based investor may want to include his or her specialty in the analysis. In the example provided, a healthcare oriented investor can assess the development and need for maternal care in a region. Any other specialty can be similarly integrated depending on investor focus.

NOTES FROM THE FIELD

In 2005, while I was working for Citigroup, we were looking to fund investment in a certain Eastern European country. The investments would be mortgage related and required a high degree of certainty regarding contract enforceability and bankruptcy protection. As part of the deal team, we noticed that the laws were very loose in these regards. We engaged in local country due diligence and met with federal government officials who told us, "Don't worry, we will be changing those laws in the next few months." After a lengthy plane ride home, we sat around a conference table the next day, and someone asked the best follow-up question, "If they can change the laws in just a few months in our favor, can't they change them just as quickly against us?" The investment was never made.

---

[2]While many immediately look to the emerging markets as the source of impact investments, there are investment strategies that focus on areas in need within developed economies, such as the East London Bond (www.eastlondonbond.org).

Data Aggregation and Weighting

Once the data are loaded, it should be aggregated on a single sheet. The Data Agg sheet does just this by listing all potential countries with the relevant rank to the right. Note that there is a guide to the rankings in row 6, called Target. This is to keep track of whether a high or low number indicating a weak or strong rank is desirable. For instance, a country with a low score for contract enforcement means that it has a high standard of contract enforcement. This is desirable for most investors. However, a low HDI rank indicates a very developed economy and may not be the best country for an impact investor. Figure 2.1 shows the top part of the data aggregation.

Once the country data are aggregated, a weighting method can be applied to layer in the investment thesis preferences. Effectively, a weighted average score is needed. However, one needs to be cognizant of whether a high value or low value is desirable. In this example, for five of the six metrics it is desirable to have a lower score. To work with the weighting method of having a higher percentage influence a higher rank converting the low scores to a high score is necessary. Conversion can be done by subtracting the count of countries for each data set by the rank for all of the factors except HDI. With the correct ranking figures, a weighted average can be calculated by multiplying the weights by the ranks.[3] Figure 2.2 provides an overview of the weighted calculations.

Controlling the Analysis

The weights can be adjusted depending on an investor's investment thesis. A scenario selector system is ideal for setting up various weighted cases.

Target	Low	Low	Low	Low	High	Low
	Insolvency	Investor Protection	Starting a Business	Contract Enforcement	Human Developmen t Index	Maternal Mortality
Afghanistan	115	189	24	168	175	23
Albania	62	14	76	124	70	129
Algeria	60	98	164	129	93	76
Angola	189	80	178	187	148	25
Antigua and Barbuda	80	34	92	65	67	No Data
Argentina	97	98	164	57	45	85

FIGURE 2.1 Country rankings are aggregated and prepped for weighting.

---

[3] Advanced Excel users will notice that some of the formulas have complex look-up functions and refer to the Mapping sheet occasionally. This is because the data sets used countries with names that differed slightly or recognized countries that the other list did not.

Weight							
10%	20%	10%	25%	35%	0%		

Insolvency	Investor Protection	Starting a Business	Contract Enforcement	Human Development Index	Maternal Mortality	Weighted Value
7.4	0	16.5	5.25	61.25	0	90.40
12.7	35	11.3	16.25	24.5	0	99.75
12.9	18.2	2.5	15	32.55	0	81.15
0	21.8	1.1	0.5	51.8	0	75.20
10.9	31	9.7	31	23.45	0	106.05
9.2	18.2	2.5	33	15.75	0	78.65

FIGURE 2.2 The aggregated data and a weighted value for each country are calculated.

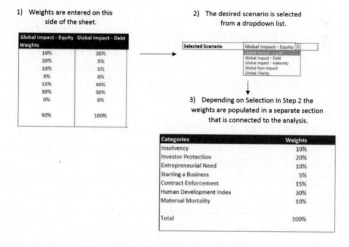

FIGURE 2.3 A scenario selector system allows the user to enter investor preferences and toggle between scenarios.

Figure 2.3 exemplifies such a system, which will be used in other analyses throughout this book.

Results

Once a scenario is selected, the Data Agg sheet calculates the appropriate statistics based on the weights and the results can be summarized. The Summary sheet shows the top 25 countries that are produced from the combination of the weights selected. Additionally, a heat map of the relevant

Top 25	Country	Score	Insolvency	Investor Protection	Starting a Business	Contract Enforcement	Human Development Index	Maternal Mortality
1	Rwanda	152.3	5.2	33.4	18	37.25	58.45	0
2	Thailand	146.1	11.1	45.4	9.8	41.75	46.05	0
3	Tajikistan	135.7	10.8	33.4	10.2	37.5	43.75	0
4	Mongolia	133.0	5.6	33.4	16.4	39.75	37.8	0
5	Malaysia	131.2	14.7	37	17.3	39.75	22.4	0
6	Azerbaijan	130.6	10.3	33.4	17.9	40.25	28.7	0
7	Kyrgyz Republic	130.3	5.7	33.4	17.7	29.75	43.75	0
8	South Africa	128.6	10.7	35.8	12.5	27.25	42.35	0
9	Ghana	128.2	7.3	31	6.1	36.5	47.25	0
10	Kazakhstan	127.5	13.5	33.4	15.9	40.5	24.15	0
11	Georgia	127.0	10.1	34.6	18.1	39	25.2	0
12	Mauritius	127.0	12.8	35.4	17	33.75	28	0
13	Singapore	125.1	18.5	37.4	18.6	44.25	6.3	0
14	Moldova	123.5	9.8	21.8	10.8	41.5	39.55	0
15	Hong Kong SAR, China	122.2	17	37.2	18.4	45	4.55	0

FIGURE 2.4 The selected countries are summarized, along with a heat map of the relevant statistics.

characteristics is displayed so a user can see what is driving the results. Figure 2.4 shows the top 15 results for a global equity impact investing scenario.

The most noticeable feature of Figure 2.4 is that there are some affluent geographies on the list, such as Singapore and Hong Kong. Even though the HDI is heavily weighted, there are still four other factors that favor developed countries. For this reason, it is necessary to take a closer look at the heat map that shows how the rankings were created. It is clear that there are trade-offs with each country that was selected. For instance, the first choice is Rwanda, a country that is very favorable because of a high development need based on HDI and acceptable scores on investment protection and contract enforcement. Insolvency and ease of starting a business are not very good, but the other factors still outweigh the low scores.

The trade-offs are evident when Singapore is examined. It has the lowest HDI score of the top 15 countries shown, but makes it to the top 15 because of very high scores for contract enforcement and investor protections. It also has high scores for the ease of starting a business and insolvency mitigation.

Investors can customize the weightings depending on the focus of their investment strategy. For instance, a debt investor may put more emphasis on insolvency protection and contract enforcement given the first lien position of debt on the assets of a company. Change the scenario selector on the sheet to Global Impact—Debt. When this is done, the results change and Ethiopia takes the top spot, primarily because of a more favorable insolvency mitigation score, which is important for debt investing.

Keep in mind that this is only a method to start building a framework for geographic suitability and that each country should be examined in detail. For instance, Ethiopia as the top choice for Global Impact—Debt has a high need for development and a good insolvency mitigation score, but compared to the mean investor protection score amongst the top 25 (6.256), its investor protection score of 1.6 is very low. Depending on the risk appetite of the investor, this combination may not be suitable. Individual analysis is always required. Also, the data sets chosen here are not exhaustive or completely indicative of a perfect investment environment. Local due diligence should always be undertaken to vet country risk.

Finally, impact investing does not have to only be done in emerging markets. There are many companies that are domiciled in developed countries that have focuses abroad or, as mentioned in Chapter 1 earlier, even in areas domestically that demonstrate need. However, investors in companies that are domiciled in developed markets and do business in emerging and frontier markets should still do a country risk analysis of the primary operational regions. Indirect risks can disrupt cash flow and quickly put stress on the viability of the company as a whole.

COUNTRY ECONOMIC ANALYSIS

Although the previous analysis on country suitability included many investment related characteristics, economic indicators were notably missing. There are many economic indicators one could look to but two important ones that capture multiple subrisks are business cycle and foreign exchange. Even if a country is suitable for investment, the timing might not be right because of these two factors.

Business Cycle

History has shown economists and businesses that there is a relatively standard pattern in the economy that creates a *business cycle*. Economies move through periods of growth, contraction, and back to growth. The time of each point in the cycle can vary widely, but this pattern is evident. Figure 2.5 depicts the standard business cycle.

Countries can exhibit their own unique business cycles or be correlated to other countries that may influence their economies. For this reason, an investor should always gather economic data on the country in mind to understand the business cycle. Sector specific investors must think about their sectors vis-à-vis the business cycles and their expected evolutions. For example, a housing project company may look attractive during the growth phase shown in Figure 2.5 since the economy will be getting better, discretionary spending will be higher, and credit will be loosening. However, during a recession phase credit might tighten up, making mortgages difficult to obtain and consumers focus on savings.

Timing investment with the business cycle can be important given the holding time of many impact investments. Most equity impact investors hold

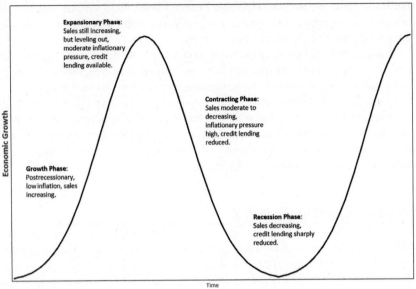

FIGURE 2.5 The standard business cycle is important for investors to understand.

on to their investments for five to seven years, if not longer. Debt investors average from one to three years for their investment horizons. The business cycle at investment and exit can have profound impacts.

An ideal situation would be to identify the early part of the growth phase for an economy. This can be difficult, as statistics that are being shown will be based on the recession phase. However, these statistics are where opportunity can exist. Businesses will generally be down and business valuations may have decreased. Investing at this stage could lead to a low entry price and future increase in performance. For debt investors, it would also be an opportune time, as sales will increase that should cover all or some debt service.

The contrary situation would be investing during a contracting phase. In this situation, the business valuations could still be very high, as they would be reporting data from the expansionary phase. Soon after investment, the economy could begin to shrink, sales could decrease, and credit could tighten. The combination of decreased sales and tighter credit can put a substantial amount of stress on an early stage company. If the company is unable to generate or obtain working capital, it will need more cash from equity or debt investors. Investors in these situations may find themselves funding the company until a growth phase begins.

Debt investors need to pay special attention to the inflationary aspect of the business cycle. If debt investors offer a fixed-rate product, they could introduce the concept of basis risk, defined as a risk caused by a mismatch between fixed and floating interest rates. For instance, if the investor is a local debt fund that pays its investors a floating rate return, but offers fixed rate debt to investees, there could be a mismatch, depending on how the business cycle evolves. If debt was issued to an investee at the bottom of a recession, when interest rates might be very low in order to spur growth, and then the growth phase proceeds quickly where rates start rising, the debt fund will incur margin compression. The yield from the investee will be fixed low and the amount the debt fund must pay its investors will increase. Most funds would invest in hedges, but these can be expensive.

Foreign Exchange Risk

Whether globally or locally based, investors often have to contend with *foreign exchange* (forex) risk. This is the risk that movements in currency exchange rates may impact the investor directly through a conversion into or out of a currency different than the one the investor is funded in, or indirectly through the invested company's operational exposure to foreign exchange.

Direct forex risk can occur at multiple points in an investors' investment horizon. For equity investors, it can occur at the time of investment and at the time of exit. For debt investors, it can occur at the time of investment, during interest payments, and during principal amortization. Debt investors typically hedge against forex risks, but equity investors have a difficult time. The difficulty for equity investors to hedge foreign exchange risk is caused by the fact that they do not know the duration or how much to hedge against. Equity investors may have to hold their investment for many years until exit, making long-term hedging extremely costly. Also, since an exit amount can vary wildly from investment to investment, the exact amount to hedge for exit is difficult to pinpoint. An equity investor can easily be over or under hedged.

If an equity investor does choose to take on direct currency risk and invest in a currency that is different from its funded currency, then she should research the foreign currency volatility and how future movements might affect returns. To understand this better the following two points of direct forex risk for an equity investor should be analyzed in detail: investment and exit.

Direct forex risk at investment can occur when an investment is agreed upon and analysis done at an exchange rate that changes between the time the funds are actually disbursed. Often, after agreeing on an investment valuation and ownership stake it could take a number of weeks before definitive documentation is negotiated and finalized. During this time, if a foreign currency is volatile, there could be risk of loss.

To understand this further, open the file FX_IRR.xlsx from the website and select the Investment sheet. Starting in C11, there are data on the Brazilian real from August 2013 to the end of October 2013. The Brazilian real was noticeably volatile during this time. The example that has been set up is an equity investor that agreed to invest BRL6 million assuming an investment valuation and ownership percentage set on August 4, 2013, but did not finalize and transmit funds until September 29, 2013. The equity investor would have completed return analyses at the August rate of BRL2.450 to USD, but would have actually invested at the September rate of BRL2.181 to USD. At BRL2.450 to USD the investor would have to convert USD2,449,170 to make the investment; however, after eight weeks the exchange rate has moved such that to invest the same BRL6 million the investor would have to invest USD2,751,511. Immediately, the investor has lost USD302,342. From an IRR perspective, ignoring exit exchange rate risk, if the investor assumed they could exit in 5 years for USD5 million, they would have immediately been down 2.65 percent IRR (i.e., difference between a potential 15.34 percent IRR assuming that was how much was converted, versus a 12.69 percent IRR caused by having to use more USD for investment due to the rate change) because of the exchange rate. Figure 2.6 shows the situation from the worksheet.

Direct forex risk at investment can be mitigated in a number of ways. It can be eliminated from the investor's point of view altogether by agreeing to an investment amount in funded currency (USD, in the example) for the same ownership stake. However, this puts the investee at risk of raising less funds than expected. Alternatively, it can be shared between parties through a forex risk-sharing mechanism. Specifically, each party could agree to bear a certain percentage of the risk by purchasing forward contracts and effectively locking in the exchange rate. That hedged exchange rate would be the one used in the return analysis.

Loss Summary

$ Loss	
Investment Sizing at Agreement	2,449,170
Investment Required at Close	2,751,511
Loss	(302,342)

Annual IRR Analysis

	No Rate Chg	Rate Chg
	15.34%	12.69%
0	(2,449,170)	(2,751,511)
1	0	0
2	0	0
3	0	0
4	0	0
5	5,000,000	5,000,000

FIGURE 2.6 Between agreement and closure, the BRL appreciated causing a loss to the USD-funded investor.

For equity holders, a similar direct forex risk issue presents itself at exit, but is more pervasive given the long time frames between investment and exit. To understand this, select the Exit tab in the same file FX_IRR.xlsx from the website. In this example, an investment structure is assumed where an equity investor has made a USD3 million investment into an Indian company in 2010. The investment is in local funds and converted at the 2010 rate of 45.7 INR to USD. Six years later, the investment can be exited for a 3x multiple, but must be converted back to USD. Unfortunately, as assumed by the INR to USD rates in column D, the INR has depreciated significantly over this time frame. Instead of receiving a 3x return in USD, the investor receives 1.96x USD invested. A further comparison can be done to look at the value of the investment if it was done purely in USD, which would return a 20.09 percent IRR over the six-year time frame, as compared to an 11.86 percent IRR if the investor had to convert to INR and back to USD. The example is captured in Figure 2.7.

The worksheet provided also shows why it is so difficult to hedge an equity investor's position. The variables that can change after investment are time, as expressed by exit year, and value, as expressed by money multiple. Without knowing time and value, a hedge can become a very expensive guess, particularly for volatile currencies.

Assuming the investor is able to avoid direct forex risk, they should still be cognizant of indirect forex risk. This occurs when an investment is made into a company that has a mismatch of revenues in one currency and

Initial Investment	3,000,000
Currency	USD
Investment Year	2010
Exit Year	2016
Money Multiple	3.00x

Non-Convert IRR	20.09%
Convert IRR	11.86%
Difference	-8.24%

			Non-Converted	Invest in INR and Return in USD	
Year	INR to USD		Cash Flow in USD	Cash Flow in USD	Cash Flow in INR
2008	43.6		0	0	0
2009	48.4		0	0	0
2010	45.7		(3,000,000)	(3,000,000)	(137,100,000)
2011	45.8		0	0	0
2012	53.5		0	0	0
2013	68.0		0	0	0
2014	70.0		0	0	0
2015	72.0		0	0	0
2016	70.0		9,000,000	5,875,714	411,300,000
2017	65.0		0	0	0
2018	60.0		0	0	0

FIGURE 2.7 Having to convert from a funded currency to a local currency and back incurs direct foreign exchange rate risk, as shown in this example.

costs in another. For example, a company that sells products in India might manufacture in China. Revenue would then be earned in INR while expenses would be in CNY. If the INR depreciates significantly against the CNY, it will take more INR to cover the same costs and margins will decrease. This concept will be explained in more detail in Chapter 3, when a corporate entity is picked apart in significant detail.

Given either direct or indirect forex risk, it is evident that a successful sourcing methodology must account for the ability to mitigate forex concerns. If a currency is extremely volatile and local investees are not willing to negotiate over mitigating forex risks, then it might make sense to avoid such a region altogether. For debt investors the ability to hedge is also based on volatility. The more volatile the currency is, the more expensive the hedge will be. At some point, the cost of hedging reduces returns to the point where investments in alternative locations may be preferable.

BEYOND GEOGRAPHY AND ECONOMICS

Thus far, an active method for approaching sourcing has been introduced based on geographic and economic considerations. This serves as a guide to direct attention to countries that will have the highest probability of success once an attractive company is found. Actually finding those companies is a core part of the day-to-day work of the investor. More seasoned investors have networks that lead to a slew of potential investments. Newer investors might want to try the following (see Table 2.1), all with advantages and disadvantages.

NOTES FROM THE FIELD

On one particular sourcing trip to Southeast Asia, I attended a traditional conference that was not focused on impact investing. During this trip, a fruit juice/puree company that had USD10 million in annual sales garnered my attention, as it seemed to source from rural areas. I asked the company representative where they sourced their fruit from and how they secured their supply chain. He proceeded to tell me how the company sourced from rural farmers, provided them loans when necessary, and gave them technical assistance to grow better fruit. Instantly, this virtually unknown enterprise, which had almost no contact with competing investors, was put on my map as a high-potential impact investment.

TABLE 2.1 Multiple Sourcing Methods Exist with Advantages and Disadvantages

Method	Advantage	Disadvantage
Impact Investing Related Conferences	Many investees freely available to discuss their businesses in detail.	Competing investors have most likely already looked at the potential investment or are already engaged in the investment process at this point.
Non-Impact Related Conferences	Less competition from similar investors and ability to differentiate investor value.	Less likely to find investees that meet impact-related requirements.
Sector Specific Conferences	Less competition from general investors and investee companies aligned with investor's sector strategy.	Potentially limited investments, given sector specificity.
Capital Advisors	Prescreened investments presented in an organized format with highly relevant information.	Best investments depend on relationship with capital adviser. If new to capital adviser, their best investments may have already been provided to other investors and the ones being shown are left over.
Existing Investees Recommendations	Regional analysis already completed and sourced from a trusted individual.	Existing investee may be doing friend a favor and not providing best sourcing.

SOURCING FOR IMPACT

Impact investors must also contend with level of impact, the third critical aspect mentioned earlier in this chapter. Before one starts looking for impact investment opportunities, it is crucial to have a well-defined impact strategy: What is the social purpose of the investment? What are the investor's impact criteria? What is the investor's risk/return profile, and should that be adjusted for an impact investment?

The better investors know who they are and what they are looking for, the greater the chance of successfully sourcing quality investments. For example, an impact investor focused on growth-stage companies in healthcare might come across an attractive rural investment opportunity, but if the impact is not related to healthcare, the investment should be quickly discarded. The better an investor targets the sourcing, the more effective the investor will be in reducing costs for both parties.

Sector-agnostic investors have a wider pool to source from. What helps limit the pool is the risk/return profile, the type of instruments available, and the maturity of the companies, which are all interdependent factors. For instance, a major commercial impact investor, Bamboo Finance, defines itself as a *commercial private equity firm specializing in investing in business models that benefit low-income communities in emerging markets*. This clear positioning helps the company focus its sourcing efforts, and it helps companies searching for funding to narrow their search for investors.

Specialized impact investing networks and services such as Impactbase or the Global Impact Investing Network (GIIN) or Toniic may provide helpful resources during the sourcing stage.

SCREENING PROCESS

With a sourcing strategy initiated, numerous potential investments must be assessed. A systematic approach should be taken to reduce the number of companies that move on to the next investment phase. Basic questions regarding social impact, investment thesis, business strategy, operational plan, and financial viability should be answered. Beyond covering these questions and possible answers to them, this section will begin the simulated experience of being an impact investor working through an investment. Three theoretical companies will be presented, the screening process will be implemented to eliminate two, and one will be chosen to move forward with.

Screening Questions

Having a systematic approach to screening can help ensure that each investment is measured objectively. Clearly, there will be unique questions to specific investments, but creating a basic set of questions to ask about each investment opportunity will assist in filtering out unsuitable or undesirable investments. The following questions focus on a company's social impact, business strategy, and operations, and the specific investment at hand. Of the three sections, unique to impact investing is the creation of a social impact map to help guide this questioning process.

Screening for Social Impact through a Social Impact Map

The impact investing sector uses different tools and methodologies to identify and capture the long term change that results from an intervention. Some refer to the *theory of change*, others to a logical framework, an impact map, and so on. All have in common a linear causality chain. On the one end, an impact investor has the intentions, goals, and inputs; on the other end is the change resulting in people's lives.

The *impact map* clarifies the causality and helps understand attribution. Impact is defined as change—change in people's well-being, whether positive or negative. It can be an increase in revenue, safety, security, knowledge, skills, or behavior. The better the building blocks are aligned, the higher the chances are of delivering the expected impact. The overall steps involved in an impact map are shown in Figure 2.8.

At the screening stage, we can sketch an impact map to assess the probability of achieving the intended long-term impact. This exercise, along with the following questions, will help an investor understand how well structured and documented the company's impact strategy is.

Step 1: Mission

What is the institution aiming to achieve? What social or environmental challenge is the organization addressing? Is the objective to improve access to healthcare? Access to education? Access to renewable energy? Affordable housing?

Normally, this is captured in the institution's mission statement and its social goals. A good mission statement[4] contains three elements: the target clients, the expected social outcome for the target clients, and a reference to how the institution will meet the needs of the target clients.

An example of an effective, concise mission statement: "To increase access to higher education for low income students in Mexico through affordable loans."

FIGURE 2.8 Overall steps to create an impact map.

---

[4]On the necessary elements of a good mission statement (and general good social performance practices), see the Social Performance Task Force, *Universal Standards for Social Performance Management (USSPM)* (June 2012), a comprehensive manual to help financial institutions achieve their social goals.

Step 2: Social Goals

What are the institution's social and/or environmental goals in the short and mid-term?

Ideally, an institution should set specific, time-bound social goals aligned to the target population and track progress in meeting these goals over time. But very often social goals are vague and not time bound. Microfinance institutions (MFIs), for instance, often quote grand social goals such as poverty reduction. Yet traditionally, they have not measured poverty and thus do not know if they are delivering on this goal. The Mix market, the leading microfinance business information provider, conducted a survey with over 405 MFIs.[5] The survey's findings indicated that while over 84 percent of surveyed MFIs quoted poverty reduction as a social objective, only 10 percent could provide data.

An example of an effective, SMART (Specific, Measurable, Achievable, Relevant, and Time-bound) social goal is: *To increase by at least 30 percent the net farm income of smallholder coffee farmers in Nicaragua by July 2015.*

Step 3: Inputs

What is the organization investing in to achieve its goals?

Input refers to the resources invested by the company (human resources, capital, and materials) in the pursuit of its activities. Again, a look at the means will tell an investor the likelihood of arriving at the intended ends. Additionally, it's important to understand the level of resources that are invested in monitoring and evaluation (M&E). This will indicate how serious this specific activity is.

Step 4: Activities

Here we examine questions such as these:

How well organized is the company's management and board to deliver on the objectives? How adequate are the products/services to the target clientele? How suitable are the distribution and payment mechanisms? How well do the company's data collection systems actually perform?

---

[5]Micol Pistelli, Anton Simanowitz, and Veronika Thiel, "State of Practice in Social Performance Reporting and Management, A Survey of 405 MFIs Reporting to MIX in 2009-2010," Imp-Act Consortium (July 2011). www.themix.org/sites /default/files/MBB-%20SoPinSPReporting%20and%20Management_FINAL_0.pdf.

Steps 5 and 6: Output and Outcome

What output indicators will capture the essence of the impact?

Understanding the difference between output and outcome is important. Output refers to direct results of the company's activities, the number of treatments offered, loans disbursed, or solar lamps sold. Outcome instead relates to the difference this makes on the life of the customer, the impact of the loan, or the solar lamp or the treatment.

Output indicators of course depend on what the organization aims to achieve. For the company just mentioned, that promotes access to education for low-income students, it needs to report the number of student loans disbursed; yet, as its focus is loans for *low-income* students we need to monitor the number of and changes in student loans per socioeconomic category. At the screening stage, we will check if the organization collects and monitors data. More importantly, we will verify if the data are in the form it requires to assess if and how it is serving the segment it claims to serve.

The nonfinancial indicators that a company will monitor periodically should be clearly defined and include source of data and explanations of any underlying assumptions or calculations. Indeed, the assumptions are an integral part of the impact map. They should be supported by research, and the sources should be cited. Assumptions may be changed when new evidence is obtained, but changes in assumptions should also be documented in the impact map.

Step 7: Impact

What is the impact?

In Table 2.2, we examine a simple impact map. A more elaborate Impact Map can be found on chapter 3 and a comprehensive impact map in Excel under the Chapter 3 folder on this book's website.

At the screening phase, a rapid examination of these components will give us a sense of the organization's likelihood to achieve the intended mission. If this opportunity proceeds to the next level, a thorough due diligence will allow further validation of the underlying data collection practices and the organization's commitment to impact measurement.

There are two other components to social impact screening that fall outside of the impact map: ESG (environmental, social, and governance) policies and monitoring and evaluation (M&E) capacity. Governance and in particular board oversight of social objectives, remuneration schemes, staff incentives, and their alignment with the impact objectives are all part of ESG.

TABLE 2.2   Simple Impact Map

Mission & Social Goals	Input	Activities	Output	Outcome	Impact
Prevent HIV infection in the slums of Rio (Brazil) Social goals: To train 30% of high school children living in Rio on HIV prevention by December 2015	Human resources, condoms, training materials	Distribute condoms Impart HIV prevention trainings Collect and analyze outreach metrics	Number of condoms distributed Number of HIV prevention trainings offered Number of attendees	Men use condoms correctly Informed men and women on HIV prevention	Decrease in HIV infection rates

Although much of an ESG assessment is part of a thorough due diligence process, some sense of the policies can be observed from a screening level.

The other critical element in assessing impact at a screening phase is the organization's M&E capacity. In the example shown in Table 2.2, in order for this organization to properly assess progress, it will require a baseline on HIV prevalence in the target area prior to its intervention. Also, it will need to test how effective the trainings delivered are in reducing infection rates. The organization needs to make the budgetary provisions to cover costs of collecting data, conducting surveys, and controlling data quality as well as analyzing findings. More importantly, it must be ready to admit failure and redesign its products/services or delivery mechanisms for improvements. Similar to ESG review, a core of M&E assessment is done at the due diligence phase, but preliminary observations can help direct the investment focus at a screening phase.

Screening Business Strategy and Operations

Impact investing requires both social impact and business related knowledge to be successful. After creating the impact map and gathering enough data to screen the social mission, we turn our attention to business-related matters.

What is the company's strategy to break into its intended market? Is the company's strategy a rapid market share takeover approach or a slow, regional deployment?

Both rapid and slow deployment methods can be successful, but one strategy requires different types of investors than the other. In a rapid market share takeover, the company will burn through significant amounts of funding. Working capital, operating, and capital expenditures will spike and remain high as the market share takeover is executed. The time to profitability may take longer than expected and investors may need to contribute additional funding. Investors in companies that seek rapid expansion should be prepared for additional funding and possibly long times to break-even and profitability.

Slow, regional deployment may be easier on an investor's accounts, but it may entail competitive risks. An investor in this type of company should be engaged in the strategy closely and understand the competitive landscape in detail.

What is the company's competitive advantage in its industry? Most companies that an investor reviews will have similarities with other companies in its industry, in respect to product, service, or business plan. Normally, there will be a competitive environment. With that in mind, it is very important to understand how the company under review differentiates itself from others. Does it have a lower cost structure that allows it to operate with higher margins? Is there a unique aspect that allows it to gain and maintain a higher market share? Competitive advantage can manifest itself in many different ways. When reviewing an investment, investors need to quickly ascertain the competitive advantage; otherwise, the investment stands a good chance of being an average to low-performing company that never truly gains momentum.

What is the market size for the product or service and its scalability? The size of the market a company operates in and its ability to scale within that market often sets the cap for long-term returns. An excellent example of this is the training company Enstruct, which I founded in 2007. The company focused on training for structured products, a very specific type of financial analysis. Although successful in the field, the specific context of the trainings limited the field of potential clients, which was further reduced post financial crisis. In response to this, the company expanded the training courses offered, which opened up a number of new revenue streams. However, even with these new markets open, scalability was very difficult. Earlier trainings were done by one or two people who had created the material. In order to expand within the market, the company had to start sourcing additional trainers, managing those trainers on content delivery, and at the same time sourcing new clients. Given that the company is a closely held private entity, instead of scaling the company a conscious choice was made to derive value by focusing on existing clients and selecting new ones. For the average investor, this company should be screened away because its ability to generate return beyond primary management is limited.

What stage is the company in?   Is the company in a business plan stage, pilot testing, early stage, or mature growth? Investors need to understand the stage of the company they are reviewing for investment with their investment strategy in mind. For instance, a single, one-off investor would most likely invest very early from the business plan stage through pilot testing. Investment funds with more capital can take an early stage approach, but their portfolio strategy would likely be one where they have limited engagement in the underlying companies. As an example, imagine a USD100 million investment fund that invests in very early stage companies. First, the initial investment amounts for early-stage companies tend to be low compared to growth-stage investments (e.g., a few million compared to tens of millions). If the fund invested on average USD2 million in each early-stage company, it would have to manage 50 investments. Later in Chapter 7, we will explore fund economics, but intensively managing 50 investments with USD100 million under management might not be tenable. The important point to understand at the screening stage is that if a company's stage does not fit with the investment strategy of the investor, then it should most likely be screened away.

Is the business capital intensive or asset light?   Another concept that needs to be in alignment with investment strategy is whether the investee has a capital intensive or asset light business plan. Both are viable investment options, but a capital-intensive business plan will require different types of investors. Capital-intensive businesses require long return horizons, plenty of follow on capital, and connections to debt. The reason behind this is that the business plan itself usually requires investment each year. As this is done, the costs increase, as well as capital expenditures. This makes it very difficult to generate positive free cash flow early on. The benefit of the investment can take many years to come to fruition. Additionally, such capital-intensive business plans are better served with debt financing. If the investors do not have a long investment time horizon, limited follow on funds, or experience with debt financing, they might want to avoid capital-intensive businesses.

Where does the company monetize?   One quick screen for risk is to understand where the prospective company monetizes. Does it earn revenue directly from the consumer, from distributors, or from other companies? Does it get paid in cash or rely on credit? Investors should be sure they are capable of analyzing the point of monetization. An example of this is a home solar energy company in Uganda. Most of its sales take place in the form of consumer financing. It monetizes directly from the consumer over extended periods of time on credit. Investors unable to assess credit risk should try to avoid such an investment.

Where is value created, and how will the company control its value chain? Earlier in this chapter, it was mentioned that an investor needs to understand the company's competitive advantage. At the operational level, the company must put that competitive advantage to work in an effective process that creates value. Once created, the value chain needs to be protected against simple imitators and true competitors. Knowing early if the product or service can be rapidly commoditized and the value chain exposed can help screen out weaker investments.

Is the company an innovator or an enhancer? Investing in a company that is creating a product or service that does not exist yet is a very different prospect than investing in one that is enhancing or building on an existing product or service. If the company is innovating a new product or service additional market analysis should be done to vet the existence and depth of the market. Follow on research should focus on whether others have tried unsuccessfully to create the same or similar product or service in the past. Investors with limited resources toward market studies, sector analyses, and possibly hiring consultants should screen away innovator companies.

Enhancer companies generally will have less risk as their market is already established, but they will encounter more competition and possibly less return upon exit. Excellent examples of enhancer type companies are those trying to add functionality to solar lanterns and solar mobile phone chargers. There are a number of companies that are looking to enhance existing solar lantern and mobile phone charges by creating "pay as you go" technology. Their products or service could include: GSM-based chips that allow sellers to offer the product cheaply and then "unlock" the lantern once payment is made, cellular audio technologies that allow a lantern owner to unlock functionality via mobile phone, or USB sticks that engage the product functionality once plugged in. For these companies, the market for solar lanterns exists and does not have to be established. These companies' products enhance the solar lantern market by allowing the lanterns to be financed over time. The investment risk of this enhancer type company is dependent on who the company aligns itself with in the industry, how unique and effective the product is, and the company's overall ability to negotiate within the industry. Enhancer-type companies will be easier for investors with sector knowledge to move through their investment process.

Is there technology risk?   Whether an innovator or enhancer, a product-oriented company may encounter technology risk. This can occur in two forms: early on in the developmental phase and later in the form of obsolescence. Technology risk is the chance that building and perfecting a new technology could take longer than expected or possibly be unachievable. In the development phase, an investor taking on technology risk has to be prepared for multiple evolutions of the product, with costly failures along the way. The investor will most likely have to put in additional funding at times when the product or service seems to be not working. If an investor isn't oriented toward this potential situation, he or she should immediately screen out companies that exhibit developmental technology risk.

Technology risk, in the form of obsolescence, can creep in later after a successful product or service has been created and sold into a market. Obsolescence occurs when a new technology replaces the existing product or service and usurps partial or all market share. Returning to the solar lantern example, a number of obsolescence risks could be identified. All of the "pay as you go" companies could be made obsolete by advances in other technologies. Assume that GPS transmitters reduce in price significantly over time and a company is able to integrate them into the lanterns for less cost than other companies using different technologies to control lantern functionality. Lantern manufacturers may entirely switch to that technology, as it would also allow location services. Or a more extreme obsolescence risk is that micro-grids become very successful and heavily reduce the need for solar lanterns. Such a scenario would make both the solar lantern and all enhancer companies partially or fully obsolete. If an investor is encountering a company with obsolescence risk, the investor should have the resources to assess and monitor the potential competing technologies and time frames toward implementation.

Who are the founders, and why trust them with the investment?   One of the fastest screening elements is the comfort level with the company's founders and top management. In early-stage ventures, unless the investor is taking a majority stake and is prepared to get heavily involved in day-to-day management, an investor is effectively investing in management. Typically, some type of connection or specialized background is an important feature of the founders that positions them well to create a competitive advantage. However, there are founders who might not have such a connection with their business ideas, but are exceptionally effective entrepreneurs. Screening for entrepreneurs who will build and maintain value, prevent risks from turning into real problems, and solve the inevitable challenges that arise is one of the most important steps.

How do the top-level financials compare across the industry? At the screening stage, it is worth looking at basic financials of the company. These should be provided in a teaser or through early communication. The most important ones include:

- Historical revenue ($ amount and growth rate)
- Cost of goods sold ($ amount or gross margin %)
- Operating expenses ($ amount or operating margin %)
- Earnings before interest depreciation and amortization (EBITDA), if any exists ($ amount or EBITDA margin)
- Debt ($ amount)
- Equity ($ amount and % ownership)
- Capital expenditures

What regulatory risk exists? In a country where a product or service is offered, there is nearly always a governmental agency that regulates the sale. In some industries, there is limited oversight, but in others such as financial markets, healthcare, pharmaceuticals, telecommunications, energy, and natural resources, there can be heavy regulation. Understanding the prior, current, and future stance of government regulation surrounding a company's product or service is critical. Smaller, earlier-stage companies have limited lobbying power and must follow governmental directives. Significant changes to regulation, in extreme cases, can shut down a business.

NOTES FROM THE FIELD

Perhaps one of the most regulated investments I have worked on is a natural gas company in Mozambique that focused on rural distribution. The company is heavily regulated by the Mozambique government, to the extent where margins are controlled. Since the company purchases gas from foreign markets, being able to work within the regulations and work with regulators is extremely important to the success of the company. In this case, comfort was taken since a very influential Mozambique political figure was interested in the success of the company and could assist with regulatory affairs when necessary.

Screening the Current Investment Round

Does the investment allow for a board seat? Some investors will not invest without a directorship on the company's board of directors. Any majority and most significant minority investors should require board seats that are in proportion to their investment amount. If the company is not willing to give this up, it can be an early screening point to back away from the investment.

Who are the other investors, and what are their major investment powers? A basic understanding of the parties in the capitalization table is important early on. If there is misalignment among investors, it can lead to business disruption and potentially reduced financial and social returns. Similarly, any powerful or unique investor rights that existing investors have and will want to maintain should be known early on. For instance, if a company's primary majority investor has the unrestricted ability to drag other investors in an acquisition or sale and wants to maintain those drag rights in the new investment round, there is legitimate concern by new investors over getting dragged for a low return. Drag rights will be discussed later in Chapter 5, but at the screening phase, questions should be asked about the primary powers of other investors.

How much financing is necessary for the current round? What may seem like an easy question is actually one that can get glossed over too early in the due diligence process. To answer this thoroughly, the full due diligence process is usually undertaken, but at the screening level, the investor should generally determine whether the financing requested is enough or too much. This can be achieved by undertaking top-level cash burn and capital expenditure calculations.

As an example, a mobile money company in India that I examined was holding a round for USD10 million. The fund I worked for was interested in a USD4 million round. Over time, it became clear that it would be difficult to raise the full USD10 million. This led the company to adjust the required financing down. However, by doing that, the company adjusted the expected speed of its geographic expansion. This example starts to require a deeper level of financial analysis; however, at the screening stage if the required financing seems too low or too high, it could be a good sign to look at other investments.

How are the other investors protected and compensated? There are two concepts that an investor should look at during the screening phase: anti-dilution rights of other investors and liquidation preferences. Anti-dilution rights dictate how investors in preferred shares would be compensated if there were down rounds (i.e., rounds where the company's valuation has decreased from a previous round). Liquidation preferences are rights given to investors that enhance investments by directing cash during a liquidity event to the investor up to a certain level. New investors must analyze these mechanisms very carefully because their investment could be greatly affected by them. Both of these will be looked at in detail in Chapter 5, but knowing the basic information on these at an early stage can help an investor decide to move away from an investment.

Can an investment be completed legally and securely? When investors place money in local investments, the legality risk is usually quite limited. However, when investors begin to invest in foreign markets, the question of foreign ownership can become an issue. The rules vary widely, depending on country, corporate structure, investor domicile, investee industry, and many other factors. Any investor in a foreign market should already have an understanding or consult local legal counsel as to the legality and security of investing in a specific company in a foreign market.

What are the tax implications of the investment? Taxes can significantly impact the final return on investment. Similar to the prior question, tax rules differ, depending on a number of factors. Investors should be comfortable that they understand or will be able to understand the tax implications of bringing local money into a foreign market, owning part of a company that might earn profit internationally, and, most importantly, knowing the taxes to expect when exiting the investment at some point in the future.

A LOOK AT THREE POTENTIAL INVESTMENTS

Establishing the right questions to ask is useful, but to be effective at screening, we will apply those questions to three potential investments. Three common impact investing sectors will be introduced through this analysis: mobile money, household solar energy, and healthcare. Entrepreneurs have gravitated toward these fields as they offer immediate benefit to low-income households while being able to offer accessible pricing that allows for profitable market-based business models. While each field seems promising and a strong contender for investment, we must remember that we are investing in a company, where each one has a unique blend of strategic, operational, financial, and social characteristics. Analyzing each aspect as objectively as possible will allow us to select the best possible investment.

For each of the following fictitious prospective investments, corporate teasers are available under the Chapter 2 folder on the book's website.

Prospective Investment 1: Mobile Money (PagaPago)

Background Traditional banking has been elusive to low-income individuals in many countries. The lack of financial inclusion can be attributed to long physical distances for rural customers, formal address and documentation requirements, transaction amounts that are below traditional bank minimums, and occasionally social stigmas against low-income populations. Without a formal banking system, low-income individuals experience increased transaction costs and timing, lower savings rates, and higher risk of loss.

Early entrepreneurs of mobile money saw the prevalence of mobile phones in both rural and urban low-income communities, as well as the localized payment structure involving mobile agents, and envisioned a new method of banking. The earliest companies, such as M-PESA, evolved directly out of a telecom allowing users to load and store money on their mobile phone accounts, send money to individuals, pay for goods using their phones, and withdraw cash from their mobile accounts via local agents. The success of M-PESA has spawned numerous similar mobile money companies.

Across developing and developed countries the use of mobile phones for banking purposes has experienced exponential growth. Understanding the market fully is incredibly complex as technologies vary wildly, banking and telecommunications regulations are often unique to each country, and user habits can demonstrate regional variance. However, in the face of those factors, mobile money enterprises offer some of the strongest business models for profitability given that high frequency, low-level transactions can scale rapidly through the use of technology.

The Company The first hypothetical company we will screen is a Colombian mobile money enterprise named PagaPago. Open and review the corporate teaser found on the website. Founded two years ago, PagaPago acquired an electronic payments integration and servicing platform from an Indian firm. The CEO leveraged his connections to win a number of key contracts with large merchants in Colombia and sign them up as partners with PagaPago. Consumers can now use their mobile phones to load money, transfer funds to peers, and purchase a variety of goods and services. The primary merchants accepting the PagaPago system are mobile phone companies for prepaid service top-up, local busses and airlines, movie theaters, and select Colombian government services such as the pension system. Of particular interest to social impact related activities, PagaPago has connected local microfinance institutions so disbursements and payments can be made electronically.

The technology that PagaPago utilizes is mainly SMS based, requiring only a mobile phone that can send and receive text messages. Subscribers open an account and load funds with a local agent, create a unique PIN to manage transactions, and then freely use their loaded funds. PagaPago is looking into additional services through the growing acceptance of smart-phones.

Merchants are the primary source of revenue, as they are charged a service fee per transaction that flows through the PagaPago system. These charges currently range from 3 to 15 percent, depending on the industry and the negotiated contract. Additional fees are generated from local businesses that sign up to be agents. The agents act as the customer facing representatives of PagaPago to create accounts and accept funds. On a customer level, most transactions only cost the price of a text message; however, peer-to-peer transfers incur service charges of 1 to 3 percent.

PagaPago has sent out a corporate teaser to start discussions amongst investors for a USD8 million Series B round of investment. Previously, a British venture capital firm that invests in mobile technologies provided a Series A round financing. While PagaPago has historically operated in the Bogota area, the funds will be used to develop into many other urban and semi-urban regions. Additional investment in new smartphone technologies will also be part of the use of proceeds.

Investment Sourcing   Although the PagaPago investment was preselected, we should examine how it would fare against a rigorous sourcing strategy. First, PagaPago is based and operates in Colombia, which has a large population of over 44 million people who also have a high literacy rate of 90 percent.[6] The country has excellent mobile penetration of 95 percent and only two mobile money players outside of banks and telecoms. Interestingly, the report where these statistics are derived, IFC's Mobile Money Scoping Report: Colombia, shows an ease of doing business rank of 39. While this appears to be a good score, if we look to the business metrics presented in the market mapping exercise we find mixed information. There are some excellent ranks, such as being 6th for investor protection, but a very poor rank for contract enforcement (155th). Investors should be aware of a barbell distribution of ranking, particularly for something as important as contract enforcement. Overall, though, Colombia has many positive metrics, and the ones to be concerned about, such as contract enforcement, could be solved with thorough due diligence and local legal counsel consultation.

---

[6]Some entities believe that literacy is required for mobile money usage; however, personal due diligence of mobile money companies in India has shown that illiterate people access and use simple SMS-based systems. A Notes From the Field in the screening section for this investment relates the due diligence experience.

In regards to economic cycle and foreign exchange rates, both have positive trends. From the end of 2013 to the beginning of 2014, Colombia has been moving along with other countries in a slow global recovery. Investing at this stage in an economic cycle could be advantageous, as there is still plenty of growth to be realized and no immediate downturn threat. As for foreign exchange risk, the country's currency, the peso, has been appreciating since the early 2000s. In fact, foreign USD equity investors would have earned profit by investing in the early 2000s and exiting in 2007/2008 due to the appreciation. Figure 2.9 is a chart of the historical exchange rate of USD to Colombian pesos (COP).

The last four years of the exchange rate, in particular, have been fairly stable. While the past exchange rate is no measure of what will come, the stabilizing pattern is comforting when committing equity. It can also mean that hedging costs may have come down and some type of currency protection may be possible.

Screening   Initiating the screening process does not always have to follow a predefined order. Earlier, when the common questions were introduced there was a flow that started more general and progressed to more specific factors. The approach to take with any investment is to save time and focus first on the most probable *deal breakers*. At the screening stage, this should begin with most relevant risks given the region, sector, and company.

FIGURE 2.9   A historical look at the USD/COP exchange rate shows appreciation and stabilization.

The most prevalent risk of investing in PagaPago and mobile money companies in general is that their main competition are well established and funded telecoms and banking institutions. With virtually commoditized technology the potential investee must demonstrate a strong competitive advantage to move beyond an initial screening stage. In many countries across the globe such as India, Nigeria, and Vietnam, there are numerous mobile money companies popping up. At the same time, the regionally entrenched telecoms and banks are introducing their mobile payment systems.

Looking back at the screening questions posed earlier in this chapter, the risk at hand is determining the competitive advantage. A company like PagaPago could make a number of arguments in regards to its competitive advantage:

1. PagaPago's system is telecom and bank agnostic. The fact that it is not associated with a telecom or bank could be the strongest factor in its favor. Most of the telecom-related mobile money and payment systems require users to use the telecom's service. Many customers in developing markets have multiple telecom accounts and may prefer a system that does not lock them into a single provider. Similarly, banks that are introducing mobile money services may require the user to be a customer or have an account. Often times, obtaining an account can require extensive know your customer (KYC) processes that low-income individuals try to avoid. Simple, universal usage may be more appealing to customers.

2. Senior management may be very proficient at securing valuable merchant contracts. Part of the competitive advantage question now spills over to the question regarding the founder's and top management's backgrounds. In mobile money the key to offering services to customers is obtaining and sustaining contracts with merchants that have customer value. If the founder or management is well connected and can negotiate strong contracts, possibly long-term, with exclusivity, then the company can establish a competitive advantage.

A critical element with each question is to not just ask it retrospectively or as of today, but to think how it may evolve. For PagaPago's competitive advantage in the future, there are more threats to be concerned about. While telecoms and banks are immediate threats, there are foreign financial entities such as Visa, MasterCard, American Express, and Western Union that are well capitalized and will also become players in the mobile money scene. Additionally, technology companies such as Apple, Google, and Square have aggressively launched into developed markets and certainly have their eyes set on foreign deployment. These companies could also be perceived as potential strategic investors or acquirers, but they would only do so if PagaPago demonstrated a competitive advantage such as key contracts.

Getting comfortable with PagaPago's ability to compete against tele-coms, banks, and foreign entities is absolutely necessary to move forward with this investment. However, mobile money investments also present an additional top-level screening factor mentioned earlier, regulatory risk. The regulations that govern mobile money companies depend on country of domicile. In most countries, the regulations and ability to operate depend on the central bank. PagaPago, being based in Colombia, is regulated by three entities: the Superintendencia Financiera de Colombia (Banking Superintendence of Colombia, SFC), the Comisión de Regulación de Comunicaciones (Communications Regulation Commission, CRC), and the Banca de las Oportunidades (BDO). The most imminent concern regarding investment in PagaPago is that mobile wallets are legally not allowed in Colombia, according to the SFC.

This does not mean that mobile money companies cannot be created and operate within the existing laws. In Colombia, e-money type companies can exist, so long as they do not allow for repayable funds. It seems from PagaPago's teaser that it has figured out a way to allow for cash out through banks. Understanding how this is possible given the strict regulatory environment in Colombia is critical to progressing this investment to the next level. Overall, even if management demonstrates a clear competitive advantage with the private sector, if they are not able to navigate the regulatory environment the entire business could be threatened.

For social impact investors, the direct social impact of mobile money is another primary screening question. Studies have shown that mobile money has an impact at the community level through local economic expansion, security, capital accumulation, and business environment.[7] For low-income individuals and families, the most direct benefit of mobile money is that it saves users time that can be used for other more productive tasks. Also, it is a safe and cost-effective method of saving money, and can be viewed as a step toward financial inclusion into the formal banking system, where additional products and services could be offered. In addition to offering better cash flow, improving risk management, and promoting asset accumulation, mobile money can also have a positive impact on healthcare as rapid access to needed cash translates into access to healthcare. In addition to offering better cash flow, improving risk management, and promoting asset accumulation, mobile money can also have a positive impact on healthcare as rapid access to cash facilitates faster access to services.

---

[7]Megan G. Plyler, Sherri Haas, and Geetha Nagarajan, "Community-Level Economic Effects of M-PESA in Kenya: Initial Findings," IRIS Center, University of Maryland (June 2010); and Guy Stuart and Monique Cohen, "Cash In, Cash Out; The Role of M-PESA in the Lives of Low-Income People."

However, mobile money systems being rolled out in developing markets target varying demographics. Some appear to exclusively favor Internet and smartphone users, which would have limited appeal or access to rural, low-income users. On the other extreme are systems that originated based on servicing microfinance clients. In the middle are mobile money companies that offer multiple access points from the Internet to SMS-based transactions. A fast screen for a social impact investor is making sure the company's demographic reach is aligned with the investor's targeted population. Also important at this stage is to check the social performance standards of the company and in particular the client protection practices, including aspects such as client data privacy.

NOTES FROM THE FIELD

During due diligence on a mobile money company in India, the social impact level was a challenging topic to analyze. It was clear that the company I was looking into was better than its peers, as some of the competitors had virtually no social impact and actually were focusing on negative net social impact business lines such as facilitating lottery ticket purchases.

The challenge of demonstrating social impact in the mobile money business is that information about the individual users is limited. While their purchases might be known, we sought to know who was actually using the service. In order to get a better understanding, the transaction team utilized a classification system for populations, based on job and income. We took a geographic approach and had the company map the percentages of sales in a predefined area that was distinguished by job and income classification. This allowed us to get a feel for the percentage of sales that were most likely directed toward low-income populations.

At this point, a screening decision to progress the investment could be made based on competitive advantage, regulatory risk, and social mission. We will wait, though, until all three potential companies have been introduced before making such a decision.

Prior to looking at the next investment, we should review secondary risks that could influence our decision whether to move the investment into a further stage of due diligence:

- *Technology risk:* It has been mentioned that the technology behind mobile money payment systems is relatively commoditized. While regional integration may take some customization, the platforms can generally be bought and sold easily. There is technology risk, though, in the fact that the entire system relies on the use of mobile telephones as the monetization tool. In some countries, the argument for mobile money is backed up because of a lack of other technology infrastructures such as point of sale (POS) systems for credit cards. This is quickly changing in some countries, such as Myanmar, where credit card systems are being rapidly deployed. Alternative technologies from companies such as Square, Google, and Apple also threaten mobile money, since even the smallest merchants can accept credit cards using those systems. If those companies came out with a rural, emerging-market version of their product for merchants, it could take market share from mobile money.

■ *Future margin stress:* A risk related to the earlier screening question on basic financials is price compression. If the mobile money industry's development is likened to the mobile telephone industry's development, then price compression will occur. The 3 to 15 percent merchant fees that PagaPago is enjoying right now may come down significantly as other entities enter the competitive landscape. Any future projections should incorporate a reduction in merchant fee rates.

■ *Appropriate stage and size of investment:* If an investor is a fund or even an individual practicing a targeted investment strategy, the stage and size of the investment can be very important. The two are typically interlinked, as later-stage companies often require larger investment amounts. In this case, the company is seeking a relatively large investment size for a B round; however, it seems that they are sourcing from multiple funds.

Although it is clear that PagaPago is raising a B round, stage is also determined by the financial maturity of the company. Investors often look to revenue or EBITDA levels and margins. In many early-stage investments, EBITDA does not exist yet, but revenue can be an indicator. Mobile money, though, presents challenges for measuring stage by revenue based on global differences in reporting. For instance, in India, mobile money companies report funds loaded onto their systems as revenue and later expense the funds when a transaction is complete. This is not true revenue in the sense of most other companies, where revenue is countered by an expense of the good or service and the remainder is profit. In this case, relating to mobile money the expense can be a very high percentage of original funds loaded, if not all of it. The true revenue is the fee earned on a transaction. Measuring the company's stage in terms of this revenue is a much better method.

NOTES FROM THE FIELD

An interesting observation related to screening mobile money companies is how important it is to understand the potential market share. One filter that was used earlier in my analyses was the literacy rate of the region. A concern was that illiterate people would not use any text-based service. However, during a due diligence of an Indian mobile money company, the topic of illiterate users came up. We learned and validated that illiterate people were using basic SMS through simple, common phrases such as "I love you" to their loved ones. This suggested that simplistic SMS-based systems could be adapted by illiterate users.

Prospective Investment 2: Micro Solar Energy (Solero Lighting)

Background The solar energy industry has witnessed significant change in the last decade. Technology has advanced solar panels with multiple types now in existence: mono-crystalline silicon, poly-crystalline silicon, and thin film being the most common. Each has its own advantages in regards to efficiency and cost; however, in general, the cost of solar paneling has come down dramatically. Figure 2.10 shows the historical cost of photovoltaic (PV).

Micro or pico-solar, as it is sometimes called, is the business of creating small-scale devices powered by solar panels. Typically less than 5 watts, the most common devices include lanterns, mobile phone charging units, universal battery storage systems that power an array of devices, and basic home systems. A number of additional accessories powered by these solar devices have been developed, ranging from radios to Internet modems. Also, more common devices can be incorporated as the systems move up the wattage scale, to include televisions, refrigerators, and virtually any electronic appliance.

Social entrepreneurs have quickly adapted the technology to help alleviate the massive electricity shortage problem around the world. Any impact investor will at some point see a potential energy-related investment that will quote a statistic of over 1.2 billion people who live without or with limited electricity.[8] While that statistic is used many times, and often

---

[8] "Energy, the Facts," World Bank (2013), http://web.worldbank.org/WBSITE /EXTERNAL/TOPICS/EXTENERGY2/0,contentMDK:22855502~pagePK:210058 ~piPK:210062~theSitePK:4114200,00.html.

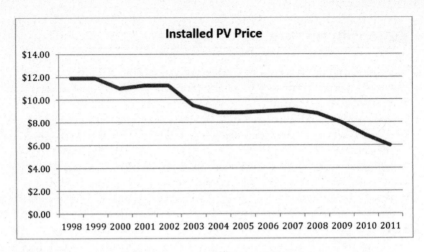

FIGURE 2.10 From 1998 to 2011, the price of installed PV has fallen by 50 percent. The cost reduction of modules has contributed to over 50 percent of this decline.

ranges a few hundred million people here and there, it is absolutely true that a substantial percentage of the world's population live with electricity shortages. Deficiencies in electricity lead to fewer productive hours per day for work and education, wasted time to acquire electricity, the use of harmful and dangerous alternatives such as kerosene, and general safety issues of reduced lighting.

The combination of lower-priced solar components, advancements in other technologies such as batteries, and a better understanding of rural and low-income consumers have made this industry flourish with entrepreneurs. Lower price points have allowed for commercially viable margins for products that have important, direct social impact. However, with all of the zeal and innovation, the basic tenets of business creation and investing must be adhered to, otherwise the risk of failure looms. This has already been seen in the industry, with a number of product failures and companies that are flirting with bankruptcy.

The Company Solero Lighting (Solero) is the next hypothetical company that we will examine. Open and review the corporate teaser, located in the same folder on the book's website as PagaPago's teaser. Solero manufactures, distributes, and sells micro solar technology products, primarily to rural communities. It offers a range of products:

- A low-cost, single-watt solar lantern
- A 2- to 3-watt solar lantern that can also charge mobile phones
- A small solar home system that provides multiple lights and USB charging

Manufacturing is done as low cost as possible in China, while verifying compliance with strict social and environmental standards. Contract manufacturers are used rather than spending funds on heavy equipment and warehouse space. Products are then shipped to two main regional warehouses: Mumbai, India, and Los Angeles, California. Within India, a Solero-run distributor system is being developed that focuses on sales to rural, low-electrified communities. Currently only large, commercial orders are taken for sales from the U.S. warehouse and occasionally direct from China.

Solero emphasizes two key features about its business: quality and distribution. Solero products have gained a reputation for their quality, which has been vetted by third-party testing institutes. Customers are able to identify the brand and have begun to trust the product. An additional component to customer loyalty is the rural distribution system.

Sales to rural customers are made through village distributors. Customers work with the village distributors directly and have a point of contact in case of problems. The village distributors are organized regionally and are heavily monitored by Solero through the use of technology and larger regional distributors. This system allows Solero to have an accurate and efficient grasp on its sales chain.

For this round of investment, the corporate teaser indicates a fundraise of USD3 million to be used for research and development, expansion into more regions within India, and international expansion to Southeast Asia.

Investment Sourcing Solero is a difficult company to pin down regarding sourcing strategy, as it already operates in three different countries: China, India, and the United States. Investors would benefit from the fact that it could accept investment in its U.S. entity, but they should recognize that a majority of its business is done in India. For that reason, we shall look to India from the lens of the market mapping exercise earlier. We can see that it scores well for investor protection. However, contract enforcement, ease of starting a business, and insolvency metrics score poorly. For social impact, it is clear that India is an excellent target country, further confirmed by the HDI score. Reinforcing the earlier thought, though, is that while India can be a challenging place to do business, many excellent entrepreneurs focus on the challenge, and thus there can be strong business plans focusing on the region.

The business cycle of India remains on a strong growth pattern versus other emerging and developed markets. While price inflation has been a problem over the last few years, recent elections in 2014 have helped bolster the economic outlook.

The Indian rupee, though, has been a difficult thorn in foreign investment strategy. India enjoyed a relatively stable exchange rate versus the U.S. dollar for many years until late 2011. At that time, the Indian rupee began a

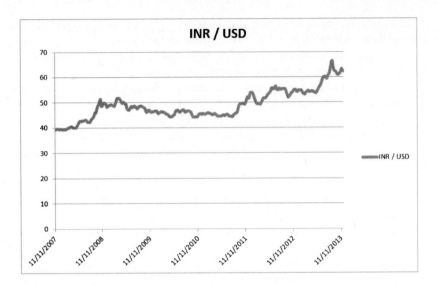

FIGURE 2.11   The Indian rupee exchange rate to the US dollar, 2007 to 2013.

path of severe devaluation. U.S. dollar investors who placed money in rupees 2006 and 2007 and wanted to exit after 2011 would have incurred significant losses due to foreign exchange rates. Figure 2.11 shows the last six years of the Indian rupee versus the U.S. dollar.

Even though an investment in Solero would be in USD, the foreign exchange issue that remains is indirect exposure to INR. Much of Solero's revenue comes from India and is in the form of INR. Pricing for products is constrained by the local market as well as the Chinese manufacturing and shipping costs. As the INR devalues, it takes more rupees to buy the same amount of dollars and therefore reduces Solero's margins. When sourcing transactions that rely on multiple exchange rates, the cross rates and volatility must be thought of, particularly in relation to investment initiation and exit.

Screening   In a field flooded with competitors, just as with PagaPago, determining competitive advantage is the initial deal-breaker point. However, there are multiple questions related to competitive advantage that differ from PagaPago and a mobile money investment, which should be asked in the case of Solero.

The first of these is not so obvious, but is the question of where value is created and controlled. If we dissect Solero's business model, we would find that there are two main value centers: manufacturing and distribution. The manufacturing component is much easier to understand, since it is a physical product that can be examined side-by-side with competitors' products, tested for performance, and reviewed by consumers. Rigorous vendor selection, contract manufacturer management, and a system for rapidly identifying and fixing problems can control quality.

Understanding the value and control of a distribution network, particularly one focusing on rural markets, is more elusive than quality. We should briefly examine the various methods of distribution that exist or have been attempted for micro solar product distribution:

- *Traditional third-party distribution*: One of the most common approaches is to sell products to a separate regional distribution company. The monetization would occur at the point of sale to the distributor and the control of the value chain ends there. The regional distributor would then sell to local distributors, which, in turn, would sell to local storeowners or small kiosk retailers. Control over pricing, product placement, and face-to-face customer service does not exist. Successful products tend to be the ones that allow for the highest margins across the distributor value chain, with limited regard to brand management and no regard to social impact.
- *Company-controlled distributor:* An approach taken by some companies is to operate the distribution business in country of sale. This is more costly from an operational perspective, but it allows the company to control the value chain better. The company then monetizes when the product is sold to local distributors or storeowners directly. The company has more control over pricing, but still must contend with storeowners pushing better margin products. Specific to rural markets is that rural consumers purchase from a very local market, which may source from a store in a close-by city. There are more points in the value chain that separate the consumer from the manufacturer. For products that might require customer service or warranty utilization, the separation makes it difficult to build brand loyalty.
- *Company-controlled value chain:* The deepest method of control is for a company to be present at every stage of the value chain. For companies focused on rural consumers, physical and cultural accessibility can be challenging to complete the value chain. Companies have been getting closer to figuring out these challenges by integrating control points up to the final sale. Investors need to be careful, though, as small differences in value chain control can make or break a business.

  For instance, imagine two companies trying to distribute solar lanterns in rural Africa. Both have their own regional distribution point, both have local distribution points, but one company has created a "shop in a box" concept where a local entrepreneur sets up business in a rural area, while the other utilizes local staff to manage individual salesmen. In the "shop in a box" case, the company monetizes when it sells the box to the local entrepreneur. Very important parts of the sales process, such as sales goals, margin analysis, maintenance, and warranty, are left up to the local entrepreneur. However, in the latter case where local staff is used to manage individual salespeople, the company can exert control further down the value chain.

- *Piggyback distribution*: Some companies strike deals with larger, entrenched companies to move their product through the larger company's distribution network. This can be an effective way to move a new product from a small company quickly to rural consumers. However, the larger company will usually have the upper hand at margin negotiation, and branding can easily be lost on consumers as they associate the product with the larger company.
- *Specialized rural distributors*: A recent development has been distributors that solely focus on rural distribution. These companies focus on creating the most efficient and effective rural distribution network. They can be excellent platforms for a company to sell products through, but margins must be heavily negotiated, it can be difficult to ensure that competing brands aren't marketed over the company's brand, and brand recognition can become a dispute as the rural distributor may try to develop its own branding.

NOTES FROM THE FIELD

During a due diligence trip on a small-scale farming equipment company in India, the time came to assess the distribution network thoroughly. Part of the business and social impact assessment focused on the end users, the farmers, where it became clear that the target consumer was not being reached. The company was unable to take the due diligence team to a truly small-scale farm that was utilizing the products. Additionally, some consumers could not recognize the correct brand of the product, since the company was distributing through a larger agricultural company. This suggested that control over the value chain was broken.

Tracing the value chain backward to the local storeowners selling the product directly to the farmers, I asked salesmen why they weren't selling to smaller-scale farms. Many of the salesmen identified the same reason: The larger-scale farms had more money and it was easier to make a sale to them. Since commission incentivized the salesmen, they would market to farmers where they would make the largest, fastest sale.

Unfortunately, this loss of control in the value chain meant that two important aspects of the business were being ignored: the volume of repeat sales to small-scale farmers in aggregate could exceed large one-off sales, and the social impact the business was marketing to investors was overstated. From a business perspective, the large farmers were underutilizing the product and only using it haphazardly, resulting in volatile sales patterns. The product was intended as a low-cost solution for small-scale farmers to use year after year. If that demographic was truly covered, then revenue would grow in a stable manner as the company geographically expanded. From a social impact perspective, the company is selling to a demographic that does not need the benefits of the product. The social impact was much more limited than originally expected.

For Solero, secondary risks that should be thought about include the following:

- *Market share expansion risk:* If the competitive advantage seems clear, thinking about how the company will expand is the next screening question. Given the number of competitors there will no doubt be overlap between companies as all of them expand to different regions. Companies that enter markets first, with a quality product, will have an advantage over others. However, expansion requires a methodical approach that can be managed as the company grows. Expanding too fast without maintaining control of the newly expanded enterprise can lead to a large organization running amok.
- *Technology risk:* Both new product risk and obsolescence are possible in the micro solar energy market. As an example, Solero intends to introduce new solar products. Each one that is introduced requires extensive factory and field-testing. In order to keep up with the competition there is limited time to test and products will need to be introduced into the market. Engineering and component problems that are not caught in the testing phase can cost the company significantly in terms of warranty returns and brand damage.

  In terms of obsolescence, the micro solar energy market is dependent on the idea that primary consumers have limited alternatives. In the broadest sense, if a previously nonelectrified community or village is hooked up to the power grid, then the market need for such devices will plummet.[9] Already, there are micro-grid solutions such as biogas generators and micro solar grids that can electrify entire villages. Additionally, electricity can be generated in other ways beyond solar, such as through wind, geothermal, or even kinetic sources. Investors need to keep a close watch on how the market develops.

- *Margin risk:* Looking at the projected financials Solero expects to have healthy gross and EBITDA margins. These margins are in line with comparable consumer electronic companies. However, as we have learned about details of Solero's operations, we can see that there are specific margin risks that could derail profitability. For instance, we know that the company must ship goods from China to far-off locations. Shipping is normally done by sea freight, which takes time. If inventory is not controlled properly, then air freight might have to be used, which is significantly more costly.

Warranty utilization is another area that affects the margins of most consumer electronics companies. Expectations for returns are usually incorporated into financial projections, but many events outside of Solero's control can cause an increase in warranty utilization and reduce margins. Such events could include component supplier quality reduction, new product design flaws, and contract manufacturing quality problems.

Prospective Investment 3: Healthcare (Mtoto Clinics)

Background Low-income individuals, whether from developed or developing countries, all contend with the challenge of finding affordable, high-quality healthcare. Most countries have government-sponsored health plans or state-run medical facilities, but these frequently come up short in providing timely, quality care. The private sector has been slow to address this gap in the market. Traditionally, private hospitals and clinics, many of which offer higher-quality care than their state-run counterparts, have not focused on lower-income demographics, believing that their services were unaffordable or not desired. Innovative entrepreneurs have begun to alter the traditional models by focusing on cost control, through asset-light business plans, standardized services, tiered services, or a combination of all three in order to bring affordable, high-quality healthcare to low-income populations.

---

[9]This risk is somewhat mitigated by the fact that even electrified rural areas in developing economies often have long periods of down time, or periods when electricity is not being provided by traditional power grids.

Cost of goods and services are the obvious hurdles to overcome for healthcare. Higher-quality healthcare normally requires well-paid doctors, and as technology advances, more expensive equipment. The infrastructure surrounding a medical facility, from the facility itself to the equipment within, can require significant capital. The more disruptive and attractive business plans have focused on cost cutting and control on every level.

Asset-light development has focused on taking over existing clinic or leasing building space that can easily be converted to a medical facility. This allows the medical company to avoid costly capital expenditure of brand new buildings. Within the building, the equipment can easily run into the millions of dollars, which is why entrepreneurs catering to lower-income individuals have favored standardized clinics. As we will see with Mtoto Clinics, focusing on standard maternal care and referring specialized cases to other clinics allows the company to operate with basic equipment that can provide service in most situations.

An alternative approach that entrepreneurs have tried has been to allow for more specialized services, but to offer tiered-income patient care, where procedures are of the exact same quality for rich or poor. Only the room amenities vary, depending on the price a patient is willing to pay. As an example, in some rural hospitals in India, an inpatient can have the following options depending on income:

1. *General ward*: Least expensive option where multiple patients occupy beds that are placed in a large room, separated by curtains.
2. *Semi-private room*: Middle-priced option where patients can share a room with one or a few other patients. Often additional enhancements such as televisions or air-conditioning might be available.
3. *Private room*: High-priced option where patients have their own individual room, typically with standard amenities such as television, air-conditioning, places for family to sleep, etc.

The advantage with a tiered pricing system is that the doctors can service all types of patients, while higher-priced options bring in better margins and profitability for the business.

The Company Mtoto Clinics (Mtoto) is the last hypothetical company that we will examine for investment. Mtoto has created a chain of branded, maternal healthcare facilities throughout Nakuru, a tier II city in Kenya. The company has been successful in creating three clinics that operate near profitability through a combination of asset-light strategy, standardization, and tiered services.

Mtoto has been very strategic on where and how it opens its clinics. Management conducts detailed studies of city districts to ascertain catchment area, competitive atmosphere, and potential site locations. Controlling capital expenditure for a particular site is especially important in executing its expansion strategy. Mtoto looks to renovate existing clinics or source buildings that are conducive to its standard layout.

Standardization in general is another strong operating strategy that Mtoto has been employing. Mtoto offers pre- and postnatal services, but only for standard natural and Caesarean section births. Any specialized care required pre- or post-birth is referred to a nearby private clinic, or government clinic if affordability is a problem. This allows Mtoto to require lower capital expenditure per clinic, require less expensive medical staff, and keep working capital low through less specialized supply purchases. Additionally, pricing is relatively standardized and with only having to offer lower priced procedures and services, there is less default risk on payment compared to higher priced, complex procedures.

Tiered services allow customers to select a level of service that fits their income level. Mtoto reinforces that the same high-quality procedures are done by the same nurses and doctors for all patients—however, the patient living quarters can differ. This is akin to tiered services on airplanes, where safety is paramount for all passengers regardless of class of service, but a first-class seat provides more luxury than an economy seat, and much more profit margin.

Mtoto's strategy allows it to offer low-cost care that is preferable to free, government alternatives. While many countries offer these free services, the quality of care, timing of care, and living quarters are typically very poor compared to an Mtoto-type clinic.

The current investment round seeks to raise 175 million Kenyan shillings to build six new clinics in neighboring municipalities and provide for working capital while the new clinics move to EBITDA breakeven.

Investment Sourcing Mtoto is clearly a foreign investment and bears the full risk of investing in Kenya. These risks can be significant for a foreign investor when we look at how it scores on the market mapping exercise. For most of the basic investment metrics, it is above 100, indicating difficulties with starting a business, recourse during insolvency, and particularly with contract enforcement. There is significant developmental need, though, in the country with an HDI of 145, and particularly for maternal mortality with a 30 maternal mortality ratio.

The requirement to invest in Kenyan shillings could also be a detrimental factor. Looking at the KES to USD exchange rate for the last 10 years, we

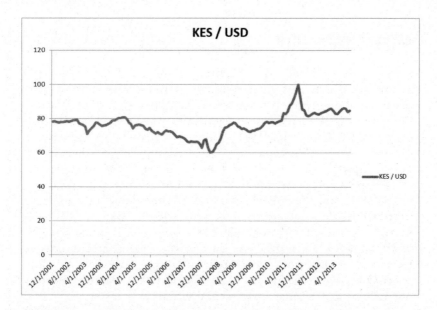

FIGURE 2.12 The Kenyan shilling exchange rate to U.S. dollars, 2001 to 2013.

can see that if we placed an investment in 2008 and had to exit in 2013, there would be significant loss due to a depreciating Kenyan shilling. An estimate of the loss would be assuming investment in April 2008 at about 60 KES to USD and having to exit in December 2013 for almost 85 KES to USD. This would result in a 29 percent loss on investment due to currency fluctuation. Figure 2.12 shows historical USD/KES exchange rates.

Screening Typical healthcare businesses require investment in infrastructure and equipment for expansion. However, Mtoto believes that significant capital investment is not necessary for its business plan, given its asset-light orientation. By taking over existing infrastructure and keeping services limited to basic procedures, capital expenditures can be significantly lower than competing maternal health clinics. An investor in Mtoto should be able to assess the company's ability to source adequate properties and economically convert them to profitable facilities. In particular, the investor should have the ability to understand local Kenyan commercial real estate drivers, the cost of retrofitting a building for maternal clinic use, the cost of having to dismantle one, and the time it takes to get one up and running.

NOTES FROM THE FIELD

During a due diligence on a maternal healthcare clinic in India, it became clear that a large part of the success of the business plan relied on the ability to open new clinics in areas with patient demand. This company also had an asset-light strategy and sought out existing buildings to retrofit. However, finding such properties was not a very easy task. Various sourcing strategies only yielded a handful of potential properties. One stress in my mind during the due diligence was extending the projection timeline for opening new clinics.

Additionally, the limited selection of properties seemed to occasionally force the company to choose properties that were not ideal and had difficulty becoming profitable. These properties eventually had to be shut down and incurred significant closing costs related to broken leases and employment termination payments to staff that could not relocate to another facility. All of these factors were incorporated into our analysis and eventual investment decision.

Another screening question that is pertinent to an investment in Mtoto is how value is created and controlled. Beyond the utilization of an asset-light model, the company has detailed how it only offers basic, standardized procedures. An important benefit that management identifies is that human resources, such as nurses, can be hired for lower cost since they need not be as skilled as other facilities, where more complex procedures are undertaken. However, employment churn is a risk that is borne out of this strategy. Junior staff may use Mtoto as a means of gaining experience and training, and then move on to a better-paying clinic. Employee churn of this nature could increase costs due to time and resources spent on hiring and training.

Secondary risks that should be considered:

- *Basic operating data and financial information:* the data provided in the corporate teaser shows an aggressive increase in clinic openings, but only a modest build in EBITDA margin. In fact, EBITDA margin reaches a maximum of 25 percent in the final projection year. While this would be a decent margin if realized, the issue is that corporate teasers are often idealized versions with very aggressive projections. As we will see in Chapter 4, when we delve into scenario analysis, corporate projections are normally very aggressive. Any scenario analysis with even medium stresses to costs will make for a fairly unattractive EBITDA margin.

■ *Regulatory and competitive risk:* On June 1, 2013, the president of Kenya, Uhuru Kenyatta, stated, "My government has made adequate budgetary arrangements to enable all pregnant mothers to access free maternity services in all public health facilities ... "[10] Any due diligence of a Kenyan maternal care clinic business must take such a statement and policy change into account. The risk is clear that the competitive landscape could change with the price point for public health facilities dropping to nothing. However, the quality of care remains a factor and a differentiator between government-run facilities. This type of identified risk would then shift the focus of part of the due diligence to understanding how Mtoto clinics are perceived in terms of quality for lower-income individuals who might otherwise go to a free government clinic.

MOVING FORWARD WITH AN INVESTMENT

Just as any investor is constrained by time and must make a decision, to progress through the investment simulation we must decide on an investment to move deeper into the investment process. In reality, an investor could choose to move forward in the investment process with one, two, all three, or none of the investments. We will impose a bit of restriction and force a decision on just one of the three investments presented.

Each one has its advantages and disadvantages. An excellent method of organizing thoughts on the investments is to create a combined strengths, weaknesses, opportunities, and threats (SWOT) analysis. From there, we can identify any potential deal-breaking weaknesses or threats, or check if the strengths and opportunities outweigh the negatives.

For PagaPago the scalability is very tempting. If it were able to penetrate the Colombian market and become a leader in mobile payments, the revenue and profit increases would be staggering. Additionally, it has the potential to integrate numerous business lines into its system and have a significant social impact by offering services that are easily accessible by lower-income segments. However, much larger local and foreign entities realize this as well, and will be competing for the same market. Additionally, the regulatory risk seems like it could hamper efficient business plan rollout. The combination of the competitive threat and regulatory risk for PagaPago doesn't seem to outweigh the potential strengths and it will be turned down for this simulation.

---

[10]Bosire Boniface, "Kenyan Hospitals Slow to Comply with Waived Maternity Fee Directive," *AllAfrica* (June 5, 2013). http://allafrica.com/stories/201306060239 .html.

TABLE 2.3 A Multi-company SWOT Analysis Is Useful for Comparing Companies

	PagaPago	Solero	Mtoto Clinics
Strengths	Highly scalable product/service Deep existing mobile penetration	Product demand and economics are strong Unique ability to control distribution	Strong business case for standardized, tiered services Asset light model is beneficial to investors
Weaknesses	Potential for fee compression Challenging regulatory environment to work through	Complicated supply chain where problems could easily affect margins	Adequate property sourcing can be difficult Maintaining quality staff and services with limited budget
Opportunities	Integration of new industries to mobile payments Potential acquisition by bank or telecom	Roll out distribution system to other geographies Introduce new items into distribution system	Regional and country-wide expansion Potential acquisition by a larger healthcare enterprise
Threats	Highly competitive environment with well capitalized competitors Possible technological obsolescence	Technology risk with micro-grid and other innovative energy sources Numerous competitive companies	Competitive facilities such as government run clinics Larger healthcare companies offer low-cost pricing plans

The next investment to make a decision on is Solero. The main risk we examined was the innovative distribution strategy and whether it will be effective. Combined with distribution is the complexity of the value chain, which could lead to margin problems. However, the market for such products is clear and it has been demonstrated that low-income populations will pay for these products. The social impact for Solero is also very clear, with direct benefit upon purchase and return on investment for purchasers in about half a year. One additional benefit is that the investment can be made in USD, which eliminates direct foreign exchange risk. The risks in this case seem like they could be mitigated by proper due diligence and analysis. Given the excellent balance of business potential, social impact, and potentially manageable risks, we will move forward with analyzing Solero in more detail.

Unfortunately for Mtoto Clinics, it is now obvious that we have not chosen to move forward with it. The decision, though, is no less difficult than the other two. Mtoto has an excellent business plan with aspects such as asset light development and tiered services that present a strong business case. Ultimately, though, the scalability of the business seems like it can easily be hampered by difficulties sourcing the right properties, challenges with maintaining low cost, high-quality staff, and threats from regulatory change.

CONCLUDING THOUGHTS ON SOURCING AND SCREENING

While these analyses are ideal to work through, the realities of the market may require discretionary use. Those active in the impact investing industry know that on a sourcing and screening level, there is a scarcity of investments that present a strong business and social impact case. This causes many investors to chase the same investments and lower their sourcing and screening criteria. By no means is it advisable to simply abandon criteria and analyses for the sake of placing investment money, but at the same time, just because an investment doesn't quite pass all analyses with flying colors does not mean it should be screened away.

Investors must be able to know what risks are immediate deal breakers and what risks further analyses or investment structuring can mitigate. For deal breakers, there is no simple generic answer since different investors can all have differing risk tolerances. However, for risks that can be tolerated, they must be thoroughly understood and prepared for. As we progress with Solero through the investment process, we will start to pick apart individual risks and explore methods for properly structuring an investment.

CHAPTER 3

Investment Analysis and Valuation

While the company Solero made it through a rigorous sourcing and screening exercise, it is still at a nascent stage in the overall investment process. The next phase is to perform a bottom-up analysis of the company to understand business drivers and how the company would be expected to perform under various scenarios. This process leads investors to determining their opinion on the valuation of the company and investment structure, which is critical to the negotiating phase.

INFORMATION EXCHANGE

The inception of the *pre–due diligence* phase is marked by a deeper level of engagement between the investor and the potential investee. As the frequency and depth of information exchange increases, it is very important for both parties to understand the level of commitment each party is bringing to the process. Often, allusions to marriage are used for the relationship between an investor and an investee. This metaphor is actually fairly accurate, as leading up to the big commitment there is a period of courtship and dating. The further each party moves along the courtship, the more time and energy are invested in the relationship. However, for investors and investees, the consequences of breaking off the relationship can be more material than a broken heart.

Investors are looking to place their money in an efficient manner. The longer it takes to invest that money, the more drag there is on potential return. Exiting investments often take a number of years from the point of investment, so if it takes many years to place funds, then there is a reduction in return due to the time value of money. Particularly for fund-based investors that are using investors' money, there is even more pressure given management fees and whether funds have been called or not. These concepts will be explored further in Chapter 7.

Investees often get the short end of the stick, with delayed or failed investment potentially causing a serious stress on the business. Normally, the companies are small and inherently short on capital as they are fundraising. Engaging with an investor can be very time consuming with constant communication, providing information, creating analyses, answering questions, hosting meetings, and so on. The entire time, though, the company must maintain operations and continue to grow. As investments get delayed cash becomes more and more in need. If an investee works with only one investor and that investor backs out then the investee could be in a serious liquidity situation.

Realizing these consequences is important for both parties and is the impetus for transparency. Investors should determine what other financing options the investee is looking at, the timeline the investee has with those options, and the expected timeline for an investment from the investor. Investees should be able to understand where their investment stands with the investor and if engaged with a fund, the timeline and method for decisions with various committees within the fund.

NOTES FROM THE FIELD

An industry colleague of mine, who is the CEO of a successful renewable energy product company, called me one day asking advice about his situation with an investor. The investor had been significantly engaged with his company and made it through the investment process up to a signed term sheet.[1] However, the CEO was frustrated that they didn't seem to be moving forward, even though calls with the investor never resulted in a rejection. My advice to the CEO was to pin down the investor and ask specifically where the investor was in the investment process, whether anything else should be done by the CEO, and when to expect finalization. On the next call, the CEO did just that and found out that the investor had put the CEO's company as a secondary priority and was looking at other companies. The CEO had to lay off three employees the next day and back out of moving to a larger location, as he was expecting funds to come in soon. Luckily, the company found financing through other means, but it came dangerously close to having a severe liquidity crisis.

[1] The *term sheet phase* of the investment process will be discussed in detail in Chapter 5.

Nondisclosure Agreement

As two parties initiate and progress through the investment process, legal documentation is standard to prevent misunderstandings and also to protect parties' interests. To begin to assess a company for investment and build a bottom-up analysis, a significant amount of information, some very crucial and proprietary to the investee's company, must be exchanged. For that reason, the first document that many encounter is the nondisclosure agreement (NDA), otherwise known as a confidentiality agreement. It is an agreement between two parties to not disclose confidential information to third parties. Normally, an NDA is requested by an investee company at an early stage, as an investor does not often share sensitive information with the investee. While it seems relatively simple in concept, NDAs can cause controversy.

An investee has the more obvious need for an NDA. They will be providing private information to the investor. If their competitors or other parties seeking to start similar businesses obtain this information, it could be detrimental to the investee's ability to be competitive. In some cases, very crucial information like proprietary processes or technology will be disclosed, which should absolutely remain private.

An investor will rarely push for an NDA as they will usually not share proprietary information. Very thorough investees may request financial or performance information about the investor, which may drive the investor toward seeking an NDA.

The controversy surrounding an NDA typically boils down to the language and scope of the NDA. Investees will seek to make sure everything discussed and disseminated is protected for as long as possible. Occasionally, language that restricts the other party's activities given certain information finds its way into an NDA. Since investors normally look at many different companies they are reluctant to sign anything that could inhibit their ability to assess multiple investments. Some well-known, highly successful investors refuse to sign NDAs altogether.

A basic NDA has the following elements:

- Clarity on the specific parties involved. This sounds obvious, but the investor could be part of a fund that has outside committees or technically separate companies that they must share information with.
- Definition of what is considered proprietary and confidential.
- Agreement to not disclose the information to third parties.
- Term of the agreement.
- Possibly an intellectual property clause that makes it clear who owns the information that is exchanged.
- Standard contract language regarding the governing law, assignment, survivability, and so on.

Desktop Due Diligence: Financial and Operating Information

With an NDA in place, the investee will typically send over the prior year's financial statements and data sets that demonstrate how key drivers enable the business to generate profits. The term *desktop data* or *desktop due diligence* is encountered here because the information that is sent over is normally analyzed without onsite visits. The reason for this goes back to signaling the depth of the relationship and seriousness of resource commitment. An investor needs enough information to be able to take a deeper look at the viability of the investment, but should not consume significant resources to get that information at this stage.

Desktop due diligence can lead to deal breakers on the investor end, which will save time and resources if reviewed in an orderly manner. For example, the historical data may reveal weaker operating margins than previously thought. The margins projected into the future would then be lower and the expected returns could be below the investor's minimum threshold.[2] The investor could save time and not expend resources on onsite due diligence by ending the investment process. Similarly, an investee should not be burdened with organizing multiple onsite meetings only to find that an investor will turn it down based on reasons that can be garnered from prior financial statements or historical operating data.

Even though the parties must be careful about signaling commitment levels the desktop due diligence phase of the investment process requires a robust, bottom-up analysis. The term *bottom-up* refers to the idea that one should analyze the business from the most fundamental building blocks that build cash flow, assets, and eventually returns. This is opposed to a *top-down* analysis where cash flow and assets are projected from historical levels and ratios. Figure 3.1 depicts the difference between the two methods.

A bottom-up analysis is a critical first step at getting detailed insight into the company's operational capabilities and potential for growth and return. Additionally, this analysis forms the basis for multiple types of valuation methodologies, which are critical when it comes time to negotiate valuation.

---

[2]As we will see later in this chapter, there can be more interplay between an investor and investee on certain deal breakers. In the case where an investor believes there is less value in the company than originally anticipated the investee could lower the agreed on valuation or offer mechanisms such as liquidation preferences.

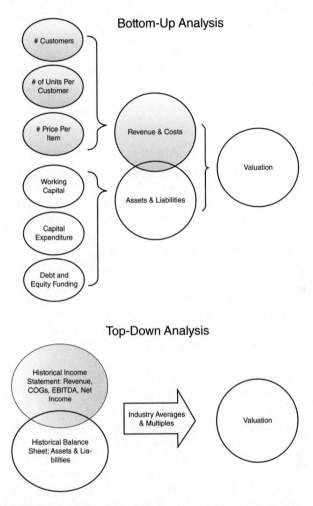

FIGURE 3.1 At the desktop due diligence stage, a more detailed bottom-up analysis is preferred over a top-down analysis.

SOLERO BOTTOM-UP ANALYSIS

To continue the simulated investment process with Solero, we will complete a bottom-up analysis using data the company would have provided: three years of historical financial statements, a data log of distributor sales, and a technical specification sheet of the products. This information, combined with other assumptions, will allow us to establish a bottom-up analysis that will lead to a base case and various stress scenarios. All of Solero's due-diligence documents can be found on the website in the Chapter 3 folder. It is recommended to open these and review them as they will be used in the following analyses.

Pricing Analysis

Understanding the composition of revenues and costs is an excellent place to start with any company, as it usually forms the basis for many stress scenarios. Two key data sets related to the revenue and cost build are the distributor log and the technical specification sheet. Let's take a moment to think about the different facets of a rural distribution business. At the core, there are items being manufactured (the solar lanterns), which are sold to distributors and eventually sold to consumers. At each stage, there can be different costs and revenues. For instance, Solero will purchase components from suppliers that will be used in the manufacturing process. The aggregation of those component costs, design costs, and labor create the cost of goods to be sold. Solero then must ship manufactured goods to various locations that will incur shipping, insurance, and taxes. These are further costs that must be tracked. A distributor will then purchase a lantern from Solero at the distributor cost. This is precisely where Solero monetizes and is a critical metric, since their gross margin (i.e., revenue less costs) is established here.

The distributors will then sell the lantern to rural consumers for a higher price and create their own margin. While Solero already monetized at the distributor level, it is important to be aware and track the consumer price to ensure that distributors are not attempting to overcharge and erode Solero's reputation. Additionally, the employment of distributors and their wages are an important part of Solero's social impact. Investors should be aware of whether the margins are fair and how they may evolve in the future. Figure 3.2 summarizes the cost and revenue chain.

Solero's Product Specification Sheet, which is available under the Chapter 3 folder of the website, helps us determine the manufacturing costs and sales prices. Open this sheet from the Chapter 3 folder. For each product type, there is a manufacturing cost, distributor price, and consumer price provided. This is an excellent starting point for costs and prices, but may later require breaking down into even more detail. For instance, we know the manufacturing price, but we may want to get even more detailed to understanding what parts of each product are driving the price. Are any components of the lantern a significant percentage of the total cost? Are there any concerns in the supply chain of these components?

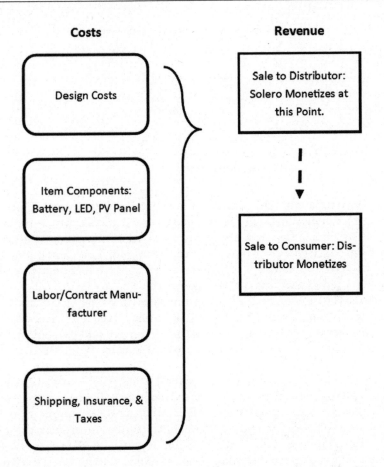

FIGURE 3.2 Solero's chain of costs and revenues from manufacturing to final consumer sale.

Also, one should always understand what other costs may be involved in getting the product to its final destination. For Solero's business, this involves shipping, insurance, and taxes. Given that these costs are not necessarily related to a per unit calculation nor unique to Solero's business, the information can be obtained from industry sources.

Volume Analysis

Knowing pricing information alone is only part of the story for a manufacturing and distribution company. Revenue is built from price and volume,

Identification	Region	Date of Sale	# of Mini Sold
A1	Region 1	1/10/2013	1
A1	Region 1	1/14/2013	1
A3	Region 1	1/21/2013	1
A3	Region 1	1/22/2013	1
A2	Region 1	1/29/2013	1
A2	Region 1	2/5/2013	1
A4	Region 1	2/6/2013	1

FIGURE 3.3 The distributor log provides sales information for different distributors.

with the distribution component conveying the volume expectations. To facilitate an understanding of Solero's distribution system, we are provided with a Distributor Log, that shows historical sales from different distributors by product type over time. Solero's Distributor Log can be found as the file Solero_Distributor_Log.xlsm in the Chapter 3 folder on the website. Figure 3.3 shows a section of the data provided.

In the Distributor Log, there are four fields per type of lantern: Identification, Region, Date of Sale, and # of Product Type Sold. The way this data can be interpreted is as follows: Distributor A1 sold two Solero Mini lanterns in January 2013 in Region 1 (one on January 10 and the other on January 14).

On the most basic level, we can see total volumes sold since 2013. With dates presented, we can also determine the monthly and yearly volumes sold. While this aggregate information is useful, to do a proper bottom-up analysis we want to understand how an individual distributor performs and how many distributors can be added per region over time. In theory, a new distributor may encounter a learning curve, whereby over time they learn how to sell the product more efficiently. We would therefore expect a distributor with more history to sell more products over time.

To help make sense of the information, an analysis of the Distributor Log data has been provided in the Chapter 3 folder on the website. Open the file Solero_Distributor_Log_Analysis.xlsm. Here we have manipulated the original Distributor Log information in order to create distributor level information. First, the information has been split by product type, with each product type moved to a separate sheet. Looking at the first sheet labeled "Mini," we can see the original distributor information has been copied with the addition of a few new columns that break apart the date. See Figure 3.4 to follow along with the analysis explanation.

Solero Distributor Log - Mini Sales

Identification	Region	Date of Sale	Day	Month	Year	# of Mini Sold
A1	Region 1	1/10/2013	10	1	2013	1
A1	Region 1	1/14/2013	14	1	2013	1
A3	Region 1	1/21/2013	21	1	2013	1
A3	Region 1	1/22/2013	22	1	2013	1
A2	Region 1	1/29/2013	29	1	2013	1
A2	Region 1	2/5/2013	5	2	2013	1
A4	Region 1	2/6/2013	6	2	2013	1
A6	Region 1	2/8/2013	8	2	2013	1
A6	Region 1	2/10/2013	10	2	2013	1

FIGURE 3.4 The data have been split by product type and the dates picked apart for flexibility in aggregation.

Next, an area has been created to calculate distributor level statistics over time. This area seeks to answer the following questions:

1. How many active distributors[3] are there? How has the number of active distributors evolved over time?
2. Is there a sales pattern for new distributors versus seasoned distributors?
3. Over time how many of each product are distributors able to sell?

These questions can be answered by first calculating the number of sales per month for each unique distributor. Figure 3.5a shows an excerpt from the Mini sheet starting in column K.

Notice that the data are organized by each unique distributor, with the number of sales per month. We must be very careful with how we think about organizing the data as we want to be able to build off the data for a projection model. Organizing the data in this way allows us to see how many active distributors there are and the aggregate number of lanterns sold each period. We will come back to the quantity sold, but right now we should calculate how many active distributors there were each period. This can be done by using a count function for each period, for each distributor that had at least one sale in a period. Figure 3.5b is a cut of the region starting in cell K132 on the Mini sheet that shows the total number of active distributors.

---

[3]In rural distribution businesses it is important to differentiate between "active" and "inactive" distributors and to understand the definition of active. In some cases, it can be a distributor that has sold a product in the last six months, one year, and so on. It is much better to have a conservative criteria for active distributors by keeping the time frame to one or two months.

Pd Ct		1/1/2013	2/1/2013	3/1/2013	4/1/2013	5/1/2013	6/1/2013
		1	2	3	4	5	6
		2013	2013	2013	2013	2013	2013
A1	1	2	3	3	3	4	4
A2	1	1	2	2	3	3	4
A3	1	2	3	4	4	5	5
A4	2	0	2	3	3	3	4
A5	2	0	1	2	2	3	3
A6	2	0	2	3	4	4	5

FIGURE 3.5a The number of sales of Mini lanterns by distributor, each month.

Active Distributor	3	6	10	15	19	23

FIGURE 3.5b Total active distributors for example.

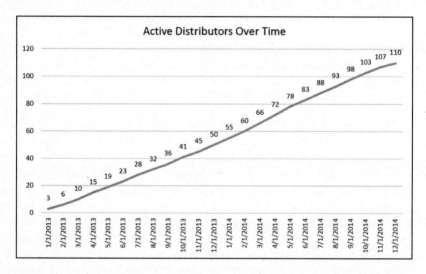

FIGURE 3.5c Active distributors over time, Jan. 1, 2013 to Dec. 1, 2014.

Looking at the formula for these numbers, you can see that this counts the number of distributors who had at least one sale. If we project this out as a chart, as shown in Figure 3.5c, we can see that there were a total of 110 active distributors after two years of operation. We also know that these were all from Region 1. This helps us understand how a particular region may develop as new regions are entered into.

While the number of active distributors is an important component to the revenue build, the next step down is looking at how an individual distributor would be expected to perform. After a distributor decides to work for

ID	0	1	2	3	4	5	6
A1		2	3	3	3	4	4
A2		1	2	2	3	3	4
A3		2	3	4	4	5	5
A4		2	3	3	3	4	4
A5		1	2	2	3	3	4
A6		2	3	4	4	5	5

FIGURE 3.6 The distributor sales are now reorganized so they represent the sales in the month since starting work for Solero.

Solero they would exhibit what can be termed a *sales performance curve*. At first, the distributor would sell a low quantity of the product. As she figures out the best sales techniques, she would begin to sell larger and larger quantities. At a certain point, she would hit saturation where sales would remain at an average level. Depending on whether the product becomes outdated or if the distributor focuses efforts on other Solero products, sales could go down. Additionally, at some point a distributor may decide to leave Solero and do something else. This distributor attrition is very important, as the replacement distributor would be expected to start at the beginning of the sales performance curve.

In order to look at individual distributor performance and create a sales performance curve from the time a distributor begins working for Solero, we have to reorganize the historical data to see how each distributor performs from the first period he or she began selling. This means that we will want to see each distributor's performance, one month from starting, two months from starting, and so on. Then we can calculate the average performance for a distributor in the first month, the second month, and so on.

In the example distributor log analysis workbook (Solero_Distributor _Log_Analysis.xlsm), we can see in cell O136 the reorganized data. The mechanics of how this is done can be seen in the formula for cell O136. Figure 3.6 shows a section of the data.

We can then average the number of sales for each period. The average is calculated starting in cell O247 on the same sheet. The graph of the average sales performance curve for a distributor is shown in Figure 3.7.

Once we know how an individual distributor would sell product, the number of distributors that can be originated each period in a region, and the product economics, we can start setting up a method to project sales and cash flow. The financial statements have not been forgotten about, but will be used later in the projection model. At this point, we should open the Solero Projection Model, located in the Chapter 3 folder on the website (Solero_Model.xlsm). This is a professional level corporate valuation/operations analysis model that is set up for Solero. In the next few sections, we will show how the historical data integrate with this

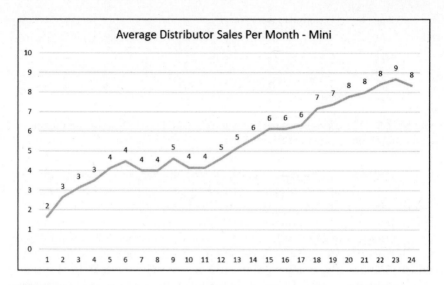

FIGURE 3.7   Each distributor is expected to sell the Solero Mini in the quantities shown over a two-year period.

model, how projections are created and valuation calculated, the process for establishing a base case valuation, alterations to the base case for stress sensitivities, and finally the valuation range and investment structure that we would be comfortable entering into with the investee.

THE SOLERO PROJECTION MODEL

At first glance the Solero Projection Model (*projection model*) can be intimidating given the size, volume of data, and calculations. It is important throughout this section for a reader to have this financial model open as there will be a number of references to the file. A reader should be able to move between the text and the model easily to follow along. To help facilitate movement through the model, we should take a moment to get an overview of how the projection model works. Figure 3.8 depicts a map of the projection model's major components and connections.

The Inputs sheet is the main sheet where assumptions about the company are stored. There are additional inputs on the Vectors sheet, with the differentiating factor being that the Vectors sheet stores curve-based assumptions or an assumption that changes over time. The combination of the Inputs and Vectors sheet create the production curves for each distributor, the distribution system as a whole, and the combination of all items

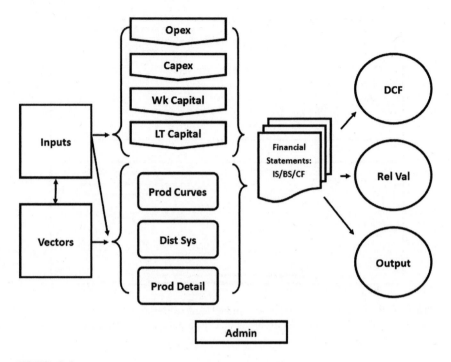

FIGURE 3.8 An overview of the Solero Projection Model.

that lead to detailed product sales data. At the same time we need to make assumptions about how the company is funded and how it manages its business. This is done on the Opex, Capex, Wk Capital, and LT Capital sheets. The combination of those sheets plus the earlier ones on production provide enough information to create a projected income statement, balance sheet, and cash flow statement. From there we have enough information to establish a *discounted cash flow* (DCF) valuation, a *relative valuation*, and a summary sheet labeled Output.

Inputs: Setting the Model Up for Flexibility

One of the particularly elegant attributes of a highly developed model is the ability to quickly test out scenarios. Since there are many parts of a business that contribute toward value, having the ability to quickly set up scenarios is a major advantage. A very efficient method is to store all assumption data for every scenario on the Inputs sheet and reference it using a scenario number. As we get to new scenarios we will discuss the content and reasoning behind the scenario, but for now we should just understand that the Inputs sheet

Scenario:	1						
Base Case			Scenario 1 is selected populating the data from Scenario 1 to the active column				
				Selected		Scenario	
Scenario Number				1		1	2
Scenario Name				Base Case		Base Case	Increased COGs
Product 1		Solero Mini					
		Initial Manufacture Cost - USD	$	5.00	$	5.00 $	5.00
		Annual Man. Cost Inflation		1.00%		1.00%	2.00%

Scenario:	2						
Increased COGs			Scenario 2 is selected populating the data from Scenario 2 to the active column				
				Selected		Scenario	
Scenario Number				2		1	2
Scenario Name				Increased COGs		Base Case	Increased COGs
Product 1		Solero Mini					
		Initial Manufacture Cost - USD	$	5.00	$	5.00 $	5.00
Notice the change ➡		Annual Man. Cost Inflation		2.00%		1.00%	2.00%

FIGURE 3.9 Changing the scenario number loads different information to the active column. Notice that inflation has increased per the scenario assumptions for the Increased COGs scenario.

lets us select a scenario by entering the scenario number in cell C3 on the Inputs sheet. This populates data from the selected scenario into column F on the Inputs sheet, which is connected to the rest of the model. Only column F flows through to the other sheets, so cell C3 controls what is in column F and column F controls what is being run through the model. Figure 3.9 shows the difference on the Inputs sheet when the scenario number is changed.

Globals

Now that we have a basic operational understanding, we will start working through the projection model to explain conceptual and mechanical components. The first place to start is the top of the Inputs sheet in cell B11. This Inputs section is labeled "Globals" since the inputs here have very fundamental effects on the model as a whole. The relevant inputs with explanations include:

- *Period 0 Date:* This input sets what can be thought of as the current period. One period after this date is the first projection period. One period before this date is the last historical period.

- *Currency 1:* The primary currency of the model. This is particularly important to keep track of for impact investing, where, as we saw in Chapter 2, many business models have direct and indirect exposures to foreign currencies whose movements can impact returns.
- *Currency 2:* If another currency influences the model it should be identified here.
- *FX Vector:* On the Vectors sheet there could be multiple exchange rate assumptions. This identifies the foreign exchange vector that is to be used.
- *Corporate Tax Rate*: Companies as a whole are generally taxed at a standard rate depending on domicile.
- *Capital Gains Tax:* Depending on the region and form of investment, an investor may have to pay a capital gains tax upon exit or dividend receipt. This assumption stores the tax rate that an investor may need to pay, which reduces net return.

Income Statement: Revenue and Cost Build

Perhaps the easiest way to conceptualize a company's financial viability in the future is to look at it from an accounting point of view, with the two most important analyses being a projected income statement and a balance sheet. The income statement seeks to project out cash flow over a given time period. That cash flow, though, can be achieved in many different ways, by leveraging up a company, investing heavily in capital expenditures, and so on. The cash flow that the income statement shows is produced with a certain capital structure in mind. This capital structure can change over time and can be represented by projecting out a balance sheet. The income statement and balance sheet interact with one another to give a cohesive picture of the firm's finances. We will first start with the income statement and then move to the balance sheet.

Moving down to the Inputs sheet to cell B19, we can see product-related inputs. We should lay out the inputs that describe the product economics. Earlier from the Product Specification sheet we saw basic costs and pricing. We could also source from the company or third parties the estimated shipping, insurance, and tax. Additionally, costs normally inflate over time. The concern with cost inflation is that the ability to raise prices may be constrained by price elasticity. Flexibility on each cost and price's inflation rate is important to build in. Figure 3.10 shows the inputs for the first product.

Scrolling down to row 74 on the Inputs sheet, a model user can see that product economics and inflation rates have been created for each of the three existing product types and a fourth new product, which we will discuss later in this chapter.

Revenue & Cost Build

	Product 1	Solero Mini		
		Initial Manufacture Cost - USD	$	5.00
		Annual Man. Cost Inflation		1.00%
		Initial Shipping Expense - USD	$	0.50
		Annual Shipping Inflation		1.00%
		Initial Taxes - INR	₹	50
		Annual Tax Inflation		0.00%
		Initial Distributor Price - INR	₹	450
		Annual Dist. Price Inflation		1.50%
		Initial Distributor Expense - INR	₹	50
		Annual Dist. Exp. Inflation		0.50%
		Initial Consumer Price - INR	₹	550
		Annual Cons. Price Inflation		1.00%

FIGURE 3.10 Cost and price economics and inflation rates should be entered for each product.

Just as we analyzed historical volumes after pricing, we should lay out volume based inputs for distributors. Starting in row 77 on the Inputs sheet we can see the assumptions for a distributor. On the Inputs sheet we can build a sales performance curve for a distributor by starting with an initial sales volume, factoring in an annual growth rate, and tapering the growth at an expected stabilization period. The curve that is created from this should be based on the data from the historical analysis.

With cost, price, and volume inputs entered, calculations can then be entered to build out the expected cost and revenue over time. These calculations begin with the Prod Curves sheet, where each product type has a cost and pricing curve over time. A snapshot of this sheet is shown in Figure 3.11. This sheet is important for calculating cost and pricing evolution over time, depending on the scenario being run.

A critical element to be aware of that interacts with the pricing is the foreign exchange curve. We can see from the labeling that some of Solero's costs are in USD, while much of their revenue is in INR. Margins can be

Product Curves

		#	1							
		Name	Solero Mini							

Period	Date	Manufacturing Cost - USD	Shipping Expense - USD	Import Taxes - INR	Distributor Price - INR	Distributor Expenses - INR	Consumer Price - INR	Distributor Margin	Corporate Margin
0	12/31/2014	5.00	0.50	50.00	450	50	550	9.09%	15.56%
1	1/31/2015	5.00	0.50	50.00	451	50	550	9.06%	15.60%
2	2/28/2015	5.01	0.50	50.00	451	50	551	9.03%	15.64%
3	3/31/2015	5.01	0.50	50.00	452	50	551	9.00%	15.69%
4	4/30/2015	5.02	0.50	50.00	452	50	552	8.97%	15.73%
5	5/31/2015	5.02	0.50	50.00	453	50	552	8.94%	15.78%

FIGURE 3.11 The Prod Curves sheet lays out projected cost and pricing data.

Geographic Expansion (Date Based)							
Region 1 - Base	Region 2 - Base	Region 3 - Base	DM - Base	Region 1 - Stress	Region 2 - Stress	Region 3 - Stress	DM - Stress
110	0	0	20	110	0	0	20
115	0	0	22	115	0	0	21
120	0	0	24	120	0	0	22
125	0	0	26	125	0	0	24
130	0	0	28	130	0	0	26

FIGURE 3.12 The geographic expansion is a projection of the number of distributors per region.

compressed depending on foreign exchange assumptions and will definitely be a scenario to run and understand impact. Since we may want to try out multiple foreign exchange rate assumptions we should store them on the Vectors sheet. These can be seen by going to the Vectors sheet (columns E and F). Column D is the currently selected foreign exchange vector assumption, which is controlled by the value in cell F15 on the Inputs sheet. With this setup, we can quickly toggle between foreign exchange assumptions.

The Prod Curves sheet combined with foreign exchange vectors project out pricing and margins over time, but volume expectations are reserved primarily for the Dist Sys sheet (columns G, H, and I). On that sheet, the most macro level of projection is a region, where there is an option to project out the number of distributors that are expected to sell in a region. Geographic expansion is normally a fairly uncertain variable and one that should be sensitized. To facilitate the sensitivities we create vectors on the Vectors sheet (columns H through O) to store possible geographic roll out scenarios. The geographic scenario that is active is selected by the model user from rows 88 through 92 on the Inputs sheet. Figure 3.12 shows a section of the geographic expansion from the Vectors sheet.

Back on the Dist Sys sheet there are a number of sections that should be explained:

> *New Distributors*: The geographic expansion is projected through a cumulative count of distributors. However, given the sales performance curve described earlier, where distributors are expected to get better over time, it is important to know the count of new distributors each period (columns K, L, and M). This is just a simple subtraction of the current period less the prior period. Note that theoretically the cumulative number of distributors could decrease, in which case an alteration of the formula would be necessary, as there can never be a negative count for new distributors. Also, be aware that certain sections on the sheet are "date based" meaning

that rows refer to the dates in column C, while other sections on the sheet are "period based" meaning that rows refer to the period in column B. A date is a specific point in time, while a period can reset depending on the reference point. The labeling in row 5 describes whether a section is date or period based.

Distributor Efficiency: For volume assumptions thus far, we know the number of distributors expected per region. The next step down from that level is how much of each product each distributor is expected to sell each period after being hired (columns O, P, Q). Recall that this was analyzed historically, so it will be interesting to see what the base case future assumption is as we sensitize this input later.

Distributor Attrition: In theory, we could build in attrition into the cumulative number of distributors, but this doesn't completely capture the concept that some distributors will leave after time. Distributor churn requires that new distributors be sourced and trained. Not only is there additional cost in sourcing distributors, but new distributors reset on the sales performance curve and do not sell the volumes that an experienced distributor does. Columns S, T, and U have functionality that creates an assumption for the period a new distributor will leave the company. The distributor attrition vectors are stored on the Vectors sheet (columns Q to V) and selected using the Inputs sheet (rows 94 to 97).

While there are still more data on the Dist Sys sheet, we should jump to the Prod Detail sheet to get a glimpse at how all of the data are coming together. The Prod Detail sheet is laid out with each future month having its own row. Each month is representative of when a set of new distributors gets hired. We can see, then, the columns are the periods after each set of distributors gets hired. The reason for this setup is to take advantage of the bottom-up analysis's level of detail; in particular the sales performance curve. Volumes being sold for each product start in row 9 on this sheet. We can see that the calculation takes the number of distributors for the given month, multiplied by the number of sales based on the value from the sales performance curve for the period. This layered method creates the total volume expected for each date in the future. A snapshot of the Prod Detail sheet is shown in Figure 3.13.

An important concept that is factored into the Prod Detail sheet is attrition. In distribution models, particularly rural ones where individuals most likely have multiple jobs, salespeople often leave the business. We see the

Product Details Over Time

Product 1 - Total Volume

Period		0	1	2	3	4	5
	Date	12/31/2014	1/31/2015	2/28/2015	3/31/2015	4/30/2015	5/31/2015
0	12/31/2014	770.00	834.17	903.68	978.99	1,060.57	1,148.95
1	1/31/2015	-	35.00	37.92	41.08	44.50	48.21
2	2/28/2015	-	-	35.00	37.92	41.08	44.50
3	3/31/2015	-	-	-	35.00	37.92	41.08
4	4/30/2015	-	-	-	-	35.00	37.92
5	5/31/2015	-	-	-	-	-	35.00

FIGURE 3.13 The Prod Detail sheet takes in many of the assumptions to calculate volumes, costs, and revenue.

ability to select an attrition assumption from the Inputs sheet on rows 94 to 97. The actual attrition assumptions are stored on the Vectors sheet in columns Q to V and referenced on the Dist Sys sheet in columns S to U. These assumptions represent the number of months that a distributor is expected to stay active. The real functionality of these assumptions takes place in the Prod Detail sheet in the volume sections (starting on row 9), where the formula checks the starting date of each row against the number of periods that have transpired and cuts off volumes if the number of periods exceeds the attrition assumption. This would effectively cut off all sales after the attrition date, as the distributor is assumed to have stopped selling.

Once we know the volumes each period, we can then project out the costs and revenue. Still on the Prod Detail sheet, jump down to row 137. This section takes the previously calculated volumes for the periods and multiplies them by the appropriate manufacturing cost on the Prod Curves sheet (column F). We can now see how complicated the rural distribution business has become. There are constantly evolving assumptions for the number of distributors, the efficiency of each distributor, and the cost and pricing assumptions. The method employed here attempts to bring order to the chaos.

To finish off the Prod Detail sheet there are the following sections:

Shipping Expense and Taxes: Similar to calculating the manufacturing cost, but for shipping and taxes. This starts on row 265 on the Prod Detail sheet and references column G on the Prod Curves sheet. Notice, though, that the formula on the Prod Detail sheet for this section is adjusted for the fact that shipping is in USD, but import tax is in INR. The latter part of the formula references the Vector sheet to convert INR to USD.

Revenue from Distributor: Starting in row 393 on the Prod Detail sheet is the calculation for revenue. Similar to import taxes, the pricing is in INR and must be converted to USD.

Distributor Margin: The distributor margin is calculated starting on row 521 of the Prod Detail sheet. It is also converted to USD.

These sections are done for each product type. For example, on the Prod Detail sheet if we jump to column DW we can see the calculations for Product 2, the Solero Standard. The revenue from the three products that we have examined: Mini, Standard, and XL (calculated on row 514 of the Prod Detail sheet) are then added together and summarized on the Inc Stmt sheet, starting in row 12. The cost of goods sold (COGs) and shipping and tax expense is also added up on the Inc Stmt sheet and referenced in a similar manner from the Prod Detail sheet. This process forms the basis for calculating a very important figure, the gross margin of the distributors.

Gross margin is important because it is the starting point for profitability. Officially, the gross margin formula can be expressed as a dollar amount or a percentage:

$$\text{Gross margin} = \text{Sales} - \text{Cost of goods sold}$$

or

$$\text{Gross margin percentage} = (\text{Sales} - \text{Cost of goods sold}) / \text{Sales}$$

Firms try to maximize gross margin in a couple of ways—either by increasing prices beyond cost inflation or by reducing costs. Typically for a startup company, the easiest method is to reduce costs per unit of sales, since the inception of a business normally has many inefficiencies.

Moving down the income statement, starting in row 21, there is a section that seems repetitive. The section is different, though, as it is for calculating revenue and costs for the fourth product type called *DM* or developed markets, which is an expected sales channel where Solero sells directly to consumers through online and special order. Given that there are no distributors for these types of sales, the calculations are done differently. The calculations work with assumptions on the Inputs sheet, row 62, and the Vectors sheet, columns K and O. There are also product economics on the Prod Curves sheet starting in column AJ and extending through column AQ. However, there is no calculation or interaction necessary on the Dist Sys or Prod Detail sheets as the revenue calculation is done directly from the volumes in either columns K or O and the pricing on the Prod Curves sheet. With the DM revenue and costs we have projected out the gross margin expectations for Solero for the given scenario.

NOTES FROM THE FIELD

A number of social enterprises have attempted to supplement their revenue by selling their products in developed markets. Solar lanterns as an example are excellent for camping or occasional household use. Developed market sales, though, need to be approached very differently than rural markets. One solar lantern company that I worked with had limited success in developed markets, largely because the product marketing design that appealed to rural customers did not work for developed market purchasers. Board-level discussions ensued on whether it was worth making a specific developed markets version that would be accepted by major retailers. Going down this path can be risky for a company that has found success in a rural client base, as it would have to focus time and corporate resources on the developed market. Additionally, there could be social mission drift if a majority of the business shifted to developed markets.

Operating Expenditures (Opex)

While gross margin shows us the immediate profitability of selling a product, there are still many more costs incurred running the business. If we move up a level from the granularity of the distributor level, we could conceptualize the regional level as the next unit. For a rural distribution network that is expanding into new regions, there is a layer of regional management and marketing that is required. Hiring these managers and buying advertising media are costs that are de-linked from the product sales. For this reason, we have to project these costs separately and factor them into the analysis.

Jumping back to the Inputs sheet, to row 118, we can see that there are regional costs, both fixed and variable. The idea behind bifurcating the two costs is that some costs will be fixed, such as regional marketing, while others will scale more closely with regional growth, such as local management costs. Fixed costs are easier to integrate as they can be created off of a schedule of expected costs. This is done per region starting in row 122 of the Inputs sheet.

Variable costs are more challenging in that they are typically expressed as percentages of revenue. These percentages can change over time and are normally increased for inflation. One of the critical analyses that an investor must look at is whether the cost inflation can be passed on through to pricing.

Especially for a social enterprise where customers are very price inelastic, the ability to counteract cost inflation is important to understand. To do this, we lay out initial percentages and cost inflation expectations on the Inputs sheet (rows 118 to 120 and rows 105 to 116).

Both the fixed costs and the variable costs initial assumptions and inflation rates are evolved over time on the Dist Sys sheet. In column W we can see that annual inflation expectations are converted to monthly figures, columns Z to AB start with the initial percentages and then use the monthly inflation rates to determine the growing variable cost percentages each period, and, finally, columns AD to AF lay out the monthly fixed expenses per region.

An entirely separate sheet named Opex is created to calculate the actual costs in dollar terms each period. This is done by taking the monthly information from the Dist Sys sheet and multiplying the variable cost percentage by the expected revenue for all regional products, and also directly referencing the fixed costs for each period. Rows 10 to 22 of the Opex sheet store these calculations and summarize the total regional operating expenditures.

The next level of decreased granularity, from the regional level, is the corporate level. There are costs associated with the core operations of the entire company and the executive management running it. In particular, during a venture stage these costs can represent a large part of the total cost of the company and are probably a major reason why the company is fundraising. The promoter's salary, travel expenses, other professional staff expenses, and office expenses can quickly add up.

Corporate costs are primarily fixed, but there can be elements that are variable. For instance, as the business scales there could be more auditing requirements and administrative functions that depend on the level of business. Both the fixed and variable cost assumptions are laid out on the Inputs sheet in rows 164 to 171. These costs are then carried over and calculated on the Opex sheet in rows 24 to 32. The sum of all operating expenditures is totaled on the Opex sheet in rows 34 to 36 and then referenced on the Inc Stmt sheet on rows 31 to 34. A section of the Opex sheet is shown in Figure 3.14 on the following page. A common metric to calculate after doing this is the operating expense margin, which is the total percentage of operating expenditures relative to sales. We will see later that this should reduce over time as economies of scale are achieved.

Once we have the operating expenditures complete, we can calculate the earnings before interest, taxes, depreciation, and amortization or EBITDA. EBITDA is one of the most important calculations to understand over the projection period, since it represents the company's ability for the product or service to generate profit, irrespective of the capital structure. It can be thought of as a pure metric of the profitability of the product or service. This

Corporate Cost				
Rent	3,000	3,000	3,000	3,000
Executive Compensation	8,000	8,000	8,000	8,000
Office Compensation	6,000	6,000	6,000	6,000
Travel	4,000	4,000	4,000	4,000
Add'l Office Costs	4,000	4,000	4,000	4,000
Total Fixed Corporate Costs	25,000	25,000	25,000	25,000
Total Variable Corporate Costs	748	837	933	1,037
Total Variable Costs	3,243	3,628	4,045	4,494
Total Fixed Costs	26,250	27,083	27,083	27,083
Total Opex	29,493	30,712	31,128	31,578

FIGURE 3.14 The operating expenditures of a new company can be substantial and must be projected separately from sales.

is why it is frequently used with multiples for relative valuation. The standard formulas for EBITDA are:

EBITDA: Sales revenue – Cost of goods sold – Operating expenses

or

$$\text{EBITDA \%:} \quad \frac{(\text{Sales revenue} - \text{Cost of goods sold} - \text{Operating expenses})}{\text{Sales revenue}}$$

Unfortunately, many companies with great products or services can generate excellent EBITDA, but underperform because of poor capital structures. The way a company funds its large capital expenditures and working capital, through debt and/or equity, can make or break a company. For this reason it is important to project out a balance sheet of the company. For a bottom-up analysis we will break apart the balance sheet components in detail, lay out the assumptions, and project them over time.

Capital Expenditures and Depreciation

The easiest place to start calculating balance sheet–related items is to estimate the capital expenditures of a company. Capital expenditures are usually large, capital intensive expenditures that a company must invest in, in order to maintain or grow operations. Often, investment rounds will be done in order to fund capital expenditures, thus making the analysis very important. For instance, in the Solero example, at some point the company may require specialized manufacturing equipment. This is a very expensive expenditure that may need financing, as we will see later in this chapter. Additionally, capital expenditures are in real assets, which depreciate over time. This depreciation provides a tax benefit to companies and should be integrated into the analysis.

As with most of the other sections, the Inputs sheet controls the capital expenditure assumptions. In the Solero model, we can see starting in row 173 a section for capital expenditures. To keep it simple, there is one capital expenditure for an injection molding machine. The most critical elements in order to project out the financial effects are the cost of the machine, the useful life of the machine, and the salvage value or how much the machine will be worth at its useful life. Also, the anticipated time of purchase is required in order to fit the expenditure in the right time period. Figure 3.15 shows the inputs required for the injection-molding machine.

Once the assumptions have been created, an effective method is to lay out each major capital expenditure over time and calculate the associated depreciation schedule right beneath it. This method is done on the Capex sheet in rows 10 to 20. The sum of the capital expenditures and depreciation can then be referenced in the balance sheet. This is done in a straightforward manner on the Bal Sht sheet. In rows 18 to 20 we can see Gross PP&E (property, plant, and equipment), Accumulated Depreciation, and Net PP&E. The total capital expenditures add to Gross PP&E, which is a cumulative figure. Periodic depreciation is accumulated and reported as Accumulated Depreciation on the balance sheet. The difference between Gross PP&E and Accumulated Depreciation is known as Net PP&E. Only when assets are sold or they hit their useful life will the gross PP&E and associated accumulated depreciation decrease. Otherwise, the net PP&E is calculated and counted as a long-term asset.

The income statement is also affected by capital expenditures, through depreciation. Looking at row 38 on the Inc Stmt sheet we can see that depreciation is deducted from EBITDA. This is done because most accounting methods allow depreciation to be removed from earnings for tax purposes. Although not a cash item, depreciation reduces the effective pretax income for the period and tax expense saved. With depreciation removed EBITDA becomes earnings before interest and taxes (EBIT).

There are two concepts related to capital expenditures and depreciation that are not demonstrated in the Solero model: maintenance capital expenditures and intangibles. Maintenance capital expenditures are costs that occur

Capital Expenditures

Injection Molding Machine	10,000
Useful Life	4
Salvage Value	1,500
Acquisition Date	1/31/2016

FIGURE 3.15 Capital expenditures must be accounted for and funded properly.

every period, which are required to keep the business running. An example might be a company that builds and sells biogas generators, which are relatively large-scale pieces of equipment. The machinery used to produce the generators would require investment each year to maintain functionality. This investment would usually be depreciated over time.

Additionally, some investments are not tangible, which is the definition of an intangible item. These could be purchases, acquisitions, or creation of patents or trademarks. Intangibles also lose value over time like capital expenditures, but instead of the term depreciation, amortization is used. Amortization would be removed from EBITDA similar to depreciation in order to calculate EBIT.

Working Capital

As we pick apart the components of the valuation and move through the balance sheet a number of items fall under the concept of working capital. The standard definition of working capital is the difference between current assets and current liabilities. However, the true understanding required when analyzing working capital is that it elucidates the immediate cash requirements of a company. For early stage ventures that are burning cash each month, this calculation and understanding is paramount.

It's easiest to break down the components of working capital to truly understand its importance. On the asset side, only short-term or current assets are incorporated. Using the Solero example, we can see from the Bal Sht (rows 12 to 14) that there are three current assets: cash, accounts receivable, and inventory. The cash account is typically ignored for working capital purposes, as it can be a product of many parts of the business that are not regular or for modeling purposes used as a catch all account in projections. Therefore, non-cash working capital is usually calculated.

Accounts receivable is one of the main current assets that are part of working capital. Receivables are generated when someone purchases an item or service, but does not pay for it immediately. While sales are clearly a good thing for a company, not receiving payment is a problem since the company must operate and costs have and will accrue. Therefore, the greater the percentage of sales in accounts receivable and the longer the expectation is for payment, the more constrained the business becomes. Increases in accounts receivable from period to period reduce working capital, while decreases in accounts receivable from period to period indicate customers paying down their accounts and an increase in working capital.

The inventory account on the balance sheet is another critical component to working capital. The dollar amount in that account represents all finished goods, work in process, and raw materials. Increases in inventory from period to period mean that more items have been produced, which costs money. This reduces working capital. Decreases in inventory from period to period mean that items have been sold and working capital increases.[4]

On the liability side of the Bal Sht we can see two items in row 29 and 30: short-term debt and accounts payable. Short term debt is similar to cash in that it can be part of many parts of the business and is a catch all on the liability side of a projection model. Accounts payable, though, is a working capital item from the liability side. When a company buys a good or service without immediately paying for it a payable is generated. Increases in payable accounts each month indicate less cash being used and is an increase in working capital. Decreases in payable accounts each period indicate cash has been used to pay off the payable and is a reduction in working capital.

To summarize the movements of working capital, we will walk through a quick example and how it affects the cash of a company. Figure 3.16 is used for reference in this example.

The example in Figure 3.16 shows a situation where accounts receivable is increasing, which means the company is selling items, but not receiving cash. Inventory is increasing so the company is producing more goods than are being sold, which requires cash. Accounts payable has decreased, meaning that the company has paid suppliers, which requires cash. The net effect between these two periods is a reduction of $45 of cash. To operate from period 1 to period 2, the company would need to draw down $45 from either its cash reserves, short-term debt, or get equity funding. When companies run out of sources of cash and have negative working capital changes, illiquid situations occur and bankruptcy can be imminent.

Current Assets	Period 1	Period 2	Change in Cash
Accounts Receivable	100	125	-25
Inventory	50	60	-10
Current Liabilities			
Accounts Payable	45	35	-10
Working Capital	105	150	-45

FIGURE 3.16 Working capital is calculated by taking the difference of current assets and liabilities. The change in working capital is important from a cash perspective.

---

[4]Do not always assume that a decrease in inventory means that a sale has occurred. Occasionally, there could be extraordinary circumstances such as theft, spoiled inventory, or even sales that were later returned.

Working Capital Timing and the Cash Conversion Cycle

An interesting aspect of each of the working capital items, accounts receivable, inventory, and accounts payable, is that they are balance sheet items linked to income statement items (revenue and cost of goods sold) and have a time element. For instance, while the accounts receivable account is reported periodically on the balance sheet, the derivation of the accounts receivable is from sales. The time element is caused by the fact that there is a measurable time lag between the generation of the receivables sale and the payment of the associated receivable. Similarly, inventory is captured by cost of goods sold on the income statement and after production can be sold over a certain period of time. Lastly, accounts payable is linked to cost of goods sold and has a time element similar to a receivable.

Parsing time into days is the standard for working capital–related accounts. For accounts receivable, this is called days sales outstanding (DSO), for inventory it is called days inventory outstanding (DIO), and for accounts receivable it is called days payable outstanding (DPO). The standard approach is to look historically at the day counts for each working capital account and project out in the future toward the industry average. For instance, if a company currently takes 100 days on average for DSO, and the average industry DSO is 50 days, then it would not be unreasonable to expect the company to project a reduction of 10 days per year for five years.

Going back to the Solero example, we should do the same thing and check the historical values for each working capital account to see how that matches up with the projections. This is now the time to utilize the prior financial statements of the company. Open the Excel file that contains the financial statement for 2014, Solero_FS_2014.xlsx, within the Chapter 3 folder on the book's website. Let's calculate the DSO for 2014 by using the following formula:

$$\text{Days sales outstanding} = (\text{Accounts receivable}/\text{Total credit sales})$$

$$* \text{ Number of days in year}$$

A few points to make on this are that total credit sales may not be available, so often total sales are used. The number of days in a year is frequently 365 unless a special convention is being used. For 2014, we have the following values: accounts receivable 21,532 (cell C7 of the Balance Sheet), revenue from distributor sales 75,732 (cell B5 of the Income Statement sheet), and 365 for an actual year day count. This produces the formula (21,532 / 75,732) * 365 = 103.78 days. We should do this for each prior year that we have data, but we can see quickly that in 2013 there were very few receivable sales and in 2012 there were none. Still, we have a starting point of roughly 100 days and can go off that.

Now, open the Solero projection model and go to X4 on the Vectors sheet. Here we see the base case projection for DSO starting at 60 days and dropping to 45 days over time. This is fairly aggressive, but not uncommon to see if the company provided the base case projections. Companies will often argue that as they gain experience selling their product they are learning how to minimize the time it takes to collect receivables, maximize their payables, and decrease the number of days items stay in inventory. We will see later in this chapter as we go through stress cases that we might not believe the company's assumptions and will try more conservative ones to see the potential effect on valuation. We can repeat the process done for DSO for DIO and DPO. Keep in mind, though, that for inventory and payables, while the formula is similar, the denominator should be the cost of goods sold and not sales. The Vectors sheet contains assumptions for each of these over time in columns Y and Z.

While the Inputs are useful to see expectations, the real value is how the days are used for future projection. Since we know the calculations behind the day counts from the historical analysis, it's not too difficult to modify the formula so we can take a day count and produce a value. Go to the Wk Capital sheet in the model, where all of the working capital calculations are stored. We can see in row 11 that the DSO is referenced from the Vectors sheet, in row 12 the total credit sales are referenced from the Inc Stmt sheet, and row 13 contains the important calculation for converting DSO to a value. The formula for DSO can be modified to:

$$\text{Accounts receivable} = \frac{(\text{Days sales outstanding} * \text{Total credit sales})}{\text{Number of days in year}}$$

We can then see this same formula implemented in row 13, which is how receivables are then projected. A useful additional metric to compare against industry levels and comparable companies is to divide the accounts receivable amounts by the total sales each period.

The previous process can be repeated for DIO and DPO with COGs replacing Total Credit Sales in the equation. Notice, though, that row 19 shows one new concept on the working capital sheet that we should examine in more detail. It is labeled Inventory Turnover and is calculated by using the following formula:[5]

$$\text{Inventory turnover} = \text{COGs}/\text{Inventory}$$

---

[5]Technically, the inventory should be averaged, but given that we are looking at it from a monthly point of view, the calculation is acceptable.

Inventory turnover represents the number of times inventory is completely churned. The higher the number the better since it means that goods are being sold quickly and not causing a drag on the company by lingering in inventory. This is another metric that is good to understand versus industry levels and comparable companies.

Now that we have projections for the key working capital accounts and the flexibility to change them quickly based on a day count basis, we should think about the full implications of these three core accounts. Two of the accounts represent cash inflows: DSO and DIO, while DPO represents a cash outflow. If we added the days for the cash inflows and subtracted the days for the cash outflow, we would get an idea of how long it takes to convert its operations into cash. This is known as the cash conversion cycle and is represented by the following formula:

$$\text{Cash conversion cycle} = \text{DSO} + \text{DIO} - \text{DPO}$$

This metric is good to know for early-stage companies since cash burn is directly related to investment requirement. A company that has a very high figure leaves a lot of cash tied up in credit, has slow inventory turn, or does not take advantage of supplier credit. These types of companies may encounter liquidity issues faster than companies with faster cash conversion cycles.

Long-term Funding: Debt

At this point we have covered all of the items on the asset side of the balance sheet and current liabilities. We have seen the importance of each element towards valuation and will explore valuation impact further in this chapter when we run sensitivities around balance sheet items. All that remains prior to summarizing the balance sheet is to go through long-term funding sources and how to set these up for analysis in a projection model.

Long-term funding is critical to a nascent company since a bulk of operations require cash to operate. While debt and equity can be used, early-stage companies often have a high reliance on equity, since debt can be difficult to obtain. However, since debt is easier to model from a projection point of view, we will integrate that first in the Solero model.

All funding is calculated on a separate sheet called LT Capital. Rows 12 to 29 allow for two separate layers of debt. There can be unlimited layers of debt in a company, but most companies will maintain an overall leverage amount that is consistent with the industry or comparable companies. The "layers" can be caused by sourcing debt that is senior and debt that is subordinate, meaning that if there is a cash shortfall, the senior debt would get priority over the cash flow. There can also be multiple layers of the same seniority debt, but with different characteristics. For these reasons, it is useful to create multiple debt schedules as can be seen in rows 12 to 29, where there is space for two separate debt issuances.

The assumptions for the long-term debt are stored back on the Inputs sheet starting in row 182. The critical components for each layer of debt include:

Initial Balance: The opening balance of the loan.

Funding Date: When the loan is issued. This should line up with a date in the model.

Interest Type: Debt can either have a fixed rate of interest or be based off of an index.

Fixed Interest Rate: If the debt has a fixed rate of interest, the rate expressed as an annual percentage.

Floating Index: If the debt is floating rate, the index that the base rate is calculated off of.

Spread: If the debt is floating rate, this is the additional interest above the base rate.

Term: The length of time the debt is outstanding.

Amortization Type: The method of principal repayment. The options in the Solero model include straight-line, which evenly spaces out principal repayment, or bullet, which is a method where greater amounts of principal are due toward the end of the term.

Back on the LT Capital sheet, the debt is scheduled, with a beginning of period balance, the current period's interest rate, the periodic interest due, the principal due, and the end of period balance. This is repeated for the second layer of debt. The total interest and principal, and end of period balances, are totaled in rows 27 to 29.

Debt impacts both the income statement and the balance sheet of a company. On the Inc Stmt sheet, we can see in row 42 that part of the formula is referencing the LT Capital sheet, where total interest is calculated. Recall that we left off on the income statement last calculating EBIT, after removing depreciation and amortization. Part of the step to get to earnings before taxes (EBT) is to remove interest expenses and add any interest income.[6]

---

[6]Row 41 contains a calculation for interest income. Nonfinancial, early-stage companies rarely have a significant amount of interest income; however, it is generally calculated based on the interest earned off of cash.

Utilizing the debt schedule from the LT Capital sheet is the best method to integrate the interest expense adjustment.

On the balance sheet, debt takes the form of a long-term liability. Go to the Bal Sheet and look at rows 33 to 36. There we can see the end of period balances for both layers of debt and a sum of the total debt, for every period.

The equity section of the model is fairly complicated, particularly since we are taking the viewpoint of an early-stage investor. That being said, the approach will be to explain the general items that compose equity and how those items are used on the balance sheet, and then later come back to the more complicated details that reside on the LT Capital sheet in the model.

Looking at the Bal Sht sheet, the equity section is stored on rows 40 to 45. There are five items there:

Common Equity: Common equity is the most basic shares of a company. At an early stage, typically the friends, families, and the founders will split up the common equity, depending on contributions and perceived value additions to the company. A portion of common equity is typically retained for future employee stock option programs (ESOP).

Class A Pref: When an early-stage outside investor invests in a company, the investor normally requires certain preferences, hence the term *preference shares*. These preferences will be discussed in detail when going through the example term sheet in Chapter 5.

Class B Pref: Often, there are multiple rounds of early-stage investment. These rounds are indicated by a lettering system with the first round being A, the second round B, and so on.

Warrants: Warrants are options to purchase shares of a company. In early-stage ventures they may be given to debt investors as part of a debt-financing package to compensate for the risk.

Retained Earnings: Net income that is generated each year builds value for the company. The asset side of the balance sheet will grow either through cash or some other type of asset, while the retained earnings will increase. This can be thought of as equity in the company until it is released as a dividend. Keep in mind, though, that in early-stage companies there can be negative retained earnings, as net income might be negative until operations become profitable. Negative retained earnings must be balanced out by other parts of the balance sheet.

The total equity is then summed up on row 46 of the Bal Sht sheet.

Finalizing the Income Statement

We last left off on the income statement explaining EBT. There are only two concepts left to finalize the income statement: taxes and dividends. Corporate taxes can be very complicated, depending on the entity's domicile, and should be thoroughly discussed with local accounting experts. However, most accounting regimes allow businesses to carry forward previous losses, which can be very valuable to an early stage company and incorporated into the valuation.

The loss that occurs when a company fails to make a profit can often be accrued and "carried forward" for use in the future when it makes a profit. This concept is referred to as net loss carry forward and is normally integrated in a valuation model prior to tax calculations. The most efficient way to incorporate it is to include the following calculations:

> *Net Loss Carry Forward Beginning Balance*: Since the net loss can grow or diminish from period to period, it can be thought of as an account. Such an account will have beginning and ending periods. We should start each period by knowing what the beginning balance of the net loss carry forward is. This can be seen on the Inc Stmt sheet in row 45.
>
> *Net Loss Carry Forward Creation*: If a loss is incurred, it should be recorded. Note that in the Solero model, the negative loss is converted to a positive value in row 46.
>
> *Net Loss Carry Forward Use*: When there is a profit at some point in the future, the balance of loss carry forward could be used. This is calculated in row 47.
>
> *Net Loss Carry Forward Ending Balance*: The net loss carry forward beginning balance plus the creation and less the use is the ending balance. This is calculated in row 48.
>
> *Taxable Income*: The actual use of the net loss carry forward is the loss amount that offsets the EBT. Thus, the taxable income is the EBT less the net loss carry forward use shown in row 49.
>
> *Tax Expense*: Once the taxable income is known, the tax expense is the rate of tax multiplied by the taxable income.

With the net loss carry forward calculated and the tax expense known, net income can be calculated by subtracting the EBT from the tax expense. Dividends are the final item before Net to Retained Earnings and are declared by the board and paid out. If any amount is left over after paying dividends,

	(670)	(18,923)	(18,133)
EBT	(670)	(18,923)	(18,133)
Net Loss Carry Forward Beg Bal	68,804	69,474	88,397
Net Loss Carry Forward Creation	670	18,923	18,133
Net Loss Carry Forward Use	-	-	-
Net Loss Carry Forward End Bal	69,474	88,397	106,530
Taxable Income	-	-	-
Tax Expense	-	-	-
Net Income	(670)	(18,923)	(18,133)
Dividends	0	-	-
Net to Retained Earnings	(670)	(18,923)	(18,133)

FIGURE 3.17 The end of the income statement incorporates value for prior losses, removes dividends, and sends the rest to retained earnings.

it can be considered part of retained earnings. The final parts of the income statement are shown in Figure 3.17.

Overall Organization and Functionality of the Income Statement and Balance Sheet

Thus far, we have approached core elements of the income statement and balance sheet in detail separately. At this point, it is worth understanding how the two statements are organized in the model, interact with each other, and function for projections. We will see later in this chapter that these two projected statements provide a majority of the information required for valuation.

The income statement we have seen build up from a very granular level of detail explains revenue and cost generation, from operations to more general corporate items that reduce or possibly increase cash flow. One thing to notice is that we have focused on the projections. Column D (highlighted in green) on the Inc Stmt sheet contains the historical data for what has actually transpired prior to the projections. In the case of Solero, we have the financial statements from 2014, located on the website in the Chapter 3 folder, and can enter the appropriate data directly. Although it is useful in some cases to gauge growth direction and levels from historical periods, it is also absolutely necessary in situations that require prior account balance data such as net carry forward loss.

The balance sheet has the same historical data in column E. The data can also be sourced from the historical financial statements. It is more imperative to have prior financial data for balance sheet items, since the change in accounts is indicative of cash flow movements that will be accounted for in the valuation.

NOTES FROM THE FIELD

Early-stage social enterprises in both developing and developed markets can struggle with keeping adequate financial data and paying for properly audited statements. In a number of cases, historical financial statements were either not looked at by auditors or only "reviewed" without a proper opinion. In some exceptional cases, such as a due diligence I conducted on a company in Vietnam, the prior financial data was riddled with inconsistencies, financial data that did not tie to historical operational data, and entanglements with other entities the company had stakes in. We spent over two full days trying to pick through the historical statements and still could not get proper explanations on some items. For this reason and a few others, we ultimately could not get comfortable with an investment.

Whether looking at a series of historical financial statements or projected ones, there are important linkages between the income statement and balance sheet. These linkages are vital to transferring asset and liability amounts to cash flow and vice versa. Key linkages include:

- *Net to retained earnings and equity*: Once cash flow has made its way down the income statement and has not been allocated, it becomes part of the company's equity. This explains the Retained Earnings section (row 45 on the Bal Sht sheet) in the Solero model, where the current period's net to retained earnings from the income statement are added to the prior period's retained earnings on the balance sheet.
- *Working capital items and sales and COGs*: We saw previously in this chapter that the working capital items such as inventory are connected to cost of goods sold, accounts receivable connected to sales, and so on.
- *Capital expenditures and depreciation*: Similarly, capital expenditures are balance sheet items that are connected to the income statement through depreciation. Intangible assets are connected via amortization.
- *Debt, cash, and interest*: Debt and cash are balance sheet items that create income statement items through interest.

Interactions not only occur between the income statement and balance sheet, but, in the case of the balance sheet, within them. The cardinal rule of accounting, that assets must always equal liabilities plus equity, needs to be maintained throughout all projection periods. This is why in the Solero model on the Bal Sht sheet in rows 55 to 57 there is a check to make sure the assets total the liabilities plus equity.

The way the Solero model is set up, though, the assets will always equal the liabilities plus equity because there are two *plugs*. These are required because when we set up custom projections there is no guarantee that we will perfectly balance the balance sheet. In cases when there are more assets than liabilities, it means that we have created assets, such as capital expenditures that have not been paid for. Theoretically these assets could be financed by any source of capital; however, if we have already entered our expectations for long-term debt and equity, the standard vehicle to fall back on is short-term debt. In the case of the Solero model, short-term debt will always plug any shortfalls in funding. When the opposite occurs, where liabilities are greater than assets, it means there is excess funding. The typical plug when this occurs is to allocate the excess toward cash. Rows 12, 29, and 50 to 53 on the Bal Sht sheet show this reconciliation.

The Cash Flow Statement

The cash flow statement is the third core financial statement; however, it is composed entirely of items from the income statement and balance sheet. That being said, it is important to create and properly calculate a cash flow statement to ensure that all items from the other statements have been accounted for and that the sheets are integrated properly. Reconciling cash movements is the check that can be done. Working through the cash flow statement we see the three key areas:

Cash Flow from Operations (CFO): This is cash generated or lost from operating the company. It starts with the net income from the business, adds back noncash items such as depreciation and amortization, and then accounts for changes in working capital.

Cash Flow from Investment (CFI): This is cash spent or earned from nonoperational components such as capital expenditures.

Cash Flow from Financing (CFF): This is movement in cash caused by capital fund raising or pay down.

Valuation: Discounted Free Cash Flow

There are a number of different valuation options once the projected financial statements have been completed. Many jump quickly to a *comparable company* methodology and look at utilizing the margins and operating metrics garnered from the bottom-up analysis to create a relative valuation.

Others take a fundamentalist approach and utilize the bottom-up analysis to project future cash flows that could be returned to an investor. Both approaches have their merits and faults, but since we have just finished projecting the financial statements, we are in a good position to create a free cash flow analysis.

The term *free cash flow* originates from the idea that cash is required to run a business, but at some point successful enterprises will generate more cash than is required. This excess cash can be thought of as "free" and could be returned to investors. Investors can analyze these expected returns by discounting them to the present day to calculate an expected value. This common technique known as discounted free cash flow (DCF) analysis has a number of intricacies to do correctly.

First, there is a critical distinction on who owns the free cash flow. There are two primary methods for calculating free cash flow: free cash flow to the firm (FCFF) and free cash flow to equity (FCFE). The distinction is that FCFF is free cash flow available to all investors in a firm, while free cash flow is what is available to only equity. Newcomers to finance often question who these other investors are, and the answer is fairly simple: debt holders. Lenders are technically investors in a firm, but investing for less risk and return than equity. FCFF is calculated to see how much cash is available to both debt and equity holders. The standard calculation for FCFF is:

$$\text{FCFF} = \text{EBIT} - \text{Tax} + \text{Non-cash deductions} - \text{Capex}$$
$$- \text{Working capital requirements}$$

Unfortunately, this formula causes confusion, as it is repeated in many different ways by different sources in the finance industry. To clarify, it is worth examining each item and the intention of it in the formula.

EBIT: FCFF starts with the cash that is available from the operations of the firm. This is normally the earnings right before paying interest or taxes. Occasionally, this calculation is started with net income, but since FCFF is from the viewpoint of both debt and equity investors, interest would have to be added back. It's much easier to begin with EBIT.

Tax: Free cash flow calculations focus on removing necessary cash uses and taxes are one of them. Keep in mind that there could be net loss carry forwards, as shown in the Solero model, which can reduce tax liabilities. One unique consideration with impact investing is that paying tax can be thought of as a social benefit, although on its own not enough to designate a company as an impact investment.

Non-Cash Deductions: Items such as depreciation and amortization were removed from EBIT. These are not cash items and should be added back.

Capex: Any planned capital expenditure is clearly a use of cash and should be removed from potential free cash flow.

Working Capital Requirements: This is often the most confused part of free cash flow calculations. Working capital requirements mean that there is a negative change in working capital from period to period. The calculations of this were shown earlier in this chapter. If there is excess cash from working capital between periods, then it should be added.

In the Solero model, we can see the calculation for FCFF on the DCF sheet beginning in row 4. The calculation follows the above formula to get us to the FCFF in row 21. Notice that FCFF can be negative. Most early stage companies, particularly social enterprises, will be losing money early on. This is clear from a negative FCFF, meaning that the company is not earning enough for operations, it is burning cash, and it will need outside funding if cash is not sufficient.

NOTES FROM THE FIELD

The Gyapa fuel-efficient cookstove in Ghana is an excellent example of the importance of free cash flow. The project began in 2002 and it has grown into one of the largest carbon-financed projects globally. As part of the board of directors with Relief International that is involved with the Gyapa project, I was able to witness the financial success of the social enterprise. The carbon credits produced cash in excess of the needs of the project, which is effectively free cash flow. This cash flow could be used for reinvestment, other projects, or split amongst both.

For equity investors in early-stage entities, FCFF is not the appropriate valuation calculation since the equity investor does not get any return from the debt. For this reason, a different calculation, FCFE, is done. FCFE is focused on determining the value of a company for an equity investor and is calculated in the following way:

FCFE = Net income + Non-cash deductions − Capex

− Working capital requirements + New debt − Debt repayment

It's clear that a number of items remain the same; however, there are three distinct differences. The first is that instead of EBIT, net income is the starting place. This makes sense because an equity investor's cash flow is normally always subordinate to the interest payments to debt holders. The second difference is there is an addition of new debt. If the board and shareholders allow it and there are no covenants against it, an equity holder could be allowed cash flow due to an increase in cash from debt. However, any repayment or amortization to debt holders must be removed, which is the third key difference in the formula. Companies with little to no debt will have very similar FCFE as FCFF. The Solero model details an FCFE calculation on the DCF page, starting in row 32 to 51.

NOTES FROM THE FIELD

While at Citigroup, we encountered a company in Latin America that was looking for debt financing. After diving into its financial statements, it became interesting that it was able to consistently dividend out large sums to equity holders year after year, even though the company was not very profitable. When we looked further into how this was done, it became clear that it was borrowing debt from many different sources with very few equity restrictions. Effectively, the equity holders were pulling free cash flow out of the company, but at a dangerous risk of leveraging the company up and stressing its ability to meet all debt obligations.

Terminal Value

We can see from the Solero model that calculating FCFF and FCFE is an intense process built up with many underlying assumptions. The DCF sheet lays out the free cash flow projections for 10 years and then finishes with column O, called Terminal Value. The terminal value is a calculation aimed to capture the going concern nature of the firm. If we just stopped at year 10 and only used those 10 years of cash flow to value the company, we would be saying that the company simply vanished and no value remained. In reality, we invest in companies that will be in business for a long time, hopefully in perpetuity. For that reason, we need a calculation to capture such value.

Perpetuity and Exit Multiples are the two most frequently used methods of calculating terminal value. A perpetuity calculation takes an expected long-term cash flow and estimates what the value would be of receiving that cash flow in perpetuity. This is done using the following formula (which can be seen implemented in the Solero model on the DCF sheet in cell O22):

Terminal value (perpetuity method)

$$= \frac{\text{Long-term FCFF or FCFE}}{(\text{Long-term WACC} - \text{Long-term growth rate})}$$

The numerator of this formula is either the long-term FCFF or FCFE. This can be calculated by growing the final projection year's figures and making adjustments so that they represent an ongoing long-term situation. The Solero model shows these calculations on the DCF sheet in O8 to O20. A particularly important part of this calculation is to make sure all of the items reflect a viable long-term situation. Notice in the Solero model on the DCF sheet that long-term capex (cell O19) has a custom formula. This is because during the projection periods there could be very specific expectations of capital expenditures that were scheduled on the Capex sheet. In the long term, there will probably be a base level of capex required to keep the company growing at the long-term growth rate. This is typically different than the early stages of the company. The same is true for depreciation, since the projection period schedules tie to the Capex and also for working capital accounts since they can stabilize in the long run.

The long-term weighted average *cost of capital* (long-term WACC) is the first part of the denominator. We will discuss WACC in detail later in this chapter, but basically, it is the funding cost for the company. Note that if FCFF is used in the numerator the WACC is used, which is a combination of debt and equity, while if the FCFE is used in the numerator the long-term *cost of equity* is used instead of the long-term WACC. Finally, the long-term growth rate for the company is an estimate of how much the company will grow in perpetuity.

An important point is that if the FCFF is used in the numerator with the long-term WACC in the denominator, the terminal value for the entire firm is being calculated. If instead the FCFE is used in the numerator with the long-term cost of equity in the denominator, the terminal value for equity is being calculated. It is important to keep everything consistent and understand whether a firm or equity value is produced.

The Cost of Capital

In order to get the firm or equity value as of today, future values of expected return, whether they are periodic or terminal values, must be discounted. The reason behind this is the time value of money and the idea that money in the future is worth less than today due to the cost of capital. Determining the costs of capital, particularly in the field of impact investing, is one of the more challenging aspects of valuation; it is also one of the most important when trying to create risk adjusted returns.

The cost of capital is the rate at which a company can fund itself. It is composed of the cost of debt and the cost of equity if there are both debt and equity investors. The costs are the rates at which a lender will lend and the rate of return expectation an equity investor would have in regards to the entity. Lenders will typically accept a lower return than equity holders since they have priority over cash flows, particularly during a liquidation scenario. Equity investors size their required rate relative to the risk of the company.

Prior to discussing the specific issues with the cost of capital and impact investing, we should go through the rationale for how investors determine the cost of debt and equity. For mature companies the cost of debt is typically associated with the credit rating of the company, as measured by one of the nationally recognized statistical rating organizations (NRSRO). For younger companies the cost of debt will be at a premium, which reflects the default risk of the company. Whether a fixed or floating rate issuance, the cost of debt should reflect a benchmark cost plus a spread. The benchmark is normally linked to the weighted average life of the debt,[7] while the spread is reflective of the credit risk of investment.

The cost of equity is a much more complicated figure as its calculation exceeds pure default risk. Equity investors do not get fixed payments like debt investors, are subordinate to debt holders, and therefore have a number of other considerations to account for in their required rate of return. The capital asset pricing model (CAPM) was introduced in 1964 to quantify the return required to invest in the equity of a company. The formal definition of CAPM is:

$$\text{Cost of equity} = \text{Risk-free rate} + \text{Market risk premium} * \text{Beta}$$

At the most basic level, this definition implies that an equity investor must earn at minimum the risk-free rate of interest that exists plus a premium for an equity investment multiplied by a factor that reflects how the specific company performs relative to all other equity investments. More formal definitions for the above equation include:

- *Risk-free rate*: Most practitioners consider a global risk-free rate such as U.S. Treasuries. Local risk-free rates are sometimes used, but debate exists around using these.

---

[7]Weighted Average Life (WAL) is a standard debt metric calculated by multiplying the periodic principal amortization amounts by the cumulative day count factor of each period, adding up the products, and then dividing that entire amount by the principal returned. It is usually expressed in years.

- *Market risk premium*: The market risk premium is the spread of equity returns over default free securities.
- *Beta*: A measure of systematic risk that is typically calculated as the covariance of the investment under consideration's returns versus the equity markets, divided by the variance in the equity market. Extensive debate surrounds determining an adequate beta, particularly in markets or industries with little to no data.

Equity investors in impact investments often have a difficult time with the standard CAPM model because of frequent emerging market domiciles and the early stage nature of investable companies. To help refine CAPM elements for equity impact investing, the following thoughts on each component are offered.

Risk-Free Rate

Most market practitioners default to a global risk-free rate. For USD investment, the common choice is to utilize a Treasury rate, while EUR investments sometimes reference Euribor. For Treasuries, the US 7- or 10-year rate is typically chosen for private-equity investments given the holding period of the investment. Others argue that a local risk-free rate should be used, creating models such as the Local Capital Asset Pricing Model (LCAPM).[8] The thought that certain emerging markets are truly risk free is sometimes hard to believe. As an example, even though India may issue highly rated local debt, the sovereign default risk can be high and not considered risk-free. Humphrey Von Jenner in his work footnoted below also cites this issue with using LCAPM.

Market Risk Premium

Fixed global market risk premiums are often used with large firms because larger, liquid investments in developed markets are more standard for those companies. For USD investments, particularly those in the United States, the common practice is to use the S&P 500 as the index to base the market risk premium. Other common practices internationally are to use the MSCI or an index with underlying global firms.

Two other considerations are the calculation method and scope of data. In regards to calculation method, there is sometimes a debate on whether to use the arithmetic or geometric mean when analyzing historical rates. The arithmetic mean seems more appropriate, since it assumes stable, non-correlated distributions of returns and will therefore consistently produce

---

[8] Mark Humphery Von Jenner, "*Calculating the Cost of Equity in Emerging Markets,*" *JASSA* 4 (2008): 21–25.

returns greater than the geometric mean.[9] As volatility in returns increase, which is increasingly being seen in markets, the geometric mean will deviate lower than the arithmetic mean. Given the contention around using both methods and the points just made, it seems more conservative to use the arithmetic mean since it will produce a higher market risk premium, which creates a higher cost of equity, and after the rate is used in discounting, a lower valuation.

The time frame of the analysis is the other issue that arises. If a large number of years are used to calculate the market risk premium, more economic cycles will be captured. This is good in that the market risk premium should span economic cycles. However, if the current economy has fundamentally shifted and the markets are not performing as they have been historically, the longer time frames will skew future expectations.

Beta

Beta can cause confusion and difficulty for many analysts trying to ascertain the beta of an early stage company given that little to no returns exist. Without such data, a comparable approach can be taken, but a number of other factors make the estimation more tedious: the time frame for analysis, levered/unlevered, using actual returns, sector returns, comparable companies, comparable sectors, or country-level betas.

A common approach is to select comparable companies in the local market. If there are none then a secondary tactic is to use comparable companies in foreign markets within the same sector. Since the betas of comparable companies reflect the capital structures unique to those companies the beta should be unlevered using the following formula:

$$\text{Beta unlevered} = \text{Beta levered} / (1 + (1 - \text{Tax rate}) * (\text{Debt}/\text{Equity}))$$

The median beta or the weighted average using market capitalization as weights should then be calculated. The resulting figure should then be levered to the capital structure of the company under analysis, using a rearrangement of the unlevered beta formula:

$$\text{Beta levered} = \text{Beta unlevered} * (1 + (1 - \text{Tax rate}) * (\text{Debt}/\text{Equity}))$$

With beta, the basic CAPM formula is in place, but by no means is the discount rate complete for early stage investments that may be in emerging

---

[9]Unless returns are identical each period.

markets. Country risk, entity size, and control premiums are other considerations. Each of these concepts attempt to adjust the valuation for a separate, distinct risk.

Country Risk

There tends to be inherent risks in certain countries due to politics, economy structure, and country specific market factors. One method of accounting for these risks is to add a country risk premium to the cost of equity. A standard approach is to analyze bond default spreads for a sovereign rating identical to those of the country, over the default free government bond rate. Some practitioners simply add this amount. Others, such as Aswath Damodaran, calculate a country risk premium with adjustments.[10] His method takes the country rating, estimates the default spread based on that rating, and then multiplies that spread by 1.5 to get the country risk premium. The logic behind the 1.5 multiplier is based on his calculation that equity markets are about 1.5 times more volatile than bond markets. Given that the market risk premium is already adjusting for equity volatility vis-à-vis bonds, an argument can be made for not multiplying the spread by 1.5.

If we look up India on Damadoran's table of default spreads and country risk premiums, we can see a 2.20 percent[11] default spread based on a Baa3 sovereign rating. This 2.20 percent can be added to the cost of equity in order to capture the sovereign risk of investing in India. Keep in mind that this is purely sovereign risk and should not be confused as a compensatory factor for foreign exchange risk. Such risks can be investment specific and have been discussed in Chapter 2.

Size

Smaller companies are typically riskier than larger companies. Management is not as developed, excess cash is virtually nonexistent, and smaller companies are beholden to their customers much more so than larger ones. The difference in company size is one reason that smaller companies have higher borrowing costs than larger companies. If this is the case then equity holders should demand similar compensation for the risk. Ibbotson Associates has done many studies on size premiums based on market capitalization. The size premium percentage is directly added to the cost of equity.

---

[10]Aswath Damodaran. "Country Default Spreads and Risk Premiums," (January 2014). http://people.stern.nyu.edu/adamodar/New_Home_Page/datafile/ctryprem.html.
[11]Ibid.

Concept	Rate	Source
Risk Free Rate	2.79%	http://www.marketwatch.com/investing/bond/10_year
Equity Market Return	11.64%	http://en.wikipedia.org/wiki/S&P_500
Market Risk Premium	8.85%	Calculated
Beta	1.7	Calculated using comparable companies
Cost of Equity	17.84%	
India Defaut Spread	2.20%	http://pages.stern.nyu.edu/~adamodar/New_Home_Page/datafile/ctryprem.html
Size Premium	4.00%	Ibbotson Associates historical data
Control Premium	0%	Assumes minority rights
Final Cost of Equity	**24.04%**	

FIGURE 3.18 The cost of equity using CAPM, factors specific to early-stage/emerging market companies, and the sources of the data.

Control Premium

Most impact investors are taking minority stakes in companies. Certain rights are given up with minority investments. Said another way, majority investors who have control of the company have stakes that are more valuable than minority investors. This concept is somewhat debatable, though, if minority rights are established in the investment framework. These rights will be discussed in Chapter 5 when term sheets are discussed, but basically if a minority investor has specific rights that prevent a majority investor from detracting value than an adjustment for control is not necessary.

Coming back to the Solero example with all of the above items we can try to construct a reasonable cost of equity as shown in Figure 3.18.[12]

The cost of equity as previously calculated is good for the present day and the short-term projections, but just like free cash flow the long-term estimate would change. This change could have implications for how the terminal value is calculated using a perpetuity formula. Recall that an equity terminal value is calculated using the cost of equity less the growth rate. The two most prevalent changes would be to beta and the size premium. Beta might be assumed to reduce in the long run as the company grows and stabilizes. Similarly, if the company's market capitalization has grown significantly by the time terminal value is being calculated, the size premium could be reduced. These changes generally reduce the long-term cost of equity and would increase the terminal value calculation.

The Cost of Debt

While a much simpler calculation than the cost of equity, the cost of debt assumption can become contentious. The standard method is to take the

---

[12]Note that this calculation may differ from what is currently stored in the Solero model. The Solero model has functionality to run sensitivities on the WACC and to change the underlying cost of equity and debt assumptions.

after-tax cost of debt that the company is currently paying using the following formula:

$$\text{After-tax cost of debt} = \text{Current cost of debt} * (1 - \text{Tax rate})$$

Occasionally, debate occurs on whether the company's risk profile has changed to demand a different cost of debt. This is typically seen in leveraged buyout situations where a large amount of debt is incurred to take the company private. A lower implied credit rating occurs due to the high leverage and stressed interest and debt service coverage ratios, and therefore a higher cost of debt. Over time, the company is expected to delever and improve its credit position, suggesting a higher credit rating and a lower cost of debt.

For early-stage companies a similar phenomenon could be argued. Initial debt for early stage companies is usually at a very high rate, in the mid-teens. As lenders become more comfortable with the company's ability to repay debt they may reduce their required rate.

Unique to impact investing, though, is that some entities receive very low cost debt from social funds or social finance groups that are part of large institutions. This low cost debt is sometimes non-market rate because of the fund's focus on supporting a social mission. Care needs to be taken that after the company grows and becomes more commercial, whether such low-cost debt will still be available to the company.

The Weighted Average Cost of Capital (WACC)

When people first see the formula for WACC they often become intimidated, but at its heart it is just a weighted average formula that takes the form of:

$$(\text{Cost of equity} * \text{Market value of equity} + \text{After-tax cost of debt}$$
$$* \text{Market value of debt}) / (\text{Market value of equity and debt})$$

The interesting part of this equation is that technically, market values should be used. For equity, it is much easier to get the market value; however, companies often have nontraded debt on their balance sheet at book value. The standard practice is to use the book value, but there are methods to convert the book value of debt to a market value.

The Discounting Process

Now that we have both FCFF and FCFE, the cost of equity, the cost of debt, and the WACC, we can now discount the cash flows to arrive at a value. Earlier, we calculated the expected FCFF and FCFE for 10 periods and then a terminal value. Each of these cash flows can be discounted using the following formula:

Present value = Cash flow (either FCFF or FCFE) / (1 + Rate)^time period

Five important points should be made here:

1. If a corporate value is being determined, use FCFF and the WACC for the rate.
2. If an equity value is being determined, use FCFE and the cost of equity for the rate.
3. Similar to 1 and 2 above, a terminal value can either be a corporate value or an equity value, but the cash flows involved and the rates must be consistent.
4. Be cognizant of timing. If a transaction is being executed in the middle of the year, a half year of time value of money can sometimes be significant. The time period may necessitate a partial first period.
5. To discount the terminal value, make sure it is included in the final year of the free cash flow. Even though it looks as if it should be discounted by one extra period, it should be moved to the final year's free cash flow.

In the Solero model, the discounting process takes place as shown in Figure 3.19.

Figure 3.19 shows 10 periods of cash flows and a perpetuity terminal value. Notice that the terminal value is included in the tenth period free cash flow and it is discounted back from that period. A couple of interesting points regarding the discounting process revolve around the discount rate and the cash flows. First, the discount process can have different discount rates for short-term and long-term, but some analysts choose to recalculate a discount rate each period to reflect a changing capital structure of the

Annual Free Cash Flow to the Firm												
Period	0	1	2	3	4	5	6	7	8	9	10	TV
Year	2014	2015	2016	2017	2018	2019	2020	2021	2022	2023	2024	Perpetuity
FCFF	(38,608)	(195,456)	10,832	433,478	1,347,293	2,738,479	4,534,483	6,395,372	7,988,944	9,543,424	11,073,247	11,100,074
Terminal Value												179,903,962
Cash Flows for Discounting		(195,456)	10,832	433,478	1,347,293	2,738,479	4,534,483	6,395,372	7,988,944	9,543,424	190,977,209	
Cash Flow PVs		(158,136)	7,090	229,560	577,292	948,330	1,271,795	1,451,231	1,466,701	1,417,549	22,950,740	
Sum of PVs	30,163,158											
Illiquidity Discount	3,016,316											
FCFF Valuation	27,146,842											
Capital Gains Tax												
Value Post Tax	27,146,842											

FIGURE 3.19   The FCFF to the firm for 10 periods and the perpetuity terminal value are discounted back to the present value.

company when the corporate value is being calculated. Typically, early-stage companies do not exhibit massive capital structure changes, such as companies that have just gone through a leveraged buyout.

The second interesting point is the fact that there are negative cash flows that, when discounted, are brought closer to 0. Negative cash flows occur frequently in early-stage company analyses. In fact, the sum of the nondiscounted negative cash flows that are projected could be thought of as the required investment amount. Without plugging those negatives with a short-term debt facility or other type of financing, the company would exhibit shortages of cash. In regards to discounting the negatives, it is typically assumed that this is done.

Prior to declaring the resulting sum of the present values as the valuation, there are two more steps that could reduce the value. The first is an illiquidity discount, which is often assumed depending on the liquidity of the private markets where the company is domiciled. For instance, in many emerging markets the private investment space is quite limited and companies trade at a discount to publicly traded companies. There are multiple methods to determine the value of this discount, but they generally range from 20 percent to 50 percent.[13] The discount is applied directly to the resulting value of the company.

The final calculation that one might want to consider is the capital gains tax. Depending on tax and investment regime, there could be taxes that diminish the value of the investment. Effectively, this diminishes the value of the company for an investor and should be reflected in the valuation.

FCFF vs. FCFE

FCFF is commonly used to calculate a corporate value. To arrive at an equity value, net debt (i.e., current debt minus cash on hand) is subtracted. FCFE can be calculated to see if it returns similar values for the equity position. There can be differences, as shown in the Solero model. In the case of FCFF in the Solero example, there is a different long-term leverage assumption for the terminal value. This produces a much lower cost of capital than a pure equity viewpoint. Therefore, the FCFF calculation is higher. As long as the expectation to access the debt markets and create a capital structure at the level suggested is maintained, then this method should work. If the capital

---

[13]S.P. Pratt, R.F. Reilly, and R.P. Schweighs, "Valuing a Business: the Analysis and Appraisal of Closely Held Companies," *Journal of Real Estate Literature* 5, no. 1 (January 1997).

Annual Free Cash Flow to Equity	
Period	0
Year	2014
Net Income	(43,255)
Depreciation	1,850
Amortization	-
Capex	(5,000)
Change in Net Working Capital	7,800
New Debt	-
Debt Repayment	-
FCFE	(38,605)
Terminal Value	
Cash Flows for Discounting	
Cash Flow PVs	
Sum of PVs	18,843,366
Illiquidity Discount	1,884,337
Equity Value Less Discount	16,959,030
Capital Gains Tax	-
Value Post Tax	16,959,030

FIGURE 3.20 Notice the significantly lower equity value derived from the FCFE analysis. A major difference between the FCFF and FCFE methods has been the discounting at WACC vs. cost of equity.

structure is not expected to shift, then the FCFF calculation is invalid and a more conservative capital structure expectation should be implemented, which would raise the WACC.

Relative Valuation and Comparable Company Analysis

While DCF valuation produces an intrinsic value of a company based on detailed assumptions, relative valuation seeks to produce a market value of the company through comparable company analysis. Although a comparable company analysis is easier to implement than a discounted cash flow methodology, the inputs require a deep level of understanding, particularly since relative valuation is often the dominant method used for valuation negotiations.

A comparable company analysis is done by identifying a peer group of companies that are in the same industry and exhibit similar corporate characteristics as the company under valuation. With the peer group identified a number of metrics should be calculated, with an emphasis on understanding the median of each metric. Certain metrics such as enterprise value to sales and enterprise value to EBITDA become multipliers for the company under analysis and lead to the valuation.

Selecting a Peer Group

The starting point for any relative valuation is identifying and selecting the proper comparable companies. The five primary criteria for selecting a company as part of a peer group include:

1. *Industry/sector/sub-industry*: The comparable company should be doing business or have a significant portion of its business in the industry as the company under analysis. The industry match-up should extend beyond a top-level categorization. For instance, with Solero we would not accept a comparable based on simply an industrial categorization of electronics. We should try to find companies that are focused on selling consumer electronics, including solar lighting products that are targeting rural markets. Clearly, the more narrow the focus, the fewer the potential companies there are to select from. It's best to start with a very narrow focus and slowly make it more general, until a suitable number of comparable companies are established.

2. *Market capitalization*: The absolute size of the market capitalization is important to understand since it is indicative of the size of the company. Early stage companies such as Solero have small market capitalizations. Companies with large market capitalizations are difficult to compare with smaller companies, as they are most likely larger, mature entities exhibiting different phases of growth. Such differences could produce anomalies in the metrics used for valuation.

3. *Capital structure*: A company's capital structure, namely its debt to equity ratio, can have a significant impact on growth and value. If a company is laden with expensive debt, it might not perform like a company with a lower debt burden. If an industry has a certain debt to equity ratio and a comparable company is an outlier, it may not be the best choice for a comparable company.

4. *Growth rate*: Each comparable company should be in a similar growth stage. If a potential comparable company has excessive or nonexistent growth, there could be an externality that makes it a poor choice for a comparable.

5. *Margins*: The gross, EBITDA, and EBIT margin of each potential comparable company should be assessed. In particular, the gross margins should be relatively similar. For example, if a potential comparable company has a much higher gross margin than the company under analysis, it could mean that the technologies being employed are not comparable. Therefore, many of the valuation metrics may not be properly comparable.

NOTES FROM THE FIELD

During one pre–due diligence, I was looking into a technology company that created a system of validating products' authenticity. This was primarily targeted at the pharmaceutical market in Nigeria since a large percentage of mainstream drugs, such as malarial drugs, are counterfeit. The company did this by employing a technology-based model with secure scratch-off labels that contained codes to SMS in for validation. While creating a comparable company analysis, I encountered a company that I thought was very close, but had very high margins. After looking into the other company, I found that it validated authenticity by using a DNA marker, which it created in its lab for virtually no cost per unit. Once created, the cost of goods sold for each marker was negligible and produced incredibly high margins. Ultimately, the company was not included in the list of comparable companies, as too many metrics were outliers.

Solero's Peer Group

On the Rel Val sheet of the Solero model, starting in row 29, there is an anonymous comparable company analysis of five potential companies. We can see that the sector is generally described, but should assume that a more detailed look has been taken to see what specific product category drives those businesses and how similar they are to Solero. Columns D through F show metrics that help determine suitability for inclusion in the peer group.

Working through the rationalization of each comparable company, we immediately see Company 4 with its negative growth rate and low margins. Looking further at its characteristics, we can see it has a lower market capitalization than other companies in the peer group. This is most likely an early-stage version of many of the other companies in the peer group. The concern with this company is that it should probably be exhibiting high growth if it is early stage.

Company 2 actually looks to be a similar company to Company 4, as it has a low market capitalization, but Company 2 has excellent revenue growth and strong margins. There are differences in exact industry, but it seems that Company 2 is a successful mid-sized company that is expanding.

The largest and most mature company is Company 3. It has a low growth rate, but good margins and a very large market capitalization. This company is a good indicator of where Solero might end up.

Company 1 is also quite large, but has higher margins and strong metrics. Overall, this company would be a good addition to the data set if its industrial focus is similar.

Company 5 is interesting in that it has similar metrics to Company 1, but its capital structure is unique among the peer group. We can see this by looking at the market capitalization versus enterprise value. Company 5 has very little debt based on this ratio (or a significant amount of cash). For now, we will leave it in as a comparable, but a company like this should be further investigated for peer group suitability. Figure 3.21 shows Solero's peer group.

Once we have a set of potential comparable companies, they must be reexamined for possible adjustment. Adjustments are often made for the following reasons:

- *Nonrecurring items*: If the cash flow in a given year is inflated because of something like a one-off asset sale or other reason, the cash flow should be restated. Similarly, if a one-off charge is taken that is not expected in the future, the expense should be removed.
- *Leverage changes*: If a leveraged buyout is imminent or an acquisition is expected, the capital structures could change significantly. These should be adjusted for.
- *Accounting differences*: If a company uses different accounting systems, such as LIFO vs. FIFO, either the comparable company or the company under analysis should be adjusted for consistency.

VALUATION MULTIPLES

Once we are comfortable with the peer group, the most important metrics to derive from the data set are multiples that can be applied to the company under analyses to support a valuation. The two most common valuation multiples are Enterprise value (EV) / EBITDA and EV / Last twelve month's (LTM) revenue. EV / EBITDA tends to be more popular as it reflects cost of goods sold and the operations of a business. However, in many instances, early-stage companies do not have any earnings and therefore might have to rely on revenue as a basis for a relative valuation.

A few distinctions must really be made when working with these multiples, as minor factors can have a very large impact. The first is whether the multiples being calculated are current multiples or forward multiples. Forward multiples reflect analysts' opinions of how the company might grow in the future. An analyst might use a DCF model similar to what was built in this chapter for Solero to determine the expected EBITDA and enterprise

Comparable Company Analysis

	Sector	LTM Rev Growth	Gross Margin	EBITDA Margin	Market Cap	LTM EBITDA	Enterprise Value	EV/LTM EBITDA	1YR Fwd EBITDA	EV/1YR Fwd EBITDA	LTM Revenue	EV/LTM Revenue
Company 1	Consumer Electronics	7.00%	51.00%	22.00%	700,000,000	78,145,118	950,000,000	12.16	83,615,276	11.36	355,205,082	2.67
Company 2	Solar Energy	20.00%	42.00%	15.00%	200,000,000	10,550,921	300,000,000	28.43	12,661,105	23.69	70,339,473	4.27
Company 3	Consumer Electronics	3.00%	47.00%	19.00%	1,500,000,000	166,004,891	2,000,000,000	12.05	170,985,038	11.70	873,709,953	2.29
Company 4	Consumer Electronics	-4.00%	27.00%	9.00%	145,000,000	16,033,725	200,000,000	12.47	15,392,376	12.99	178,152,500	1.12
Company 5	Consumer Electronics	9.00%	55.00%	25.00%	650,000,000	50,005,281	700,000,000	14.00	54,505,756	12.84	200,021,124	3.50
Median								15.82		14.52		2.77
Mean								12.47		12.84		2.67

FIGURE 3.21 Solero's peer group analysis used to establish valuation multiples.

value. These can be used for comparability or for structuring convertible structures, but LTM multiples are more typical for current valuations.

Another important facet of multiples is that occasionally people will mix in trading multiples with transaction multiples. A trading multiple is what we have already been calculating—multiples based on market capitalization and current metrics. Transaction multiples look to prior transactions to establish the valuation and revenue or EBITDA at the time of the transaction. Transaction multiples are often less relevant and not preferred for at least three reasons:

1. *They are difficult to get accurate information on.* Oftentimes, transactions that elucidate the value of a company are private, and precise information on the terms of the transaction or company fundamentals is difficult to obtain.
2. *Transaction multiples can be influenced by exogenous factors not related to the true valuation of the company.* Poor negotiating, synergy expectations, and so on can inflate or undervalue the calculations.
3. *Hot industries can have inflated multiples.* These lead to higher transaction multiples.

Once multiples are agreed on, the final part is deciding how to calculate the final multiple to use. In the Solero model, we can see that both the median and mean of the peer group are calculated (Rel Val sheet, row 37 and 38). The more common approach is to use a median, since it eliminates the effects of extreme outliers. Those outliers could be removed manually and the average used, but the use of the median is more standard.

Using Multiples for Valuation

With multiples at hand, the final use is to calculate a value and return analysis with them. For a present value analysis we would look to the last 12 months (LTM) of revenue or EBITDA and apply the (LTM) multiple to it. This can be difficult for early-stage companies that are expecting high growth and most likely have little to no EBITDA. From an investor perspective, one has to understand that the company's value lies in its future growth. For this reason, relative valuation should be used in conjunction with a DCF method to get multiple valuation points. In the case of Solero, its LTM revenue and EBITDA are quite low, but it has very high expectations for future growth. It is unlikely that the current equity holders would agree to a valuation with the multiples at hand and the metrics presented. The current investors would most likely look at a DCF approach, but also present a return analysis to the investor.

A return analysis is shown in the Solero model. Looking at the Rel Val sheet of the Solero model, we can see in row 11 that an EBITDA value is being multiplied by the future expected EBITDA. At first glance, this seems similar to the DCF setup where we discounted cash flows, but the valuation method here is different. We are valuing the company and equity position based on an assumed exit date, not every period. To do this, we must assume an exit year. Traditional early-stage investors seek to exit in five to seven years from investment. Many impact investments, though, seem to have longer investment horizons and are closer to at least seven years of holding time. We can see in the Solero model that the user controls the assumed exit year on the Inputs sheet in row 241, highlighted in Figure 3.22.

Guidance on what exit year to assume is investment specific, but there are general considerations to think about. If an exit year assumption is too early it may be unrealistic simply from a timing point of view, but also the company's EBITDA will not have time to grow and the valuation could be low. If the exit year is too far in the future, then the EBITDA may have hit a long-term growth level, and while the absolute return may be attractive, the IRR could be affected. We will look at IRR later in this chapter to see how timing is important, but for now we should be aware that the assumed exit year can have varying impacts on valuation.

With the timing understood, it's time to think about what value is actually created by multiplying the EBITDA by the multiple. Since the multiple was calculated using enterprise value, the enterprise value is the result of the multiplication. It is extremely important to realize that the enterprise value is inclusive of both debt and equity. In order to get the equity value of the company, we need to subtract out net debt, which is equal to the debt outstanding less the cash on hand. In many circumstances, there may be a negative net debt value. This is because cash has built up in the projections and is in excess of the debt. Therefore, when the net debt is subtracted from the enterprise value, the enterprise value grows. This is correct because the cash is internally generated funds that are available to equity after paying off debt. Row 13 shows the equity value for Solero, with the assumed exit year highlighted in gray.

For private companies, a final illiquidity adjustment to the equity value should be made. Public companies trade openly on the stock market and often have market makers to help facilitate trading. Private companies do not benefit from such liquidity. Shares in a private firm can be very difficult, expensive, and time-consuming to sell. For this reason, a private share would trade at a discount to a public share, purely based on liquidity. A number of studies have been done using different methods, but all of them suggest a private company's equity trades at a discount to a similar public company. To account for this, a final adjustment is made to the equity value, as shown in row 14 on the Rel Val sheet and the net value in row 15.

Relative Value Return Analysis

Period	0	1	2	3	4	5	6	7	8	9
Year	2014	2015	2016	2017	2018	2019	2020	2021	2022	2023
Exit Year								Exit		
EBITDA	(173,234)	74,920	780,619	2,303,101	4,492,568	7,366,802	10,154,772	12,593,395	14,969,397	17,096,432
Assumed Multiple	8.00	8.00	8.00	8.00	8.00	8.00	8.00	8.00	8.00	8.00
Enterprise Value	(1,385,874)	599,357	6,244,949	18,424,808	35,940,541	58,934,413	81,238,180	100,747,163	119,755,173	136,771,458
Net Debt	(886,766)	(931,189)	(1,425,151)	(2,784,746)	(5,548,633)	(10,131,644)	(16,611,265)	(24,731,507)	(34,463,805)	(45,793,888)
Equity Value	(499,108)	1,530,546	7,670,100	21,209,554	41,489,174	69,066,057	97,849,445	125,478,670	154,218,979	182,565,346
Illiquidity Discount	(49,911)	153,055	767,010	2,120,955	4,148,917	6,906,606	9,784,944	12,547,867	15,421,898	18,256,535
Equity Value Post Disc	(449,197)	1,377,491	6,903,090	19,088,599	37,340,256	62,159,451	88,064,500	112,930,803	138,797,081	164,308,811

FIGURE 3.22 With future EBITDA from the projection model and assumed exit multiple, we can calculate the expected enterprise value for every year in the future. The expected exit year is highlighted in gray.

Internal Rate of Return and Money Multiple

We now have a few valuations to think about: the first is the DCF method that led us to the value of the firm today, the second is a present value relative valuation if we look at the current revenue multiple and multiply that by the LTM revenue, and the third is a future value based on an assumed exit and an EBITDA multiple. Our goal so far has been to determine the value of the company and the equity, in order to enter into negotiations with the current equity holders of the firm. While the value can be substantiated through DCF and relative value techniques, an investor must look to the future and assess whether the assumed value is worth the investment.

The most common method of assessing whether an investment is worth the cost is to calculate the internal rate of return. We saw this calculation earlier in Chapter 2 and know that it produces an annual rate of return, over the life of the investment. This rate can be compared to other alternative investments to help determine whether the investment is the right choice. To determine the IRR of a corporate equity investment, we need three figures:

1. *Investment cost*: This is the amount that is invested. We know that the company is seeking investment and may take this from multiple sources. In the Solero example, USD1 million was assumed to be invested.
2. *Equity percentage*: The whole purpose of the valuation section has been to figure out the equity value of the firm and that if equity is invested, how much of the firm the new equity investor owns. In the Solero model we see that the USD1 million investment bought 4.65 percent of the company. This suggests that the company's equity value is now USD21.5 million (USD1,000,000 / 4.65 percent). Note that this is known as the post-money equity value, meaning that it is after the new equity investment has been made. The pre-money equity value of the firm was determined to be USD20.5 million (Post-money = Pre-money + New investment).
3. *Future equity value*: This is the value in row 15 of the Rel Val sheet at the assumed exit year, as discussed earlier.

Knowing these three items, we can lay out the IRR calculation, as shown in the Solero model in row 24 of the Rel Val sheet. In the current period, we put the investment cost.[14] The future equity value is multiplied by the equity percentage to get the investor's future return. The easiest way to conceptualize this is that when the company is sold, acquired, or exited in any

---

[14]This must be a negative value for Excel's IRR function to work properly.

way for the assumed value, the equity investor will get returned her percentage. In the Solero example, this comes to USD7,159,572. The internal rate of return can then be calculated using the IRR function, which comes to a healthy 32.47 percent under the base-case scenario.

Along with IRR, money multiple is the other metric that is used to consider equity investments. The money multiple is simply the gross amount returned, divided by the original investment amount. While IRR takes into account timing of investment return, money multiple purely looks at how many dollars were returned compared to those invested.

Triangulating a Value

No single value can be thought of as the absolute right answer. While the modeling process provides concrete answers, we must always take a step back and realize that a series of assumptions have been made that led us to those answers. Those assumptions may or may not be accurate. In order to help bring order to the fact that assumptions may vary, investors typically employ multiple methodologies, look at various scenarios, and run sensitivities around their valuation analyses.

We have worked through common methodologies: DCF, relative valuation, and return analysis. All of this work has been done in one static base case. The base case can be thought of as the case where management executes their plan accordingly and growth and return is as predicted. Most investors know that a base case is rarely achieved perfectly and that a number of assumptions that went into it will perform differently. For this reason investors begin to develop multiple scenarios as seen in the Solero model on the Inputs sheet, in row 10. These scenarios are usually developed and tested throughout the full due diligence process as the assumptions must be examined in detail. We will go through that further in Chapter 4.

While we will hold off on the many different scenarios, we can take a look at common sensitivities that help hone in on the valuation. On the Output sheet starting in cell D35 and D44 we can see FCFF and return sensitivities. These grids are run using the buttons to the right and take in the assumptions in blue, run the model, and export the results.[15] For FCFF the two major assumptions that have a significant effect on valuation are the long-term growth rate and the WACC. We can see there is over a USD23 million difference between the lowest valuation of USD19,360,531 (0.00 percent long-term growth and 25.60 percent WACC) and USD42,531,881 (5.00 percent long-term growth and 21.60 percent WACC).

---

[15]Note that for the buttons to operate, the user must have enabled macros in Excel, when prompted during file load.

Similarly, for return analysis we set up a grid to look at assumed exit year and varying EBITDA multiples. In this case there is a difference of nearly 14 percent IRR between the best IRR case and the worst. What's interesting about the return analysis sensitivity is that the best IRR year is 2019. One might think exiting in later years would produce a higher IRR since the EBITDA would be larger; however, the time value of money has its effect, and we can see that an earlier exit produces a higher IRR under the assumptions provided. The counter to this analysis is that the money multiple is higher under other assumptions. While we might exit with a higher IRR in 2019, waiting until 2023 would give us the absolute most amount of dollars returned. Figure 3.23 shows the sensitivities for Solero.

Using these analyses allows us to work through establishing a base-case valuation that makes sense both intrinsically and on a market-based level. We can iterate through sensitivities to see if the assumed valuation has a return proposition that is acceptable. At this stage it makes sense to progress with the Solero investment as the expected returns are robust under a reasonable exit time frame and a conservative EBITDA multiple. The valuation at this point, though, represents a management base case, since the assumptions have largely been derived from materials the company has provided. It would not be a surprise if management attempts to start the valuation discussion at USD40 million.

An investor will most likely not immediately accept such valuation. The investor must now take time to pick apart risks in further detail and establish his or her own view on the valuation. In Chapter 4, we will see how due diligence must be completed in order to establish such a view and valuation.

FCFF Sensitivities					
	LT Growth Rate				
WACC	0.00%	1.00%	2.00%	3.00%	4.00%
21.60%	25,996,651	28,400,832	31,584,326	35,999,345	42,531,881
22.60%	24,122,187	26,337,312	29,270,468	33,338,306	39,357,146
23.60%	22,400,247	24,442,541	27,146,842	30,897,295	36,446,526
24.60%	20,817,145	22,701,325	25,196,261	28,656,356	33,775,968
25.60%	19,360,531	21,099,959	23,403,221	26,597,494	31,323,792

Return Sensitivities					
	Exit Year				
EBITDA Mult	2019	2020	2021	2022	2023
4	28.94% / 3.56	27.53% / 4.30	26.03% / 5.05	24.72% / 5.86	23.51% / 6.69
5	31.10% / 3.87	29.55% / 4.73	27.83% / 5.58	26.32% / 6.48	24.91% / 7.40
6	33.13% / 4.18	31.42% / 5.15	29.49% / 6.11	27.78% / 7.11	26.20% / 8.12
7	35.03% / 4.49	33.17% / 5.58	31.03% / 6.63	29.14% / 7.74	27.39% / 8.83
8	36.84% / 4.80	34.81% / 6.00	32.47% / 7.16	30.40% / 8.36	28.49% / 9.55

FIGURE 3.23 Valuation and return expectations should be calculated for a range of sensitivities based on key drivers.

DESKTOP DUE DILIGENCE: SOCIAL IMPACT MAPPING

From a social analysis point of view, the next step is to create a more comprehensive impact map, in order to analyze the social mission of the company and whether it is consistent with the investor's investment thesis. In Chapter 2, we looked at a basic impact map and process that helps guide us during screening, but at the desktop due diligence phase, we should elaborate on that and standardize it with impact industry tools. A comprehensive impact map for Solero has been developed in Excel and is saved under the Chapter 3 folder on the website.

To accomplish the standardization, we start by integrating the Impact Reporting and Investment Standards[16] (IRIS) indicators. These indicators convey standard information that should be understood regarding a company, when analyzing it from a social impact point of view. The indicators can be seen in the first column in Figure 3.24, with the corresponding IRIS indicator code in the second column next to it. The codes link to the IRIS website for each indicator and can be clicked on when online to take the user to the IRIS website, where a description of the indicator is provided.

With the standard characteristics laid out, we can begin a seven-step process of completing the impact map.

Step 1: Mission

When drawing the impact map, we first examine the company's mission statement. As mentioned in Chapter 2, an effective mission statement contains three elements: target population, an outcome (or an output) objective, and a means to achieve it. The mission statement is a concise message that expresses how the company generates financial, social, and/or environmental value through its business activities.[17] Companies that are set up to deliver impact normally have a mission statement reflecting their social impact. Figure 3.25 shows the mission statement for Solero.

Mission lock is an additional concept related to the mission statement. Some companies ensure through a legal document (such as in their incorporation bylaws through B Corporation certification) or by adhering to a third-party commitment (GIIRs fund or B Corporation) that the social or environmental mission will be maintained over time, regardless of company ownership. An investor can also require a mission lock requiring the company to serve a specific segment of the population. Solero has a commitment to serve off-grid population; we will examine mission lock in Chapter 5, in relation to the term sheet.

---

[16]http://iris.thegiin.org/metrics.
[17]B Lab

	IRIS code	Solero Lighting Company Profile Note: Solero Lighting is a fictional company created for illustration purposes only.
Company description		Solero designs, manufactures, markets and distributes affordable, quality, solar lamps for off-grid populations.
Year founded	OD3520	2010
Legal structure	OD2999	Limited Liability Company
Ownership		Promoter: 69.77% Angel investor shareholder 1: 11.63% Shareholder 2: 4.65% Warrants: 2.33% ESOP: 11.63%
Female ownership	OI2840	Angel investor shareholder 1: 11.63%
Minority/previously excluded ownership	OI7194	0%
Address of the organization's headquarters	OD6855	No.111, M. L. Dahanukar Road, Cumbaya Hill, Mumbai 400026, India
Operational model	OD6306	Production/Manufacturing and distribution of solar lamps
Customer model	OD8350	B2C (Business to customers model)
Sector		Renewable energy, manufacturing/retail
Products		Solero Mini; Solero Standard; Solero XL; Solero Developed Markets (DM)
Distribution channels		Direct to villages; export; wholesale
Client locations	PD2587	India, USA, Europe

FIGURE 3.24 Standardizing company characteristics is a preliminary part of developing a detailed impact map.

Step 1
Mission Statement
We design, manufacture, market, and distribute affordable, quality solar lamps and solar products for off-grid populations.

FIGURE 3.25 The first step of developing an impact map is to create the mission statement.

Step 2: Social/Environmental Goals

The next step is to examine the social and environmental impact objectives pursued by the company. The IRIS framework allows you to choose from a thorough list as shown in Figure 3.26.

Social Impact Objectives	Environmental Impact Objectives
- Access to clean water	- Biodiversity conservation
- Access to education	- Energy and fuel efficiency
- Access to energy	- Natural resources conservation
- Access to financial services	- Pollution prevention & waste management
- Access to information	- Sustainable energy
- Affordable housing	- Sustainable land use
- Agricultural productivity	- Water resources management
- Capacity-building	
- Community development	
- Conflict resolution	
- Disease-specific prevention and mitigation	
- Employment generation	
- Equality and empowerment	
- Food security	
- Generate funds for charitable giving	
- Health improvement	
- Human rights protection or expansion	
- Income/productivity growth	

FIGURE 3.26   The second step is to choose from all of the IRIS standardized social and environmental impact objectives.

Step 2
Social and Environmental Impact Objectives Pursued
Social objective: • Access to energy • Employment generation Environmental objective: • Sustainable energy

FIGURE 3.27   Solero's social and environmental impact objectives can be selected from the possible IRIS indicators.

From the possible IRIS indicators we select the ones that are appropriate for Solero, which is shown in Figure 3.27.

While there are standard indicators, we should be mindful of case specific nuances. For instance, given Solero's direct sales to village model, the increase in income revenue of distributors is a better articulation of the social objective than *employment generation*.

Another useful reference to define impact objectives is the "Outcomes Matrix" presented by Big Society Capital, which was designed from a beneficiary point of view.[18]

Keep in mind that the general impact objectives above are very broad. In Chapter 6 we will examine how these general objectives are further detailed and grounded into annual SMART targets (Specific, Measurable, Achievable, Realistic, and Time scaled) in an Annual Operating Plan (or similar strategy document).

Step 3: Inputs

In this third step of building the impact map, we examine the resources, both human and capital invested, used in the pursuit of the organizations objectives. We need to assess whether the inputs appear to be in line with the organizations objectives. Solero's inputs are shown in Figure 3.28.

Step 4: Activities

The next stage of the impact map continues with the fourth stage, activities. Figure 3.29 details Solero's activities.

In this stage, we need to examine the company's activities. Each one of these activities raises specific social and environmental issues. As we analyze the company for a potential investment, we need to understand the risks and opportunities from an ESG perspective at each step. As we will

Step 3
Inputs
• Staff inputs in terms of numbers and qualifications (check organizational chart: management, design and technology team, production engineers, supplier finance, logistics, distribution, strategic partnerships, marketing, salesforce, customer finance, after sales) • Resources (budgets) • Timesheets related to activities • Client inputs in terms of time (attending information sessions, or reaching place of purchase) and money invested (credit facility and eventual costs linked to this deferred mode of payment)

FIGURE 3.28 Solero's inputs form the third part of the impact map.

---

[18]In their own words, "The outcomes matrix is a tool to help social investment financial intermediaries and social sector organisations to plan, measure and learn about their social impact." Big Society Capital, "How to use the Outcomes Matrix" www.bigsocietycapital.com/outcomes-matrix.

Step 4
Main Activities
1. Design quality, affordable solar lamps that adequately respond to the needs. (performance and pricing) of rural off-grid clients. 2. Manufacture (responsibly). 3. Set up delivery channels that meet clients' needs and preferences. 4. Manage delivery channels. 5. Build and manage brand awareness. 6. Obtain client (and other stakeholder) feedback to improve design, pricing, and distribution.

FIGURE 3.29 The fourth step of the impact map is to detail the company's activities.

discuss in the next chapter, during the due diligence we will explore how the company intends to manufacture responsibly and what percentage, for instance, of its significant suppliers it visits regularly to screen for social and or environmental malpractices.

Step 5: Output

As mentioned in Chapter 2, outputs are the direct consequence of the company's activity: loans distributed; houses built; cleft lip surgeries realized; and so on. Solero will measure lamps sold, which is the company's number one output indicator. Also, since we are mainly interested in low-income, off-grid customers, we will track three out of Solero's four products, leaving aside sales of lamps for outdoor leisure (camping) in developed markets. The outputs for Solero are shown in Figure 3.30. In a separate exercise in Chapter 6, we will build a quarterly reporting framework to capture the essence of Solero's activities and impact. The quarterly metrics will be largely based on the output metrics original data points (number of lamps sold) and calculated on the basis of assumptions (people reached, based on average number of users per lamp).

Step 6: Outcomes

Again, as mentioned in Chapter 2, outcomes are the consequence of the output. For Solero, a customer survey identified the following outcomes shown in Figure 3.31.

Step 7: Impact

Although there is no guarantee and careful monitoring will be undertaken, the outcomes listed may result in the impact detailed in Figure 3.32.

Step 5
Output
Number of solar lamps sold (total cumulative since inception and total this quarter) Hours of additional light Number of micro-entrepreneur distributors Micro-entrepreneur distributors earnings Number of countries of presence Number of communities served Greenhouse gas offset/mitigated
Assumptions Average luminosity (unit lumens) Average lifetime of lamp Average number of hours of use Average battery lifetime Conversion rate GHG per lamp Number of persons in household Number of lamps per household

FIGURE 3.30 Solero's Outputs are carefully defined.

Step 6
Outcome
Additional number of hours of study Additional number of hours of income generating activities Reduced spending on non-renewable energy sources Reduced CO_2 emissions Reduced eyestrain Reduced incidents of kerosene (and other fuels) burns, explosions (linked to fuel adulteration), and ingestion Improved indoor air quality Reduced incidents of snake bites Reduced incidents of crime

FIGURE 3.31 Companies need to define their outcomes based on survey data.

As we seek to assess impact, we face the challenges of causality and attribution. In the previous list, it could well be that the observed improvement in student performance is not only the result of increased hours of study, due to a solar lamp, but also a consequence of better schoolbooks, or a better teacher, or lower teacher absenteeism, or a campaign encouraging parents

Step 7
Impact

Improved student performance
Increased revenue
Increased savings in kerosene and kerosene lamps
Improved health (visual, respiratory)
Improved safety
Improved security

FIGURE 3.32   Outcomes lead to impact.

to send children to school. There are many things that could have led to better student performance, making it challenging to claim that it is the direct and exclusive consequence of the child having access to a solar lamp and additional hours of light. This concept is referred to as the challenge of attribution. Additionally, there is the issue of the counterfactual. We do not know what would have happened otherwise, that is, without our "intervention" selling a lamp to an off-grid household. The best way to tackle this is through RCTs (randomized controlled trials), yet these are not always feasible and can be expensive. We recommend examining the work of the Poverty Action Lab,[19] a research center that uses RCTs to test the anti-poverty effectiveness of policies and interventions.

Outside of the impact map process is the operational impact of a company. The operational impact refers to the company's policies and practices regarding social, environmental, governance and ownership issues. Formally, it is not a step in the construction of the impact map, but it has an effect on the impact created. A company's operational impact is carefully examined at due diligence when all ESG practices will be scrutinized immediately and subsequently every year or every other year, depending on the underlying ESG risk factors. If a company submits to an annual impact assessment, such as the B Impact Assessment, which is used to generate GIIRS Impact Ratings and certify B Corporations, these practices as well as the intended business model impacts will be examined. Figure 3.33 details Solero's operational impact.

Using a Third-Party Impact Evaluation Tool   The Impact Map we developed here is an internal strategic exercise connecting and aligning the building blocks that ultimately deliver impact. This exercise is excellent for a pre-due

---

[19]www.povertyactionlab.org/.

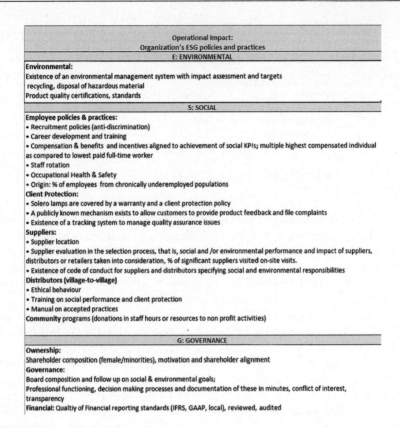

Operational Impact: Organization's ESG policies and practices
E: ENVIRONMENTAL
Environmental: Existence of an environmental management system with impact assessment and targets recycling, disposal of hazardous material Product quality certifications, standards
S: SOCIAL
Employee policies & practices: • Recruitment policies (anti-discrimination) • Career development and training • Compensation & benefits and incentives aligned to achievement of social KPIs; multiple highest compensated individual as compared to lowest paid full-time worker • Staff rotation • Occupational Health & Safety • Origin: % of employees from chronically underemployed populations **Client Protection:** • Solero lamps are covered by a warranty and a client protection policy • A publicly known mechanism exists to allow customers to provide product feedback and file complaints • Existence of a tracking system to manage quality assurance issues **Suppliers:** • Supplier location • Supplier evaluation in the selection process, that is, social and /or environmental performance and impact of suppliers, distributors or retailers taken into consideration, % of significant suppliers visited on-site visits. • Existence of code of conduct for suppliers and distributors specifying social and environmental responsibilities **Distributors (village-to-village)** • Ethical behaviour • Training on social performance and client protection • Manual on accepted practices **Community** programs (donations in staff hours or resources to non profit activities)
G: GOVERNANCE
Ownership: Shareholder composition (female/minorities), motivation and shareholder alignment **Governance:** Board composition and follow up on social & environmental goals; Professional functioning, decision making processes and documentation of these in minutes, conflict of interest, transparency Financial: Qualtiy of Financial reporting standards (IFRS, GAAP, local), reviewed, audited

FIGURE 3.33   The operational impact component covers social, environmental, governance, and ownership issues.

diligence/due diligence stage assessment of a potential investment. In addition to this, companies may wish to have a third party validation of their impact. If this is done prior to an impact investor analyzing the company it can help streamline the investment process and be a positive metric for investment assessment. One existing tool that has been used broadly[20] is the B Impact Assessment (BIA, used in the GIIRS impact ratings). This is a standard impact measurement tool that generates a set of questions and metrics (leveraging the IRIS taxonomy) that are tailored depending on a company's geography, sector, and size. The GIIRS assessment covers three types of impact data:

---

[20]As of August 2014, B Corp's impact assessments had been used by over 18,000 companies in 8 years.

Operational/ESG: data about the company's own practices and policies around governance, workers, community, and environment

Impact Business Model: data that focuses on the positive impact intent of the business with regard to products and services, target beneficiaries, and other innovative impact models

Disclosure Items: data that focuses on potentially sensitive activities or impact of the business

To fully elucidate this process, Solero has completed the B Impact Assessment[21] and gone through B Lab's data validation process, resulting in a GIIRS Impact-rating. All GIIRS rated companies and certified B Corps must complete an assessment review with the B Lab team. Solero has received a 'Platinum' Impact Business Model Rating and a 'Rated' Impact Operations Rating. The Impact Business Model (IBM) Rating recognizes business models that are specifically designed to solve environmental problems through company products or services, target customers, value chain, ownership, or operations.

The Impact Operations Rating evaluates the impact of the business in how it operates, commonly referred to as "ESG" (or Environmental, Social, and Governance) practices.

Solero's full GIIRS Rating assessment including the detailed questionnaire and improvement report can be found on the Chapter 3 website:

Sample Company - B Impact Assessment

Sample Company - GIIRS Rating Report

Sample Company - Customized Improvement Report

Overall Rating Summary

	IBM Rating	Operations Rating
	PLATINUM	Rated
Consumers	PLATINUM	
Community	PLATINUM	★
Environment	SILVER	★
Workers	N/A	★★★
Governance	N/A	★★★★

Overall Score

124

A company's overall score and GIIRS Rating are representations of their performance on the same set of standards, the B Impact Assessment.
For more details, see B Impact Report page

Company is a Certified B Corporation?   no

Becoming a B Corp

Companies that earn an overall score of at least 80 on the assessment are eligible to become a Certified B Corp.

FIGURE 3.34   Solero's GIIRS Rating Results

---

[21] The B Impact Assessment, GIIRS Impact Ratings, and B Corporation certification are run by B Lab, a U.S. based 501(c)3 nonprofit.

CONTINUING THE INVESTMENT PROCESS

A significant portion of this chapter has been a detailed examination of the company's fundamentals, possible base-case valuations, and return potential. Earlier, we called this the *pre-* or *desktop* due diligence phase because everything could be done at a desk using operating data, prior financial statements, and expectations about future development. However, much of the information has been provided by the company, particularly the growth assumptions that led us to the base-case valuation. This information is frequently very aggressive and optimistic. Although an intense amount of analysis has been done, there is still much more.

The purpose of the pre-due diligence phase is to determine whether the company and investment is worth engaging further into full due diligence. The returns that are calculated from the base case should easily meet the minimum requirements of the investor. In fact, generally speaking, the returns should be much higher than the minimum requirements because the investor will need to build his or her expected case during the full due diligence process. Building this case often means examining the company for risk, calculating the effect the risks have on the investment value, and adjusting the valuation accordingly.

Additionally, the base case gives us a basis for incorporating structures that might help mitigate risk, such as the liquidation preference that readers may have noticed in the Solero model. These types of structures should be contemplated in the full due diligence stage that leads up to their incorporation into a term sheet.

The other aspect of the pre-due diligence presented here is an initial attempt at assessing the social impact. The impact map created serves as a standard method to guide social impact knowledge. Third party tools can provide objective analysis and help standardize the impact assessment. These analyses can provide enough information to support a decision to allow or discontinue the investment process based on social impact.

From here, we will build off the analyses done in this section and move on to Chapter 4, which examines the full due diligence phase and finalizing an investment structure.

CHAPTER **4**

Due Diligence
and Investment Structuring

The due diligence phase of the impact investing process signifies a serious commitment toward investment. Both parties will have to expend time and financial resources to make the due diligence effective and meaningful. From an investor perspective, the company, its market, and its business operations will undergo intense scrutiny. Management meetings will become commonplace, interaction will occur with employees at various levels and departments, data will be requested and vetted, the operations will be observed onsite under various conditions, validation of both financial and social performance data presented earlier will ensue, and research will take place on competitive companies. The investors seek to solidify their opinions on management and validate their investment theses. Additionally, the business drivers that led to the pre-due diligence valuation will be revisited and tested, and any risks found will be incorporated into the analysis. Possible advanced investment structures might be necessary to help mitigate concerns that arise out of the due diligence.

DUE DILIGENCE

The goal of an investor completing a due diligence is to thoroughly vet the company so that the investor is comfortable finalizing the investment. The *due diligence* that we are referring to should be more specifically referred to as the *operational and business due diligence*. The distinction is made because there are other forms of due diligence—namely, legal and accounting, that also take place. However, those other two forms of due diligence are typically done after a term sheet has been signed and all precedent conditions are met. The reason for this is that the investment could fall apart at the term sheet level, and hiring lawyers and accountants can become costly affairs. At this stage, the investor is seeking to validate the business and operational assumptions and risks. The information that is communicated is assumed to be true and thoroughly vetted by professionals later.

A business and operational due diligence is difficult to convey in pure writing, as it is an iterative process that can take weeks to months to complete. To best attempt to capture this process, we will walk through general due diligence concepts first, pose critical questions, and then integrate how such concepts would be applied to Solero, where relevant.

Management Meetings

By the time a full due diligence has initiated, there is a good chance the investor has already met with management, possibly a few times. For a full operational and business due diligence, the founders and management should be prepared to "open the hood" of the business. The investor should take time to meet with each founder and senior manager to discuss the following:

Strategy: Each founder and senior manager should elaborate on the market that the company is operating in, their competitive advantage, and how their business plan will be executed. Information that was exchanged previously was probably more generic than what should be garnered at this point. Exact plans on how the value chain will be created/sustained should be clear.

Roles: An interesting occurrence is that the founders of companies are not always the best people for certain senior management roles. Some founders may have a technical background that leads them toward directing technology, while others may have a broader skill set that allows them to operate as CEO. It's imperative to discover each founder's and senior manager's strengths and ensure they are in a role that allows them to apply those skills. Particular care should be taken to assess how well management works together and whether there is any dissent that could lead to a dysfunctional management team post-investment.

Alignment of interest: It's important that the investor, founders, and senior managers are all aligned toward sustainably growing the business. Founders' motivations, their specific equity interest in the company, and future expectations of the company should be elucidated. The investor should be clear to the company on his or her anticipated investment holding period, return expectations, and preferred method of exit.

Existing Investor Meetings

The existing investors of a company may have significant influence over the funding round. In fact, depending on prior investment terms, certain decisions could require majority or supra-majority voting. Additionally, earlier investors may have negotiated specific terms, such as tag-along rights or drag-along rights that could affect the new investor's exit ability and conditions from the company. These concepts will be covered in detail in Chapter 5. Similar to founders, who may also be existing investors, it's very important to align interest among all investors.

Board of Directors Meetings and Corporate Governance

In early-stage companies the *board of directors* often exerts considerable influence over strategy and management of the enterprise. In some situations, board members may take up projects that would be considered management's responsibility in more mature companies. For this reason, it is important that a new investor is satisfied that the existing board has the depth of experience in the right areas to support management and the company through rapid, sustainable growth in competitive markets.

In particular, significant minority investors and majority investors will typically require board of directors' seats to invest in the company. As a potential new member of the board, the investor must assess his or her future role on the board and believe that participation will be constructive and additive.

To evaluate the existing board, a part of a due diligence is a review of prior board meeting minutes. Analyzing the minutes for decisions made, how the decisions were arrived at, and who influenced the decisions can provide a window into how the board and management have approached and solved problems. More interestingly, prior board meeting minutes can reveal to an investor potential board issues and discontent.

Specific to social enterprises, mission alignment, board composition, and oversight of social and environmental targets is important. How sensitive and knowledgeable are board members to the institution's mission and social and environmental objectives? Does the board monitor these objectives? What information does the board receive, and with what frequency? Do the board minutes confirm the claims of oversight? Have there been discrepancies among board members regarding vision, mission, and trade-offs (apparent or not) of social versus financial targets?

A due diligence will examine the overall governance of the institution, including aspects such as the following:

- Role and responsibilities of the board of directors in defining and monitoring the execution of the company's strategy, vision, and culture.

- Board composition:
  - A best practice is to have one to two independent board members.[1]
  - Ideally for a social enterprise a direct representative of the main stakeholder group (the target population or end customer) would participate in board meetings. In the case of Solero, this would be an off-grid rural Indian for Solero. It is rarely the case, though, that a local representative has board membership. Typically, board members claim sufficient knowledge of the target population and alignment to their needs to be able to represent them.
- Board member affiliations and a register of their interests (in order to avoid conflicts of interests).
- Legally established terms of office and rotation, clarity of voting rights, existence of a mechanism to evaluate board members, and a demonstrated practice of introducing new members.[2]
- Committees: audit, credit, risk, and remuneration.
- Frequency of board meetings and quality of minutes and documentation of board decisions.

Following the Value Chain

Outside of meetings, the onsite portion of a due diligence entails following every step of where value is built and created, otherwise known as the *value chain*. Each step should be identified and assessed for its continued viability, the level of value it produces for the company, the repercussions of disruption, contingency options in case of interruption and, unique to impact investing, the integrity toward the social mission and social and environmental objectives.

Research and Design

Before most enterprises sold their first products, they focused a large part of their time and resources on the design of their products or services. Even though a company may have grown to where it is generating revenue, the research and design process

---

[1] An independent board member is defined here as a person who is not (and has not been) affiliated with the institution or its senior executives through an ownership, employment, business, or family relationship.
[2] See "GIIRS Emerging Market Assessment Resource Guide: Creating and Improving a Board of Directors or Advisory Body" in http://www.giirs.org/storage/documents/Best_Practice_Guides/em_creating_bod_advisory_body.pdf.

should continue. The communication process between the board of directors and management's strategy and the product or service design should be well understood.

Viability: A properly functioning research and design process should be constantly improving existing products and working on new innovation or complementary products. Although this sounds simple enough, the process actually folds in a number of areas of the company. A due diligence should reveal how design decisions are made and then put into action.

Value: Research and design can increase profits in two ways: It can make or innovate products to increase sales or it can reduce the production cost of existing products, while still retaining core functionality and design. The key takeaway from assessing research and design is whether changes to the existing product builds sustainable, long-term value. What research has been done on the design to ensure that it satisfies customers' wants and needs? What is the impact of any innovation on the margins of the company? Is the company straying from its original business strategy and entering an area where management is unskilled or unprepared?

Disruption: Key man risk is the first thought that comes to mind for disruptive potential in research and development. In early-stage companies, products or services often originate from just one person. As an investor, it is critical to identify any key individual responsible for product creation and assess their level of commitment to the company. Does that person have a significant equity stake in the company? Have the intellectual property rights been properly assigned to the company, rather than residing with an individual? Is the key person interested in building out a team and disseminating knowledge?

Product issues and design failures are another disruptive element related to research and design. Has the company had any significant product problems or recalls? Were the problems idiosyncratic or systemic?

Contingency: Directly related to the last point on product failures, the follow-up is how those failures were resolved. How were the problems first identified? What feedback loops exist in order to have information regarding design issues and how long does it take to alter the design of a product? What legal risks might occur if the product or service performs adversely? What is the proper amount to reserve for warranty returns or expected failures?

Earlier under the disruption section, we also discussed key man risk. Contingency plans should exist if the primary innovator is no longer part of the company. Methodologies should be documented and subordinate managers in constant training.

Social mission integrity: As mentioned earlier, from an impact perspective the focus is on the individuals or households whose lives are meant to be impacted through the use of the product or service. Is there a full understanding of the customer's needs? Are the customer's needs adequately addressed in the product design and distribution? Is this backed by survey data, or is it speculation? Does the company integrate customer feedback into the improvement of the product or service adequately and in a timely manner?

NOTES FROM THE FIELD

While serving on the board of a solar lantern company, the question came up on how to approach a larger, more powerful lighting product designed for installing throughout a home. The design process involved a board of directors feedback loop where new products were previewed to the board and strategic discussion followed. In the case of the home system, it was noticed during field research in Kenya and Uganda that the design many rural, poor, nonelectrified homeowners wanted was one that closely simulated an on-grid experience, with little details like a wall-based switch. The board of directors assessed home system prototypes for cost, functionality, and whether market demands were met. While cost seemed to be in the right range, the functionality in meeting the market demands seemed lacking. Continuous debate ensued, and eventually earlier prototypes were scrapped for a more grid-like device. This process was essential in making sure that the correct products were being created and released.

Suppliers

Any enterprise that manufactures a product or provides a service will require suppliers of the components to the product or supplies for the service. Given the tangible products it produces, Solero's supplier requirements are clear: solar panels, batteries, and other electrical components required to build the final lighting products.

Other types of companies such as service companies still require suppliers. The maternal healthcare company that we looked at earlier, Mtoto Clinics, would need medical supplies. PagaPago, the mobile money enterprise, would require hardware for core operations, but more importantly, the telecommunication companies supply a critical aspect of PagaPago's value chain.

Viability: Many early-stage enterprises encounter stress when their supply chain has problems. Each supplier should be assessed for its ability to continue to produce the product or service supplied to the enterprise. Dialogue and analysis should take place to understand the importance of the enterprise to the supplier. Is the enterprise a significant portion of the supplier's revenue? Is the supply the enterprise purchases becoming obsolete or soon to be discontinued? Are there or have there been any quality issues related to the supply or supplier?

Value: Suppliers and supplies generate costs that are part of the cost of goods sold and affect the enterprise's gross margin. In many circumstances the prices are negotiated. Due diligence should verify whether the costs are reasonable, if contracts exist to lock in prices, the duration of such contracts, and how competitive the pricing is versus industry averages.

Disruption: Companies may have an inventory of supplies to last them through disruptions, but thinly stocked companies, companies that employ just-in-time inventory, or long disruptions could effectively shut down an enterprise. Due diligence should assess prior supply chain disruptions, the reasons for the disruptions, how long the disruption lasted, and ultimately the effect the disruption had on the company. A supplier delivering defective or poor quality supplies can also cause disruption. If this is the case, the process for resolving returns, warranty procedures, and overall level of customer service should be assessed.

Contingency: Upon supply disruption the company should have a contingency plan in place. Are there multiple suppliers of the product or service for the company to access? If so, the existing relationship the company has with those suppliers should be understood and the pricing expectation should be known.

Social mission integrity: Companies that purchase, manufacture, or assemble parts of their products in developing countries may be exposed to sub-standard social and environmental practices. As an example, with Solero, several components of the solar lanterns are produced in China. The environmental and social (E&S) practices of suppliers become an important element of the company's impact management, even when the supplier is an independent third party. A case of child labor or environmental pollution in its supplier base could devastate Solero's impact claims. It's critical to ensure that the company establishes a clear expectation regarding the E&S practices of its suppliers and lays out a plan for monitoring those practices. Does the company have such a plan or a supplier code of conduct? How often does it conduct labor and environmental audits of its significant suppliers? Is there a corrective action plan if there are poor practices occurring?

Manufacturing

For companies that produce a tangible product, the manufacturing process is essential. Manufacturing can be structured in many ways, with the two most prominent being either a capital intensive, in-house approach that allows for full process control or an asset light method that utilizes contract manufacturers. Both have advantages and disadvantages, which require assessment with the business as a whole.

Viability: The viability of the manufacturing process involves a comprehensive calculation of the cost of manufacturing, determined by the combination of the final cost of goods sold and the capital required to produce them. A strong understanding of capital intensive purchases should also be undertaken, along with depreciation policies. Maintenance capital expenditures that are expected in the future should also be questioned and understood.

Value: The value addition built by the manufacturing process should be reflected in the cost of goods sold, which should be in line with industry standards or better. If gross margins are significantly different from industry standards, while pricing is aligned, it suggests that the cost of goods sold may be very expensive. Early-stage companies may have to contend with higher costs of goods sold until economies of scale are realized. Integrating the ramp to normal margins as part of the business analysis is integral to making sure the company is properly funded as it grows.

Disruption: Manufacturing processes that are done in-house are exposed to less disruption; however, they still require due diligence. What are the primary weaknesses in the manufacturing process? Is there specialized equipment necessary to operate the business?

Who are the key personnel that run the manufacturing process? Are workers unionized, and what is the potential for employee disruption?

For companies that utilize contract manufacturing, disruption can occur if the contract manufacturer decides to no longer service the company. Contract manufacturers may drop smaller clients for larger ones who offer more lucrative, longer-term contracts. Pricing negotiations may then raise the manufacturing process costs, which will flow through to the final cost of goods sold.

Contingency: If in-house manufacturing is utilized, there should be back-up plans for potential plant, machinery, and human resource issues. For companies utilizing contract manufacturing, there should be alternative contract manufacturers identified and possibly already in use. Timelines and costs for transition should be estimated.

Social mission integrity: Many elements of social mission integrity related to suppliers are similar for manufacturing. Contract manufacturers should be reviewed for proper labor practices. One particular aspect for manufacturing companies is what happens to their products after the products reach their useful lives. Do they have established recycling programs or do the products get thrown out? If they are thrown out, are there any concerns such as dangerous waste?

NOTES FROM THE FIELD

While vetting the manufacturing process of a company that provides combination wind and solar power solutions, it became clear how important the manufacturing setup was toward competitive advantage. The company had its own factory and was in the process of expanding. This seemed counterintuitive, given the high cost of producing and testing some of the wind-related components; contract manufacturing seemed like the likely alternative. However, the majority investor had strong connections in China and was able to get much of the property granted for limited cost and low rate debt for in-country facilities. This alleviated immediate concerns around production costs, but the due diligence shifted toward the majority investor's connections.

Distribution

Companies with physical products will have to be able to get those products to end users. For impact investing companies, this is often the most challenging aspect of the business model considering emerging market focuses and a preponderance of rural customers.

Viability: A distribution system is viable if customers can reliably access a company's products and are able to purchase them at standardized prices. The critical element in the previous statement, though, is "access." Using Solero as an example, the lanterns that are produced in China must be able to make their way to foreign countries such as India, clear ports of entry legally and with minimum taxation, aggregate at regional distribution centers, find their way to local distribution centers, and eventually to village sales representatives who sell the product to customers.

Village sales representatives are often singled out as unique aspects to many social enterprises; however, their viability operates the same as many companies' sales forces. Incentive is the critical element for any sales force. Not only should the margin for the products sold be understood, but the margins of competing products that the sales force could sell must be known. Any reasonably astute salesperson will gravitate to focusing on higher margin products if they are able to sell them. Additionally, the time commitment to sell the products needs to be understood since alternative uses of time can detract from sales efforts. Finally, the timeline to hire and train a sales force needs to be assessed, since it is the foundation for revenue and sales expansion.

Value: The due diligence should focus on understanding two elements that are critical to the value of a distribution system: time and costs. Time refers to the sense of understanding how long it takes for a product to leave the manufacturing facility to when it gets to the customer. This is integral to liquidity in the company and will be revisited later in this chapter when discussing the effects of breakdowns in product distribution. Vetting the cost at each point is important because it is the underlying contributor toward gross margin. Complex distribution systems that incur cost increases can significantly affect margins.

Disruption: The distribution system is the most visible area of a business for disruption. The lack of product becomes clear to entities along the distribution network and obvious to customers when a stock out occurs. Major disruptions that prevent product from being available can damage the company's reputation amongst regional distributors, village sales representatives, and, most importantly, customers. The due diligence should reveal if disruptions in the distribution system have occurred in the past and where the most likely future breakdown of the distribution system lies.

Contingency: If the company has encountered a distribution system problem in the past, the solution should be examined in detail. Were any systemic changes undertaken to prevent such a breakdown from occurring again? What were the costs of the breakdown?

Social mission integrity: Later in this section, stakeholders will be discussed, which are important concerns related to a distribution system. Overall, it is necessary that the distribution system works fairly for every level, from the corporate leaders to the last mile distributors.

NOTES FROM THE FIELD

During the due diligence of a company that manufactured in China, but sold in India, the question of product stockouts was introduced. The company admitted to having stockouts two times in the past year. The causes and repercussions were incredibly insightful for the investment process. A lack of a strong enterprise resource planning (ERP) system was the origination of the problem, as product demand was not clearly being communicated to production. This led to insufficient manufacturing volumes. When further questioned how the problem was resolved, the company explained that it had to transport the required volumes by air, rather than by sea. This caused a drop in the company's gross margin by over 20 percent during that time period. From an investor point of view, it was clear that some of the investment proceeds needed to be dedicated to a new ERP system and software. Additionally, the valuation was adjusted after running scenarios where margins could be affected by the need to utilize expensive air transport occasionally rather than sea shipment.

Corporate Operations

Although the value chain technically ends with the final sale of the product to the customer, an undiscussed element is the corporate operations that oversees and directs the entire process. While there can be many variations depending on company focus, the core areas include human resources, accounting, and technology.

Viability: The due diligence of corporate operations should be done through the lens of scalability. The immediate viability of the corporate operations should be apparent through the current ability to hire and retain individuals, the speed and accuracy of generating financial reports, the capture and transmission of information, and management's ability to direct and learn from each department. Each area, though, should be thought of in regards to massive scaling in operations. What if there was 10 times as much business? Perhaps 100 times? How would human resources manage to hire people quickly? What accounting software is being used? If the business scales to other geographies, are there people who know the appropriate accounting rules? Can the current technology be significantly scaled? If so, how fast, and at what cost?

An additional part of the corporate operations' due diligence is a deep dive into the financial statements provided. Any unclear or irregular items should be discussed thoroughly and explained by division heads.

Value: Corporate operations are largely cost centers, which are captured in the operating expenses that the company reports. While the corporate operations create costs, value is built as the business would cease to operate efficiently and more importantly fail to grow.

Disruption: Typical disruptions that should be understood include the potential departure of key individuals who manage the various departments, the inability to handle growth with existing systems and being overwhelmed by information, and in the case of technology, outright failure that leads to a blackout in communication and information.

Contingency: Given the disruptions previously mentioned, each one should be vetted for contingency planning. Are key individuals incentivized properly and participating in employee stock option (ESOP) plans? What are the terms of their employment contracts? Do existing managers have the requisite knowledge to work through the expansion plan? What systems are in place right now, given the volume of business? Is there a data backup system or a full physical and technical disaster recovery plan?

Social mission integrity: Fast expansion may put stress on a company's social mission. Management may be unable to recruit staff that is aligned with the mission and has the proper skills to responsibly service the low income population. Staff incentive structure should be coherent to the organization's social objectives. That is, if the institution aims to sell to low income populations, the employee variable bonuses should be linked to serving exactly this target. It is important to vet the company's capacity to recruit and train staff adequately, particularly in stress situations. Conversely, a business contraction situation may cause a need to reduce staff, services, and ultimately the ability to meet client needs. In the recent Andhra Pradesh microfinance crisis, the credit crunch faced by lending institutions led MFIs to reduce lending to their clients.[3] A contingency plan to protect the client's needs in the best possible way during a business disruption situation is necessary.

NOTES FROM THE FIELD

One very successful company that I invested in was experiencing rapid growth, but going through growing pains. While this is clearly a good problem to have, real bottlenecks were beginning to form. For instance, financial reporting was constantly being delayed and riddled with errors as the accounting team was overwhelmed with data from various sources and systems. This led to delays in board meetings and management, and the board of directors having the ability to fully understand operations. Future planning was problematic until the reporting issues were resolved and a new enterprise resource planning system installed.

---

[3]In October 2010, the Andhra Pradesh (AP) Government passed an ordinance radically altering how microfinance institutions (MFIs) could conduct their business and prohibited practices that were integral parts of the MFI's business models. The AP government was responding to allegations of customer over-indebtedness and claims of coercive lending practices. The resulting local government interference effectively halted repayments by clients within AP, which in turn led to no new loan disbursements. This resulted in a general liquidity crisis in microfinance in India with MFIs at risk of defaulting on their loans, their profitability deteriorating, and customers being denied access to new credit.

Specialized Due Diligence for Social Impact Validation and Analysis: Stakeholder Analysis

A due diligence aimed at validating the impact thesis should focus on the main stakeholder impacted. The social return on investment (SROI) methodology defines stakeholders as people, organizations, or entities that experience change, whether positive or negative, as a result of the activity that is being analyzed.[4] In impact investing, the most important stakeholder is most often the end user of the product or service—for example, the woman receiving the healthcare treatment, the child being vaccinated, the family owning the new house, the child attending the school, or the loan recipient. Employees are another important stakeholder. And, when the company sources or manufactures an important amount of products/services from a vulnerable population, these suppliers may also be an important stakeholder for an impact analysis, or even the most important one.[5] If the company has a distribution system that relies on micro-distributors, these too may be important stakeholders. Other stakeholders may be investors or regulators.

Who the main stakeholder is depends on the product/service, and the distribution model. It is advisable to limit *stakeholder analysis* to the most-important two to three main stakeholders. The onsite due diligence is the most important opportunity to learn about the stakeholders and test impact hypotheses.

In the case of Solero, the main stakeholders are: (1) the end users, individuals or households, from off-grid, rural, underserved communities, and (2) the distributors. The selection of stakeholders directly responds to the social objectives of the company: to promote access to energy and to increase revenue of distributors.

NOTES FROM THE FIELD

At an SROI training, we were asked to identify the stakeholders of the Donkey Sanctuary, a large UK charity that aims to protect donkeys from abuse. We brainstormed and listed a number of stakeholders from donkey owners, regulators, and breeders, but failed to list the number one stakeholder: the donkey.

---

[4] www.thesroinetwork.org/.
[5] In fair trade, the smallholder farmers are the main stakeholder.

Stakeholder 1: End User of the Service or Product Here are some questions related to the product/service and its use and benefits:

- How does the customer describe the product and its benefit?
- How does the customer use the product? How long? What for? In what circumstances? With whom? How many products/services are used?
- Does the product/service appear to be used according to the company's specifications? Is the client optimizing its use?
- What did he/she use before? What made him/her change? What is the alternative? How satisfied is he/she with the product, its price, its delivery and after-sales service?
- Fairness of treatment: Has he/she been treated with respect? Are there signs of aggressive sales tactics, unannounced visits, or other pressure to purchase?
- Did the salesperson explain the costs of the purchase (price, commissions, and other fees) and the purchase terms satisfactorily? Were they described in a language understandable to the client? Was the product well described prior to purchase?
- Are there cancellation rights? Does the client appear to understand his rights? Was the client asked to sign a purchase contract? Does the client have a copy of this contract?
- Does he/she have any complaints about the product and or the purchasing experience? Are there appropriate mechanisms to complaint? How do they function? Has the client complained?

What do you need to know about the customer? This, too, depends on the company and business model, but often the questions below will be relevant.

- Socioeconomic segment: Low-income, poor; middle income
- Location: Rural, urban, peri-urban
- Gender: Female, male
- Age: Adult, youth, children
- Education level
- Household composition

While the previous questions are important, the due diligence should also look to how the company interacts, works with, and generally protects its customers. Customer protection is important everywhere, but it is even more important when the client is vulnerable. A poor client might be less well-informed than a wealthier customer. Although we assume clients to be rational economic actors, they can make wrong choices. The cost of a wrong purchasing decision for the poor client is more likely to have a greater negative impact than on his better off neighbor. The higher vulnerability results from less education, lack of social protection (lack of insurance, lack of savings, etc.), and overall reduced access to information. Vulnerability calls for protection. During due diligence, client protection policies and practices should be an important focus of the visit. Reviewing a complaints book will offer valuable information on client treatment.

Client protection should also extend to the due diligence process itself. It is important to create an atmosphere of trust when interviewing end users. The interviewee should feel comfortable sharing his or her opinions and telling you about himself. The objective is to assess the product or service, what makes it different from alternatives, and the quality of the sales and after-sales service offered.

A common challenge during the end-user assessment is that often times the institution presents the clients to be interviewed. This introduces a selection bias as the customers presented are the "model clients." The experience then becomes one of a staged authenticity rather than objective authenticity. To get a more exact reading, interview the customers suggested to you by the organization as well as other customers, noncustomers, and former customers. A customer book can always be requested and randomly selected customers chosen for interviews. Additionally, transport staff, hotel personnel, and the staff of NGOs working with the target population can also give insight into the company.

In social audits and impact analysis, it is important to listen attentively, demonstrate empathy, and avoid patronizing. Be aware that the desire to validate an impact thesis can cause one to selectively acknowledge information that probes the thesis and disregards data that invalidates it. The key to a successful impact due diligence is to listen actively, avoid putting words in people's mouths, and be open to hear the unexpected.

NOTES FROM THE FIELD

When visiting investment clients, I have often walked into their homes, asked many questions, and at times I have taken pictures. I normally feel welcome. Most of the time, I am accompanied by the loan or sales manager who knows the client. Back home, I realize how intrusive my visits are. Would I welcome a sales representative or banker into my house, invite him to sit and respond to his inquisitive questions? What is the validity of information collected this way? How freely will a client express in front of the loan officer or sales manager that she is having difficulties meeting her loan payments or is unsatisfied with the product?

Additional field observations include the following candid quotes from impact due diligences:

- "We secure government contracts, which are important to our business; we offer government officials a *compensation* for the contracts we get."—sanitation company in India

- "It's better to try and sell to the wealthy farmers with lots of land. They can easily afford the product. The smaller farmers do not buy as easily."—agricultural services company in India

- "We don't want the client to know the price of her loan because she will compare and our competitors have better prices." —loan officer explaining transparency of pricing in Central America

- "We've outsourced our collection services on defaulted loans to a collection agency run by former military, they are physically strong men, very persuasive, they achieve a high rate of recovery for past-due loans."—microfinance company explaining recovery practices in Eastern Europe

Stakeholder 2: Employees During due diligence, time is spent in the offices and in the field with different levels of staff, from the CEO and top management, to branch managers, and salespersons. This offers a unique opportunity to get a feeling for the organization's overall coherence with its mission and its probability of delivering the impact. The company's labor policies, remuneration policies, the overall level of staff satisfaction, staff's engagement with the company's mission, and the company's sensitivity to the client's interests will become apparent in practice. Test whether the staff appears to endorse the company's social mission and how aware they are of the social objectives. Do their incentives reflect the company's social objectives? What client-level data do staff collect? What do they do with the data?

Due Diligence by Others: Engaging Independent Consultants

Generally, investors should focus on investing in companies where they have expertise and are able to conduct a due diligence on their own. Occasionally, excellent investment opportunities outside of this expertise will present themselves. Rather than passing on such potential investments because of the inability to conduct a thorough due diligence, an investor may choose to engage a third party to assist in vetting the company, product, or service.

Independent consultants can vary from institutes that produce research papers on specific technologies to individuals who have a very deep specialization in a certain field. In the case of Solero, an actual independent consultant that could be utilized is Fraunhofer, a European application-oriented research organization. In 2009, it conducted testing on 10 different solar lanterns that were being commercially produced and sold.[6]

Qualifications, objectivity, and cost are three considerations when looking to engage an independent consultant. The consultant should clearly have a thorough history of experience in the field being assessed. More importantly, though, is the consultant's level of independence. If the consultant is an institute, the primary source of the institute's funding should be determined. The consultant's affiliations with other companies and organizations should also be reviewed. The final consideration, and typically the major decision factor in engagement, is the cost of the consultant for a particular investment opportunity. If the investment is USD250,000 and a consultant estimates a USD50,000 charge, the deal expenses have immediately swelled to a level that would make the deal uneconomical.

UTILIZING DUE DILIGENCE INFORMATION

As alluded to earlier, this chapter will apply some of the due diligence points discussed earlier to the Solero investment. The main focus will be on how to mitigate some of the potential risks uncovered by due diligence through adjustments to the equity valuation of the company. Recall that at the end of Chapter 3 we saw that management may value the company as much as USD40 million. The figures shown throughout this section are DCF valuations derived by altering assumptions.[7] The thought process is that the risks being

---

[6]P. Avato, G. Bopp, A. Cabraal, R. Gruner, S. Lux, and N. Pfanner, "Investigations and Tests of LED-based PV-Powered Lanterns," http://publica.fraunhofer.de /documents/N-142765.html.

[7]In addition to valuation figures, IRR calculations are also shown. These are based on an assumed investment valuation of USD21.5 million with a liquidation preference that will be discussed at the end of this chapter.

identified are real and it is likely that some or many of them may occur. For this reason, the investor and investee need to agree on a price that incorporates such risks. Also keep in mind that both firm value and equity value figures are being shown. Equity investors must remember that they are negotiating their investment on equity value. Clearly, there can be many issues learned from the due diligence that may require other, non-quantitative mitigation strategies, such as indemnification, but those will be discussed in Chapter 5.

Increased Costs

During the value chain section of the due diligence, we discussed the potential for a number of problems that could cause costs to increase. Alternative, more expensive suppliers may have to be used, manufacturing costs may increase, or specific issues such as having to use pricy shipping methods may arise. To account for this we should run a series of scenarios in the Solero model to see potential impact on value.

Open the Solero model and go to the Inputs sheet. Notice in column I that Scenario 2 is named "Increased COGs." In cell C3 enter "2" in order to load up this scenario. The most apparent change is a significant decrease in the valuation and IRR seen in the Quick Results section in cells H3:J6. Figure 4.1 shows a comparison of the Quick Results for Scenario 2 versus Scenario 1.

The reason for the large decrease in valuation and IRR becomes clear when the differences between the scenarios are examined. The annual manufacturing cost inflation has been doubled for every product (notice cells I22, I36, I50, and I64 moved from 1.00 percent to 2.00 percent). The effect of these changes filters through to the manufacturing cost on the Prod Curves sheet and eventually through to reducing the available free cash flow. Such sustained increases in manufacturing costs can be attributed to a number of reasons identified earlier during due diligence.

A specific issue identified during due diligence was the reliance on air shipping during stockout situations. If we know the increase in costs due to air shipping utilization, we can incorporate that into a scenario. Scenario 3 does this by doubling the Annual Shipping Inflation assumption (cells J24,

Scenario 1 - Mgmt Base Case		Scenario 2 - Increased COGs	
Quick Results		Quick Results	
FCFF Value:	$27,146,842	FCFF Value:	$19,491,553
FCFE Value:	$16,959,030	FCFE Value:	$12,382,707
IRR:	32.47%	IRR:	29.00%

FIGURE 4.1 Increasing the product cost each year has a significant impact on the valuation and anticipated IRR.

Scenario 1 - Mgmt Base Case	
Quick Results	
FCFF Value:	$27,146,842
FCFE Value:	$16,959,030
IRR:	32.47%

Scenario 3 - Increase Shipping Costs	
Quick Results	
FCFF Value:	$26,474,655
FCFE Value:	$16,557,579
IRR:	32.19%

FIGURE 4.2 Doubling the anticipated shipping expenses due to potential air freight use impacts the valuation and IRR.

Scenario 1 - Mgmt Base Case	
Quick Results	
FCFF Value:	$27,146,842
FCFE Value:	$16,959,030
IRR:	32.47%

Scenario 4 - Increased Capex	
Quick Results	
FCFF Value:	$27,107,487
FCFE Value:	$16,918,209
IRR:	32.47%

FIGURE 4.3 One-off expenses can also decrease value and return.

J38, J52, and J66). We can see that this impacts the valuation and IRR from the management base case, as shown in Figure 4.2, but not as severely as doubling the manufacturing costs.

Scenarios 2 and 3 looked at sustained costs throughout time; however, we may also have seen a need for better equipment or technology, which would be a one off, immediate cost. Recall the "Notes from the Field" where the enterprise resource and accounting systems were inadequate as the company scaled. Implementing these can be expensive one-off expenses. Scenario 4 looks at such a situation by assuming an expensive capital expenditure in 2016. This assumption can be seen on the Inputs sheet in cell K174, with the effect on valuation and return shown in Figure 4.3.

Distribution System Risks

During the due diligence, many risks were identified in the distribution system. One of the critical ones that spanned a number of parts of the due diligence were related to the village-level distributors. Their incentive based on margin, alternative employment, and, from a social impact perspective, getting paid fairly, were all important components to a functioning distribution system.

These risks translate directly into value and return in many ways. Distributors may require higher margins in order to be properly incentivized. Scenario 5 looks into such risk by decreasing the ability to pass through cost increases in price, effectively increasing the distributors' margins. As expected, this has a considerable impact on the value and expected return of the business, as shown in Figure 4.4.

Scenario 1 - Mgmt Base Case	
Quick Results	
FCFF Value:	$27,146,842
FCFE Value:	$16,959,030
IRR:	32.47%

Scenario 5 - Increased Distributor Margin	
Quick Results	
FCFF Value:	$21,580,031
FCFE Value:	$13,626,144
IRR:	29.97%

FIGURE 4.4 Increasing the margins for distributors is good for the distributors, but impacts the value and return proposition of the company.

The other risk associated with distributor incentive that can impact Solero is that it is more difficult to hire distributors than previously thought. Scenario 6 looks at this risk by scaling back the number and hiring speed of distributors that are assumed to work in Region 2. This is done on the Inputs sheet in cell M90, where Region 2's stressed expansion curve is selected. The difference between the regional expansion plans can be seen on the Vectors sheet by comparing columns I and M. The effect of this is seen in the valuation and return expectations, as seen in Figure 4.5.

Similarly related to incentive and the ability to hire distributors is the ability to retain them. Attrition rates can quickly vary, depending on alternative opportunities for distributors. In the management case, there is an aggressive assumption that distributors will stay employed for 10 years from day one. Most likely, as Solero begins to scale, distributors will probably drop off and new ones will have to be hired. This churn affects the expected productivity of distributors, since seasoned ones typically sell more than new ones. Stressing distributor attrition is done in columns T, U, and V on the Vectors sheet. Figure 4.6 shows the significant impact on valuation and return.

Another risk that can stem from distributors is assumed productivity. To assess this risk, we can lower the annual sales growth expectation for each distributor in cells O81:O86 by lowering the annual sales growth and the stabilization period. This has the overall effect of decreasing sales volumes, which lowers the valuation and return expectation as demonstrated in Figure 4.7.

Scenario 1 - Mgmt Base Case	
Quick Results	
FCFF Value:	$27,146,842
FCFE Value:	$16,959,030
IRR:	32.47%

Scenario 6 - Regional Failure	
Quick Results	
FCFF Value:	$20,601,449
FCFE Value:	$12,926,565
IRR:	28.96%

FIGURE 4.5 Incentive can lead to difficulty hiring adequate staff for the distribution system. This translates to reduced value.

Scenario 1 - Mgmt Base Case	
Quick Results	
FCFF Value:	$27,146,842
FCFE Value:	$16,959,030
IRR:	32.47%

Scenario 7 - Increased Distributor Attrition	
Quick Results	
FCFF Value:	$16,465,069
FCFE Value:	$10,790,850
IRR:	27.99%

FIGURE 4.6 Distributor attrition can severely impact the value of a distribution-focused company.

Scenario 1 - Mgmt Base Case	
Quick Results	
FCFF Value:	$27,146,842
FCFE Value:	$16,959,030
IRR:	32.47%

Scenario 8 - Low Distributor Productivity	
Quick Results	
FCFF Value:	$11,865,557
FCFE Value:	$7,640,539
IRR:	23.19%

FIGURE 4.7 Distributor productivity also affects valuation and return.

Corporate Management Risks

Risks can emerge from due diligence that come under the purview of corporate management. Ultimately, these risks translate into diminished value when business operations are impacted and cash flow is affected. Many variations of corporate management risks can exist in a company, but to illustrate a couple in the case of Solero we will focus on the cash conversion cycle and warranty expense.

In Chapter 3, we looked at the cash conversion cycle as a representation of how efficiently cash is generated. Recall that it is calculated as the number of days inventory outstanding plus days sales outstanding minus days payable outstanding. A valid concern from the due diligence is that it could take longer than expected to receive payments across the distribution system. At the same time, a change in suppliers may require faster payments to new ones. Stressing the underlying components of the cash conversion cycle can translate into real economic loss for a company. Figure 4.8 demonstrates the results from a scenario where the cash conversion cycle is stressed.

Scenario 1 - Mgmt Base Case	
Quick Results	
FCFF Value:	$27,146,842
FCFE Value:	$16,959,030
IRR:	32.47%

Scenario 9 - Inc. Cash Conversion Cycle	
Quick Results	
FCFF Value:	$26,477,416
FCFE Value:	$16,314,787
IRR:	32.23%

FIGURE 4.8 Alterations to the cash conversion cycle impact business operations, cash flow, and, ultimately, value.

Cash Conversion Cycle					
DSO - Base	DIO - Base	DPO - Base	DSO - Stress	DIO - Stress	DPO - Stress
60	80	50	80	140	30

FIGURE 4.9 Increasing the days sales outstanding and days inventory outstanding, while decreasing the days payable outstanding, lowers the cash flow and value of the company.

This scenario is created by using increased days for accounts receivable and inventory and decreased days for accounts payable. The relevant changes are made on the Vectors sheet starting in column X and partially shown in Figure 4.9.

Warranty expense is another corporate management risk that could arise from the due diligence, particularly for a distribution company. If the products have a fault and customers return them at a much higher rate than expected, not only are the sales effectively voided, but there is additional cost to process the returns. There are many ways to account for this when valuing the company, but basically revenue needs to be countered due to warranty returns and expenses relating to the returns. In the Solero model, this is done by increasing the operating expenses, as seen on the Inputs sheet in Scenario 10 (cells Q107:Q116).

The effect of this can be substantial and is shown in Figure 4.10.

Scenario 1 - Mgmt Base Case	
Quick Results	
FCFF Value:	$27,146,842
FCFE Value:	$16,959,030
IRR:	32.47%

Scenario 10 - Inc. Warranty Expense	
Quick Results	
FCFF Value:	$17,711,121
FCFE Value:	$11,309,218
IRR:	28.02%

FIGURE 4.10 Increasing operating expenditures is a method to account for higher-than-expected warranty costs.

Market-Based Risks

While the company can have many inherent risks, there are risks that a due diligence can expose that are related to the markets as a whole. During due diligence the competitive landscape, the industry, and sovereign environment should be analyzed. Unexpected change in those areas can impact the value and return of a private investment.

Changes to foreign exchange rates is an excellent example of a risk that affects the company and one that can specifically affect an investment. In Chapter 2, we introduced the concept of foreign exchange risk, when we discussed screening away companies that were exposed to significant direct and indirect foreign exchange risk. In the instance of Solero, we identified the risks, but were comfortable with the current expectation of the Indian rupee. However, post due diligence, where we now know details on the distribution systems exposure to the rupee and have more clarity on the investment round, we should try to quantify the risk.

In the Solero model, Scenario 11 utilizes an alternative exchange rate path for the Indian rupee. The two potential paths can be seen on the Vectors sheet in column E and F. Notice that in F, the rupee is expected to go from 60 INR/USD to 71 INR/USD over a 10-year period. The stress that this puts on the company and investment is twofold. First, from purely a corporate point of view, Solero's cost of goods sold is in dollars, while the products are primarily sold in India for rupees. This means that as the Indian rupee devalues, the company makes lower margins on sales since it takes more rupees to buy a dollar. Particularly in markets where the customer base is very price sensitive, it would be difficult to pass on the full effect of the devaluation.

An additional stress can also occur on the investment level. In the example in Chapter 2, we saw that an investment was made in Indian rupees, but the investor was a U.S. dollar-based investor. This means that the investor would have to exchange USD for INR at investment and then INR back to USD upon exit. If the INR devalues after investment and up to exit, the investor loses money. In the Solero model, this has been kept simple, with the investment assumed to already be in USD.

Regardless, the effect of devaluation is still substantial for Solero. Figure 4.11 shows the large decrease in value and return due to an expected devaluation.

Beyond foreign exchange, if the industry is on a weakening trend or the sovereign market is becoming more difficult for private enterprises, the investment may be harder to sell at exit. Recall that the ultimate financial

Scenario 1 - Mgmt Base Case		Scenario 11 - FX Devaluation	
Quick Results		Quick Results	
FCFF Value:	$27,146,842	FCFF Value:	$10,848,410
FCFE Value:	$16,959,030	FCFE Value:	$7,163,797
IRR:	32.47%	IRR:	23.91%

FIGURE 4.11 Direct exposure to foreign exchange volatility can impact the valuation and return prospects of a company.

Scenario 1 - Mgmt Base Case	
Quick Results	
FCFF Value:	$27,146,842
FCFE Value:	$16,959,030
IRR:	32.47%

Scenario 12 - Increased Illiquidity	
Quick Results	
FCFF Value:	$21,114,210
FCFE Value:	$13,190,356
IRR:	29.15%

FIGURE 4.12   If a private investment is more difficult to sell, the value and return that is ultimately realized will be lower than expected.

value of an equity investment is predicated on being able to exit and sell the investment. In this instance, we may want to increase the illiquidity discount that was originally assumed. In the Solero model, a 10 percent illiquidity discount was originally assumed in order to incorporate the risk that a private investment is more difficult to sell than a more liquid public investment. Scenario 12 increases the illiquidity discount to 35 percent, the results of which can be seen in Figure 4.12.

After having gone through a wide variety of scenarios for the Solero investment, a trend that careful readers may have seen is that the value of the company seems to be much more volatile than the IRR. This is because there is an advanced feature in the Solero investment, known as a *liquidation preference*.

LIQUIDATION PREFERENCES

After a due diligence, when an investor is analyzing value and return possibilities, the investor may feel the potential outcomes are extremely volatile. To help mitigate these concerns, the investor could propose a liquidation preference to the sponsors. A liquidation preference can be set up in many ways, but at the heart of it is the idea that the holder of the liquidation preference has a priority on cash flow during a liquidation event. Typically, the preference is given to investors who invest in preference shares and the preference is discussed in terms of multiples, such as 1x or 2x.

A basic 2x liquidation preference means that the investor has priority on all cash flows during liquidation, up to 2 times the investment amount. For instance, if an investor invested USD4.5 million into a company and the company realized a liquidation event where USD15 million was available for equity, then the investor would get back USD9 million and the remaining USD6 million would go to other equity investors.

The real protection of a liquidation preference occurs, though, if the company has a distressed liquidation event. If the company was sold under duress and only USD6 million was available for equity holders, the same investor with the 2x liquidation preference would claim all USD6 million and other equity holders would get nothing. In this case, the investor with the liquidation preference would get his or her original investment back, plus some return. However, if we think about the opposite situation, where the company is a home run and sells for many multiples of the original investment valuation, the investor with a simple liquidation preference would only realize a 2x return and an unremarkable IRR.

The idea of participating and nonparticipating liquidation preferences arose out of the "home run" conundrum. We previously described a nonparticipating liquidation preference where the investors only get up to the limit of their preferences. We can examine this situation in more detail in the Excel file LiqPrefs.xlsm located on the website in the Chapter 4 folder. Open this file and go to the sheet named "Non-Participating Liq Pref."

On this sheet we have two separate preference share investors who put in funding during the same round (Investor A: USD4.5 million, Investor B: USD2 million) at a valuation of USD25 million, and negotiated a 2x, nonparticipating liquidation preference. Starting in cell D8 and continuing across row 8 a series of potential exit values are displayed. When there is enough money to pay both investors their 2x liquidation preference, it gets paid and their returns complete. This can be seen in columns E through N, where there is enough money to pay both investors. The IRRs and money multiples in rows 16 and 17 stay static at 12.25 percent and 2x, respectively.

The exception is clearly visible in column D, where there is only USD10 million available after exit, but liquidation preferences totaling USD13 million. Since Investor A and B own the same preference share class, they will split the USD10 million based on the pro-rata percentages of their preference share class holding (Investor A: 69.2%; Investor B: 30.8%). This means that Investor A would get USD6,923,077, earn a 7.44 percent IRR, and make a 1.54x money multiple. This is not too bad, given the low exit scenario and compared to the fact that common equity gets nothing.

The true comparison, though, is what would happen if there were no liquidation preference and instead the investors had invested in the company with only participating shares. Rows 19 through 22 show the calculations at the same exit values. We can see that the investors would lose money until the exit value was the same as the original investment valuation (USD25 million), where they would break even. After breakeven, though, as the exit valuation potential increases the returns for investors concurrently increases. If the exit valuation exceeds 2x, then the pure pro-rata payout is worth more to investors and the liquidation preference would have been a detrimental mechanism. The chart below the calculations that is reproduced as Figure 4.13 shows a comparison of the payout possibilities.

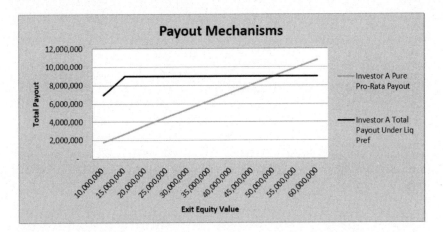

FIGURE 4.13 An investor with a nonparticipating liquidation preference will do better at scenarios below the liquidation multiple and worse in scenarios above.

Since investors would miss out on the upside of the investment, participating liquidation preferences were created. These structures allow the investors to earn their return, protected by a liquidation preference, and then share in any possible upside from a strong exit. For instance, go back to the Excel workbook, to the sheet labeled "Participating Liquidation Preference." The setup for this sheet is similar, but there are two new rows (inserted in 13 and 14) called "Investor A/B Pro Rata Under Liq Pref." These rows allocate remaining funds after the liquidation preference is fulfilled to the preference shareholders, based on the investors' total stakes in cells N4 and N5. This is clearly a very advantageous scenario for investors, since they are protected on the downside and can participate in the upside. Figure 4.14 replicates the chart for total return under various exit figures.

A participating liquidation preference is fairly aggressive, though, and is typically only seen in very risky investments, where the sponsors drastically require funding. It can also be used as a method to force other investors to co-invest during a down round. Investees would normally push back against such a structure, since the risk sharing is lop sided, with heavy investor protection.

Since nonparticipating liquidation preferences strongly limit an investor's upside and a participating liquidation preference may overly benefit an investor, other structures have been created to mitigate the extremes. A participating liquidation preference with a cap is one such structure. The cap refers to a multiple of invested amount. In the example on the sheet labeled "Participating Liq Pref with Cap," we can see that in cell E6 there is a 3. This means that the total return for the preference share

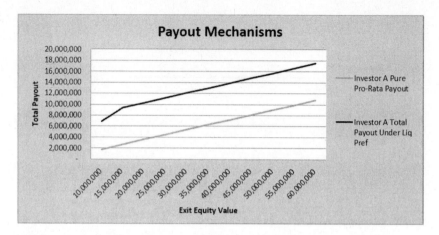

FIGURE 4.14 Under a participating liquidation preference, the investor will always be better off than investing without any liquidation preference.

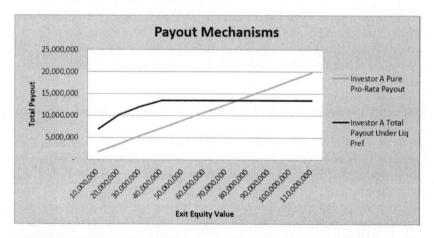

FIGURE 4.15 A participating liquidation preference with a cap allows for upside, to a certain extent.

investors will not exceed 3x. Visibly, Figure 4.15 exemplified the return potential assuming different exit amounts.

In Figure 4.15, all of the characteristics of return are evident by the changing slope of Investor A's payout under a participating liquidation preference with a cap. The first part of the slope shows the higher payout under distressed valuations. The second part of the slope is reduced and increases as participations are available. Finally, the third part of the slope is where the

Scenario 1 - Mgmt Base Case	
Quick Results	
FCFF Value:	$27,146,842
FCFE Value:	$16,959,030
IRR:	32.47%

Scenario 13 - Reduced Liq Pref	
Quick Results	
FCFF Value:	$27,146,842
FCFE Value:	$16,959,030
IRR:	29.80%

FIGURE 4.16 Altering the liquidation preference affects the IRR, but not the valuation.

cap kicks in and the investment return remains fixed. When the exit equity value goes above about USD75 million, the pure pro-rata payout is a better option. There are similarities to the first, nonparticipating situation, where the pure pro-rata payout exceeded the liquidation preference, but for this to occur in the participating preference with a cap, the exit value must be higher.

Returning to the Solero model, we can see that a participating liquidation preference has been assumed on the Rel Val sheet in rows 17 and 18. The Inputs sheet drives the liquidation preference amount, with a base case assuming 2x. Scenario 13 alters the base-case liquidation preference by using 1x instead of 2x. Keep in mind that a reduction in a liquidation preference will only impact the investor and not the value of the firm. Therefore, as expected, in Figure 4.16, we can see a reduction in return, but not valuation.

One final thought, touched on earlier, is that liquidation preferences can be used punitively. If investors are already invested in a company and the company is not performing well, there may be a requirement for additional funding. If existing investors still believe in the company, they will participate in that round of funding. However, since the company is underperforming, there is a good chance that the valuation is lower than what it was for the previous round, known as a down round. Occasionally, not all existing investors will want to participate in a down round. If some of the existing investors decide to participate, while others do not, then the participating investors may try to implement a very aggressive liquidation preference for the new round. These can sometimes be in excess of 3x. Such action is taken to incentivize other investors to participate, since if they do not they may effectively be wiped out upon a liquidity event, as the investors with the new round preference would take a large portion of the exit.

CREATING AN INVESTOR BASE AND DOWNSIDE CASE

Each of the 13 scenarios created thus far has an impact on the valuation and/or return expectations of the company. Taking a step back, the valuation

Scenario	FCFF Value	% of Base	IRR	% of Base
Scenario 1 - Mgmt Base Case	$ 27,146,842	100.00%	32.47%	100.00%
Scenario 2 - Increased COGs	$ 19,491,553	71.80%	29.00%	89.31%
Scenario 3 - Increase Shipping Costs	$ 26,474,655	97.52%	32.19%	99.13%
Scenario 4 - Increased Capex	$ 27,107,487	99.86%	32.47%	99.98%
Scenario 5 - Increased Distributor Margin	$ 21,580,031	79.49%	29.97%	92.29%
Scenario 6 - Regional Failure	$ 20,601,449	75.89%	28.96%	89.19%
Scenario 7 - Increased Distributor Attrition	$ 16,465,069	60.65%	27.99%	86.20%
Scenario 8 - Low Distributor Productivity	$ 11,865,557	43.71%	23.19%	71.41%
Scenario 9 - Inc. Cash Conversion Cycle	$ 26,477,416	97.53%	32.23%	99.26%
Scenario 10 - Inc. Warranty Expense	$ 17,711,121	65.24%	28.02%	86.30%
Scenario 11 - FX Devaluation	$ 10,848,410	39.96%	23.91%	73.62%
Scenario 12 - Increased Illiquidity	$ 21,114,210	77.78%	29.15%	89.76%
Scenario 13 - Reduced Liq Pref	$ 27,146,842	100.00%	29.80%	91.76%

FIGURE 4.17 Examine the results of the sensitivities to see which variables primarily affect the investment.

process overall has been to work with a base case created from management information, then conduct a detailed due diligence to vet data and form independent viewpoints, and then incorporate that knowledge into a model to see the effects on valuation and return. We can summarize the effects of the sensitivities in the table in Figure 4.17.

While we can see that foreign exchange and distributor productivity changes have the most impact and altering capital expenditures has very little, part of these relative differences are caused by the level of each stress. How should the scenario stress levels be determined? There is no simple answer to this question. Rather, the due diligence process should elucidate the necessary stress levels. For instance, after learning about the company in detail we can assess that the most likely increase in capital expenditures beyond their standard plan is to implement new enterprise resource planning and accounting software. A conservative estimate for this cost is USD100,000, but this can be checked against third-party software vendors if the figure is in doubt.

Other, more impactful assumptions, such as foreign exchange devaluation can be assessed based on historical performance. There are many years of history on the INR to USD to draw projections from, which was referenced in Chapter 2. We could project the INR to devalue to its worst 5- or 10-year level, depending on risk appetite. Alternatively, we could take a more scientific approach by examining the volatility over the last few years and then applying a multiple of standard deviation going forward. This could be done for many of the other assumptions as well.

Scenario 1 - Mgmt Base Case	
Quick Results	
FCFF Value:	$27,146,842
FCFE Value:	$16,959,030
IRR:	32.47%

Scenario 14 - Investor Base Case	
Quick Results	
FCFF Value:	$ 8,804,705
FCFE Value:	$ 5,820,520
IRR:	22.30%

FIGURE 4.18 An investor base case combines many of the individual stresses identified.

FCFF Sensitivities					
	LT Growth Rate				
WACC	0.00%	1.00%	2.00%	3.00%	4.00%
21.60%	8,573,250	9,275,574	10,205,556	11,495,299	13,403,624
22.60%	7,971,764	8,618,860	9,475,712	10,664,034	12,422,295
23.60%	7,418,100	8,014,707	8,804,705	9,900,310	11,521,386
24.60%	6,908,031	7,458,450	8,187,286	9,198,070	10,693,643
25.60%	6,437,741	6,945,874	7,618,717	8,551,848	9,932,523

FIGURE 4.19 The same matrix of valuations and returns should be run for the investor base case.

In the Solero model, an investor base case is created on the Inputs sheet in column U, the results of which are shown in Figure 4.18.

The investor base case took aspects of the prior 13 scenarios and incorporated them into a single case. The effects of this are substantial, of course, but the proper mindset is that the assumptions should dictate the results, not vice versa. We can see that there could be a large disconnect between management's expectations of the company's value versus what an investor should believe. To help see the range of possibilities, the matrix of valuations and associated returns should be run by going to the Outputs sheet with Scenario 14 selected on the Inputs sheet and pressing the sensitivities buttons. These results should populate in the model on the Outputs sheet and are also shown in Figure 4.19.

Keep in mind that the values in Figure 4.19 are the company values and that negotiations for equity rounds should be focused on equity value. These values suggest that in most scenarios the company is worth less than USD10 million. Also, the Return Sensitivity table seen in the Output sheet, assumes the investment took place at a certain equity value. The model is not set up to change the equity shares based on the FCFF/FCFE results. This should be done manually. The setting for the equity shares are still set to USD21.5 million of equity valuation, based on the pre-due diligence results.

Return Sensitivities					
	Exit Year				
EBITDA Mult	2019	2020	2021	2022	2023
4	22.11% / 2.72	20.45% / 3.05	18.31% / 3.24	16.58% / 3.41	14.98% / 3.51
5	23.39% / 2.86	21.73% / 3.25	19.39% / 3.46	17.49% / 3.63	15.72% / 3.72
6	24.62% / 3.01	22.95% / 3.46	20.41% / 3.67	18.36% / 3.85	16.43% / 3.93
7	25.80% / 3.15	24.12% / 3.66	21.38% / 3.88	19.19% / 4.07	17.10% / 4.14
8	26.94% / 3.30	25.23% / 3.86	22.30% / 4.09	19.98% / 4.29	17.74% / 4.35

FIGURE 4.20 Even under the stressed Investor Case, at a 21.5 mm post-money equity valuation, there are still favorable return expectations.

While we know from the management case that the investee may ask for a high valuation, we should check the return sensitivities for a 21.5 mm equity valuation assuming the Investor Case stresses. Figure 4.20 shows that even if we had to negotiate up to the 21.5 mm equity valuation, we could still have many favorable return scenarios.

One thing we haven't considered, though, is that the investor base case is still not quite that stressful. If we look at what assumptions were made, one of the assumptions that affected the valuation the most, foreign exchange stress, was left out. This and others should be added in for the investor downside case, which is presented in column V on the Inputs sheet. In Figure 4.21, we can see the compounded effects of adding in more of the most impactful stresses.

The valuation under the downside case would almost be a nonstarter if presented to many investees. The value of running this case, though, resides in the IRR. As we noticed earlier, the IRR is quite resilient. The reason behind the resiliency is that in both investor cases we are assuming that a 2x liquidation preference has been negotiated. We should check the investor downside case with a 1x and 0x liquidation preference. Figures 4.22 and 4.23 show the return matrices of these two cases.

Scenario 1 - Mgmt Base Case	
Quick Results	
FCFF Value:	$27,146,842
FCFE Value:	$16,959,030
IRR:	32.47%

Scenario 15 - Investor Downside Case	
Quick Results	
FCFF Value:	$1,981,905
FCFE Value:	$1,476,427
IRR:	14.36%

FIGURE 4.21 Combining almost all of the stresses shows a very low valuation for the company.

Return Sensitivities					
	Exit Year				
EBITDA Mult	2019	2020	2021	2022	2023
4	5.39% / 1.30	5.29% / 1.36	4.70% / 1.38	4.09% / 1.38	3.49% / 1.36
5	6.28% / 1.36	6.08% / 1.42	5.30% / 1.44	4.55% / 1.43	3.81% / 1.40
6	7.14% / 1.41	6.83% / 1.49	5.88% / 1.49	4.99% / 1.48	4.11% / 1.44
7	7.97% / 1.47	7.56% / 1.55	6.45% / 1.55	5.41% / 1.52	4.41% / 1.47
8	8.78% / 1.52	8.27% / 1.61	6.99% / 1.60	5.83% / 1.57	4.70% / 1.51

FIGURE 4.22 The IRR quickly begins to drop off in stress cases where a liquidation preference is reduced. In this table, the results are generated from a 1x liquidation preference.

Return Sensitivities					
	Exit Year				
EBITDA Mult	2019	2020	2021	2022	2023
4	-19.08% / 0.35	-13.84% / 0.41	-11.48% / 0.43	-10.14% / 0.43	-9.46% / 0.41
5	-16.64% / 0.40	-11.79% / 0.47	-9.89% / 0.48	-8.92% / 0.47	-8.58% / 0.45
6	-14.45% / 0.46	-9.95% / 0.53	-8.46% / 0.54	-7.80% / 0.52	-7.75% / 0.48
7	-12.46% / 0.51	-8.28% / 0.60	-7.15% / 0.60	-6.77% / 0.57	-6.98% / 0.52
8	-10.64% / 0.57	-6.76% / 0.66	-5.94% / 0.65	-5.81% / 0.62	-6.26% / 0.56

FIGURE 4.23 Without a liquidation preference, we can see that there are significant risks of losing money in a downside case.

The exercise of changing the liquidation preference showed us how important it was to the return expectations. Without a liquidation preference, the returns in the downside case would all be negative. Given that many of the stresses built into the downside case could occur, such as the foreign exchange devaluation, negotiating the liquidation preference into the investment structure in this case should be a strong focus and ask for the equity investor.

BRIDGING POTENTIAL VALUATION GAPS WITH CONVERTIBLE DEBT STRUCTURES

As we can see in the case of Solero, there is a large difference between what management may expect for their company's valuation and what the investor expects. Oftentimes, the gap can be closed by the investee working with multiple investors and receiving similar feedback, the investor giving ground and accepting more risk, or altering the transaction structure such as including a liquidation preference as seen in the previous section. If these attempts break down and there is still a large gap, but both parties are still very interested in closing a deal, a convertible debt structure can be a solution.

A *convertible debt structure* for a private investment works similarly to a convertible bond. To help understand how this structure works we should look at how a standard convertible bond functions. The most basic question most people ask when being introduced to convertible bonds, is what the bond converts into? A convertible bond can be structured in many different ways, but most convert from being a debt instrument into equity.

A convertible bond example has been provided in Excel on the book's website, under the Chapter 4 folder. The required elements to analyze the basic convertible structure are shown on the first tab labeled "Basic Convertible Bond," cells D4:D11. These assumptions include:

- *Debt amount*: The initial principal balance of the loan.
- *Interest rate*: The interest rate of the loan. In the example, it is a fixed rate, but it can also be a floating rate with a spread over an index.
- *Term*: The time until the debt matures.
- *Conversion ratio*: Convertible debt is often structured with a conversion ratio reflecting the number of shares that the debt will receive per bond. In this case, the USD1,000 bond would convert into 50 equity shares of the company.
- *Current stock price*: The current equity price of the company that is issuing the debt.
- *Current market rate*: The underlying market rate can differ from the debt's rate. If the market rate is lower than the debt's rate then the bond should be priced at a premium. If the market rate is greater than the debt's rate then the bond should be priced at a discount.
- *Conversion term limit*: Depending on debt structure, there can be a time limit for the debt holder to exercise conversion. In the example, it is set to two years.

To the right of the assumptions, the debt is analyzed in a number of ways. The first step is to create an amortization schedule for the debt, which is done in cells F4:J10. This shows the interest payments and an assumed bullet principal amortization. In K6:K10 the bond cash flows are totaled. By discounting those cash flows at the current market rate, we can quickly calculate the bond's present value.

If we were examining a standard debt investment, we could stop there at bond pricing; however, with a convertible we must also analyze the potential equity value. In order to do this, we need to have an expectation of the issuing company's stock price. Cells M5:M11 show today's stock price and expected future stock prices. The equity value is calculated in cells N5:N11 for each period by multiplying the number of shares from conversion by the current stock price. Given a two-year conversion period, we can see a possible cash flow scenario in cells O6:O11, where the debt holder holds the bond for two years, collects interest payments, and then converts to equity. In year 5, the bondholder chooses to sell the equity shares.

The conversion analysis shows us that the bondholder was better off converting in this scenario because the stock price rose to a level in the fifth year that made the present value of all the cash flows higher than the present value of holding the bond to maturity.[8] To understand this dynamic better, change the stock price values in M8:M10 to 21 for each year. This would mean that the stock appreciates slightly, but stays flat for a number of years. In this scenario, if sold in year 5, the present value of the equity converted instrument would be less than the present value of holding onto the original debt.

With the basic understanding of a convertible bond, we can move on to the more relevant example of investing in a company using a convertible debt instrument. The example is laid out on the next sheet labeled "Convertible Debt Investment." There are many similarities to the convertible bond example used previously. First, many assumptions are known upfront:

- *Investment amount*: This is the amount that will be invested in the company.
- *Interest rate*: Since a debt instrument is initially created, there can be an interest rate. In impact investing, the companies are usually early stage and interest payments may be structured as PIK (payment-in-kind), where interest payments may be missed and capitalized. Some structures may also not have any interest.
- *Convertible term*: The time period for when the debt can be converted to equity. Like interest, this can be structured in many ways. The term can be fixed where conversion occurs on a specific date, no matter what. The conversion can be an option where on the date of conversion the investor has the option to choose to convert or remain a debt holder. Or the investor may have the option to convert at any time period prior to the end of the conversion term.
- *Valuation multiple and multiple basis*: The two most critical and hardest negotiated components to a convertible investment is the valuation

---

[8]This assumes that the current market rate is used to discount both cash flows. Generally equity flows should be discounted at the cost of equity, while debt uses the market rate of debt.

multiple and the basis that the multiple will be applied to. These two elements play a crucial role in determining the equity percentage holding of the investor upon conversion. The multiple is usually straightforward and negotiated based on analysis of comparable companies and entity negotiating power. The multiple basis can be set on any metric, but in early-stage companies revenue is commonly used, since EBITDA may not be expected to generate for a number of years.

In order to complete a convertible investment analysis, we would also need modeling assumptions for the company's performance. As we have seen from the Solero modeling example, we can create detailed financial forecasts and investment valuation scenarios. For this example, we will create a basic revenue expectation with a potential exit scenario.

The real analysis of the convertible investment starts in cell F6, where we first assume cash flow out from investment. In cells G7 and G8, we can calculate two years of interest payments. In this example, we assume that the convertible investor chooses to convert her debt into equity and therefore does not receive a principal payment in column H.

Calculating the equity ownership is the next important step. To do this we must project out the company's revenue. In this example, we use a simple growth rate applied against current revenue. The revenue multiple that was decided on was a pre-money revenue equity multiple. The "pre-money" distinction is incredibly important since it denotes whether the valuation is pre-money or post-money. Recall that the difference between pre-money and post-money is the investment amount, so equity ownership would be very different using one versus the other. The other important qualification is that the multiple is an equity multiple, meaning that the value produced is the equity value, not the enterprise value. Column J shows the pre-money equity valuations over time. The equity ownership is calculated at year two, where the investor's investment amount is divided by the equity value plus the investment amount. Note that the pre-money equity value plus the investment amount returns the post-money equity value. The investment divided by the post-money value is the investor's equity ownership stake after investment.

The total return of the investment can now be calculated. First, an exit timing and value for the investment must be determined. In the example, an exit year and revenue multiple is assumed. The company's equity value in column J uses a formula that calculates the equity value using the exit multiple. Multiplying the investor's equity ownership stake by the equity value is all that needs to be done to determine the investor's cash return. To calculate the IRR of the investment, we must remember to incorporate the debt interest that the investor received. Cells C19 and C20 show the example scenario's IRR and money multiple.

AGREEING TO TERMS

It has sometimes been said that the best investment is one where no party is overly happy. While this may sound very pessimistic, the derivation of the statement has truths. Valuations and investment structure should be accepted by both parties through negotiation. If one party is too happy, the other may feel discontent, and as the investment progresses through the process, the other party may back out. Even worse is if the investment is completed and later discontent emerges. This could have serious effects on the operations of the company.

In order to make the terms of the investment clear and to legally solidify the negotiation, a term sheet and definitive documentation are necessary. This phase in the investment process marks a shift from a more operational analysis to a legal one where certain investment mechanics are documented in detail. Chapter 5 covers this detail, starting off by assuming the investment valuation and structure are agreed upon.

The Term Sheet and Definitive Documentation

Transactions are rarely finalized on verbal agreement alone, particularly corporate investments that could have a number of complexities that establish parties' rights and protections. Ultimately, the documents that govern the transaction are solidified in formal binding agreements and articles, but a term sheet is typically created first. The term sheet lays out the transaction on paper and creates a basis for understanding. The intent is for all parties to be in agreement on terms prior to launching resource and financially intensive legal due diligences and utilizing legal teams to craft final documents.

THE TERM SHEET

The purpose of the *term sheet* is to lay out core details of the investment so all parties understand exactly the terms of the investment. Additionally, there are legally binding clauses of the term sheet to govern certain circumstances prior to finalizing the investment.

Conventional market participants may notice a few unique clauses in this section related to impact investing. Impact investments seek to deliver a product or service to a specific segment of the socioeconomic population previously underserved. If, for whatever reasons, the company deviates from its target population and begins to serve a higher-income segment, it drifts from its original mission. Investors who invest in a company because of this social focus should protect their impact focus in various sections of the term sheet and eventually the definitive documentation.

Overview of a Term Sheet

Term sheets can vary significantly depending on transaction type and specific investment structure; however, most exhibit the following core characteristics:

- Definitions
- Transaction details
- Protective clauses for shareholders
- Protective clauses for boards of directors
- Conditions precedent and subsequent
- Board composition and governance
- Purchase, sale, and conversion rights
- Founder/management restrictions

For each section we will explain the topic, show example language, detail sections that may require specialized consideration for impact investing, and then provide viewpoints from an investor and investee.

Definitions

The start of a term sheet lays out the company, parties to the transactions, and the investment type. These are normally simple definitions, although it's not unlikely to find a controversy. For instance, some individual investees may try to avoid being named to avoid liability or investors discover that the co-investors are investing from an entity that has not been through a due diligence. The definition section of the term sheet solidifies who is involved in the transaction and identifies the type of transaction.

For readers not used to definition conventions in legal documents, a bit of explanation is useful. The main aspect to be aware of is that legal documents use defined terms throughout to avoid misinterpretation and also for reuse of documents. Defined terms have a definition in the document, are defined with quotes around them, and begin with a capital letter, such as Keith Allman, the "Investor." This means that any time Investor is used (with a capital "I") in the document, it refers to Keith Allman.

One has to be extremely careful with reading legal documents because definitions can sound very similar to one another. For instance, the Investor and Investors are two separate definitions. One refers to a single party, Keith Allman, and Investors refers to multiple parties. Also, while the convention is to define terms prior to use in a document, there are many legal documents that use a defined term, which is defined later in the document. It is critical to read all documents in their entirety. With that being said, we will move on to the beginning of the term sheet.

Example Language:

Corporate Entity: Solero, the "Company," a limited liability corporation organized under the laws of the Cayman Islands.

Existing Shareholders: Desh Mallik is referred to as "Existing Shareholder DM," Mike Loh is referred to as "Existing Shareholder ML," and both parties are collectively referred to as the "Existing Shareholders" or the "Founders."

New Investor: Keith Allman is referred to as the "New Investor."

Investors: Existing Shareholders and the New Investors are collectively referred to as the "Investors."

Existing Capital Structure: The share capital of the company, presented on a fully diluted basis, is shown in Exhibit 1.

Proposed Security Type: The New Investor shall subscribe to an investment of convertible Series A Preferred Stock of the Company, "Series A Preferred" or "Preference Shares." The rights of Series A Preferred shareholders shall be consistent with the terms and conditions set forth in this term sheet.

Investor Viewpoint The first item an investor would notice is the type of company that Solero is organized as (a limited liability company otherwise known as an LLC) and one that is incorporated in the Cayman Islands. An investor needs to know the type of entity and place of domicile that they are investing in for legal and tax reasons. At this stage an investor should seek legal and tax advice on the implications of investing in such an entity with the given domicile.

The other critical item for an investor, under the definitions section, is the existing capital structure of the company. Investors should know the current ownership structure of the company. In fact, prior to a term sheet, this topic should be known early on. The details of ownership, though, should be laid out in the term sheet so there are no surprises. Notice that the words "on a fully diluted basis" were used. If existing shareholders have options or warrants that can convert into shares, these should be presented as if they were exercised. Otherwise, an investor stands the risk of negotiating a valuation, establishing an ownership percentage, and then realizing that the ownership percentage is diluted by the exercise of options or warrants.

One potentially dilutive element that investors should be aware of and discuss with the investees is an employee stock option program (ESOP). An ESOP is a specially designed program for a company where shares are created, but not allocated, for future issuance to employees. Such shares will be necessary to attract and retain key employees in the future. If an ESOP does not exist, an investor should plan on establishing one, whether it is done as a condition prior to investment or calculated as part of the expected ownership percentage.

Investee Viewpoint   The main focus for an investee in this section of the term sheet is the Proposed Security Type. The important items for an investee to pick up in this section are descriptors of the investment type. For instance, in the above example the words *convertible* and *preferred* stick out. The term *convertible* can have a number of meanings, so the investee should look for language later in the term sheet that defines the term of the conversion.

Specific to preferred shares, conversion normally means convertible to common stock. This should not be confused with the convertible debt structures that were discussed at the end of Chapter 4. Those types of convertibles are debt that becomes equity. If a convertible debt structure was being used, the investment type would be into a debt security with a convertible option, not into preferred shares.

Returning to the idea that preference shares convert to common stock, there are a couple of key reasons for such a design. The first reason is that new shareholders who put a significant amount of capital into a company may require preferences in order to invest. These preferences can include items already discussed, such as liquidation preferences, or other protective features that will be explored later in this chapter. The second reason is that preference shares typically convert to common shares upon an initial public offering (IPO). The ratio of conversion is usually set to 1:1; however, this can change, depending on anti-dilution provisions, which will also be discussed further in this chapter.

Transaction Details

With the parties to the transaction and the investment type known, the next step is to cover the actual investment in more detail. This section should state the amount being invested, the number of shares being acquired, the valuation that corresponds to the investment round, and the investment round's effects on the capital structure.

Example Language:

As part of the Series A Preferred investment round, the New Investor will make an investment of USD 1,000,000 (the "New Investment") for 200,000 Series A Preferred shares at a price of USD 5.00 per share.

The Series A Preferred investment round is based on a USD 20,500,000 fully diluted pre-money valuation, corresponding to a USD21.5 million post-money valuation. Exhibits I and II shall set forth the pre and post money capitalization of the Company.[1]

At any time, upon the holder's discretion, the convertible Series A Preferred shares are to be convertible into Common Shares, based on the Conversion Rate.

Prior to a Qualified Initial Public Offering (QIPO), the New Investor shall convert the Series A Preferred shares into Common Shares.

Subsequent to investment, the Company will increase the ESOP pool to an unallocated 10 percent of the Company.

Investor Viewpoint The investor should ensure the terms are consistent with the verbal agreements made earlier. Notice in this case the ESOP is to be capitalized up to 10 percent of the company, post-investment. This means that the investor needs to account for an increase of wherever the ESOP allocation currently is, up to 10 percent. Most importantly, the post-investment capitalization table should reflect the expectation and agreement earlier.

The term *QIPO* is referenced in this section and is another item that an investor should understand. We will see later in this chapter that just any initial public offering may not be ideal for investors and that there are certain criteria to establish a qualified initial public offering. The use of this language is to protect the investor against offerings that do not meet a minimum standard and put the investor's return at risk.

Investee Viewpoint The investee should share similar concerns as the investor for this section. The most common confusion tends to be the ESOP pool and elements that could affect the capitalization table. Investees need to be aware that if the investor is asking for the ESOP pool to be increased prior to the investor's investment, then the existing shareholders' ownership will be diluted. In the above situation, the ESOP pool is being increased subsequent to the investment, and thus all parties will share in the dilution.

Protective Clauses for Shareholders

An investor, depending on the investment amount and risk tolerance, could require protective clauses. Generally significant minority investors (10 to 49 percent of the company) require minority rights. These rights can be expressed in different ways, such as through shareholder voting

---

[1]Note that the example calculations pertain to the Solero example and can be seen starting on row 45 of the LT Capital sheet for the New Shareholder 2.

requirements or board approval powers. There can be a number of variations on these voting rights, but often the split between the two occurs with common *shareholder rights* versus *board of director rights*.

The first type of rights we will examine are shareholder rights. These can be dependent on preference share ownership percentages and either require the vote of the investor, the majority of series shareholders, or a supra-majority of series shareholders, if there are multiple investors in the same share class. The following example language captures common preference shareholder rights:

Example Language:

As long as at least 15 percent of the Series A Preferred shares initially issued are outstanding (adjusted for reorganizations, stock splits, etc.), a majority affirmative vote of the Series A Preferred shares will be required for any of the following actions that:

1. Alters or amends the articles of incorporation or the bylaws of the Company or any Subsidiary, if such alteration adversely affects the rights, privileges, preferences, powers, or restrictions on the Series A Preferred shares.

2. Creates or authorizes any new shares, new classes or series of share, options, warrants, or other rights to subscribe for, acquire, or call for shares.

3. Decreases or increases the authorized number of Series A Preferred shares.

4. Approves any sale of assets, merger, or other acquisition or reorganization of or by the Company or any Subsidiary.

5. Approves the purchase, sale, redemption, or other acquisition of capital stock of the Company or any Subsidiary. This excludes repurchases pursuant to stock restriction agreements already approved by the Board of Directors, upon termination of an employee, director, or consultant.

6. Approves the dissolution or liquidation of the Company or any Subsidiary.

7. Encumbers or grants a security interest in all or substantially all of the assets of the Company or any Subsidiary through the commitment of indebtedness.

8. Declares or pays any dividend or distribution with respect to any Series A Preferred shares or the Common Shares of the Company.

9. Changes the number of Board Directors serving on the Board of Directors.

10. Changes the Company's or any Subsidiary's auditors.

Investor Viewpoint   Given that these are investor rights, each one has meaning and reason for an investor. These are discussed with the corresponding number:

1. The first of these rights, the requirement to approve alterations to company bylaws or incorporation documents, is the most basic and fundamental. In fact, any other right is secondary to this right, since altering the core documents of the company can change parties' powers. Clearly, significant investors should have the comfort that the company they are investing in cannot change the terms of their investments through alterations to core company documents.
2. The creation of unauthorized new shares should be obvious to both parties. This dilutes ownership of all parties and can greatly impact investment value. Wording is required, though, to ensure that the protection encompasses items that can convert into shares, such as options.
3. Similar to number two, creating additional shares of the same share class should be expressly prohibited unless discussed and agreed upon.
4. Selling the company or its assets without approval of a significant investor can cause problems, particularly if the value it is sold for provides a low return for the investor. The investor or a majority of investors should have the right to approve a sale or merger. Care needs to be taken with this clause when it comes time to writing the final version in the legal documents, as it should be understood that there are multiple ways to sell a company. For instance, selling the company in small pieces should be addressed by a clause stating that the sale of series of assets with an aggregate amount of X is prohibited, and so on.
5. Another way of changing control of the company is to sell existing shares. Number five covers this, where the sale of capital stock should require approval.
6. Similar to four and five above, dissolving or liquidating the company outside of a sale requires approval.
7. Another issue an investor has to worry about is debt. Debt has priority over equity, even preferred equity. If the company assumes debt, then this could impair the existing shareholders. Another key word that is used is "encumbrance," where the assets that equity investors are invested in are encumbered either by debt holders or by pledges from management.
8. If dividends are paid to Series A Preferred shareholders, it could be earlier than investors want. Not wanting a dividend seems counterintuitive, but there are multiple considerations surrounding such a distribution. First, the investor might perceive that the company needs

the funding for other growth related uses. Without such funding, the overall value of the company might be lowered and the full value of the investment lessened. Second, there are tax implications for receiving a dividend, and an investor should be prepared for receiving one.

9. Shareholders usually vote on the number of directors serving on a board. In the case of a significant minority investor, the board voting will matter and if more board directors are added without the shareholder's consent they could find themselves out voted on critical issues that relate to their predefined board powers (which we will see in the next section of this chapter).

10. Changing auditors might seem minor, but the auditors are an important third-party providing a transparent window into the operations of the company. If the auditors are switched to a local company or family friend of the founders there could be questions of transparency. Typically the choice of auditors is left to the shareholders.

Investee Viewpoint   The list of investor protections in the example is quite comprehensive, and the investee should realize the implications for himself or herself and his or her business. If an investor protection could impede business or is detrimental to the investee's shares, the reasoning for the investor request should be understood. The investor should present a clear and cogent reason for the protection and should never use or rely on the reason, "Because it is standard."

Let's work our way through each of the 10 points:

1. The investee should agree that it will not attempt to alter core business documents without significant shareholder approval. Much of the negotiation at the term sheet stage will make its way into the shareholders agreement, which, in turn, will modify the articles of incorporation. Any core concept introductions should be made at the time of the term sheet creation. Waiting until the shareholder's agreement stage is frowned upon as core concepts should be part of the term sheet.

2. Similar to number 1, the creation of new classes of shares should not be done without significant shareholder request.

3. Creating additional shares for the same share class is also a protection that a significant investor should maintain.

4. Significant investors should have a vote in selling the assets of a company or the company itself. However, the investees must ensure that certain large-size sales are not construed as part of this protection. This could impede the company in a normal course of business if large asset sales can occur. Carving out limits to define what a "large or substantial" size sale is, is a method to mitigate concerns of both parties.

5. Selling capital stock could be part of an investee's plan. There are likely going to be restrictions around founders and management when significant investors invest. Small carve-outs might be agreed to, but investors want to see that investees and management are still committed to the company and retain a large part of their equity.

6. If the course of events goes wrong and the investee wants to dissolve or liquidate the company, significant investors stand to share in the loss. They normally should have the right to approve a dissolution or liquidation plan.

7. Debt is another area where the investee should make sure to have some flexibility. Not allowing an early-stage company to take on millions of dollars of debt has a clear rationale, but what if the company needed USD25,000? Would it have to get the approval of significant minority investors? This could cause unnecessary time and resources spent to obtain approval, which detracts the investee from the business. There should be a threshold to the quantum of debt that requires investor approval.

8. It would be an unusual situation for an investee to pay dividends when a shareholder did not want them. This situation could occur, though, when some shareholder's want a dividend, while others do not. The company's articles of incorporation should clearly delineate the rights of investor classes on voting on and receiving dividends. The investee should make sure that this is understood by existing and new shareholders to avoid disagreements later.

9. Board seats should be settled on during the investment round. Any changes to the board would require a shareholder vote. An investee should think carefully about whom it wants on the board, in terms of contributions and added value.

10. While seemingly benign, an investee has to provide reputable, transparent information. Auditors are key to this and changing audit firms frequently can be a bad signal and also create issues with providing timely financial statements.[2]

Protective Clauses for Boards of Directors

Shareholder rights are very important, but decisions are also made at the board of directors' level. Significant minority investors will usually require

---

[2]Information availability is usually also a requirement. Therefore, any action that an investee does that could inhibit his or her ability to provide timely information puts him or her at risk of violating his or her corporate duties.

at least one voting director. On certain critical issues, a significant minority investor may ask for approval or veto rights. There is a slight distinction between approval and veto rights. Approval rights are technically stronger. It might not seem that way at first glance, but when we discuss board quorum, we will revisit why approval is better for an investor than veto.

For now we will focus on understanding what approval or veto powers an investor might ask for when joining the board of directors.

Example Language:

The Company, nor any Subsidiary, without prior approval of the Board of Directors, including the approval of the New Investor's nominated director, to:

1. Increase the number of Board of Directors serving on the Board.
2. Increase the size of the Company's ESOP or any other stock option plan.
3. License, transfer, or encumber any intellectual property.
4. Remove or modify the compensation of any executive officer of the firm, unless agreed upon in the annual Business Plan.
5. Issue a power of attorney unless part of ordinary business.
6. Amend or approve the annual business plan ("Business Plan").
7. Commit to any capital expenditure that exceeds USD500,000[3] in any one instance or USD1 million in aggregate, other than designated in the agreed upon Business Plan.
8. Commit to any debt greater than USD250,000 in any one instance or USD750,000 in aggregate, other than designated in the agreed upon Business Plan.
9. Commit to any investments in securities or purchase of material assets of a company that exceeds USD100,000 in any one instance or USD1,000,000 in aggregate, other than designated in the agreed upon Business Plan.

Investor Viewpoint We can see here that the investor cares about events that could occur in the course of managing the business. The following comment on each part of the board of director protections:

1. Increasing the board of directors through a board vote should be limited.
2. Similar to a shareholder vote, the board can vote on the ESOP, and this should be limited to avoid unnecessary dilution.

---

[3]The figures presented in the example term sheet are for demonstration purposes only. When negotiating a term sheet, these figures should be adjusted for the operational needs of the company at hand.

3. A key item in investing in any modern business is intellectual property. Particularly with social entrepreneurship, there are often new methods, services, or products being created and used. The investor attributes value to these and must be sure that the company retains them.

4. In early-stage companies, investors have largely invested in management. These are the people that they have entrusted to execute the business plan and grow the company. If some of the directors disagree and want to remove management, an investor who just invested should have discretion over it.

5. Issuing powers of attorney are sometimes viewed as a way around board powers, but clearly this should not be the intent of a power of attorney.

6. Amending and approving the annual business plan is an important duty of the board of directors. It provides the necessary oversight of management and the correct level of involvement in the company. Board directors should not be expected to run the company, but help craft the strategy around it.

7. A significant minority investor may be concerned about the use of his or her proceeds for capital investment. Investment outside of the annual business plan should be carefully regulated.

8. If the company is going to incur debt, for whatever reason, a significant minority investor should have some discretion over this, especially since any debt will be ahead of preference shares during a liquidation scenario.

9. While unusual for most companies, management should not take the funding round proceeds and use it to invest in other securities. The purpose of many of these protections is to ensure that the money provided is used as intended.

Investee Viewpoint   The investee has very clear interests in many of the aforementioned items:

1. It should be clear that the board of directors is only expanded or changed by consent. The investee should consider that a new investor is coming in with a director to represent the investor's best interests. If all of a sudden the board is changed or altered in such a way that the new investor's board vote is diminished, then many of the protections that the new investor valued could be gone.

2. Like other matters, ESOP changes should be made at the time of investment and not after.

3. When an investee creates intellectual property and an investor invests in a company that is based on it, the investee should assign the property rights to the company. While the investee may feel a deep connection to the idea, product, or service, it needs to recognize that the investor most likely perceived a significant amount of value to the intellectual property that was presented.

4. While an investor will want to maintain management, the investee should feel protected that its position is dependent on board of directors' approval. This does not suggest that the new investor director has the ability to remove management or alter salaries, but to only approve the removal or alteration to compensation if it is being considered.

5. There are times when specific powers of attorney may be necessary, but it should be clear to an investee that having unlimited ability to empower an attorney to make key decisions regarding a company is not a good practice.

6. Managing the annual business plan is where confrontation can take place between management and board directors. Some investees may be concerned that a single director could have the ability to hold up business by not approving the annual business plan. This is a valid concern, but properly structuring voting and quorum rules can mitigate it. It would be unlikely that a single board director would consistently vote against an annual business plan that other board members supported. The only instance would be if the board director is unavailable, but if quorum rules are set correctly, the investee should not have to worry.

7. The investee should negotiate a capital expenditure threshold that makes sense for ordinary business.

8. The investee should negotiate a debt-level threshold that makes sense for ordinary business.

9. And finally, the investee should negotiate an investment level that makes sense for ordinary business. The one exception to this is if the initial investment money is drawn down immediately, but not utilized for some time; a safe investment account may be a good place to temporarily keep the investment funds.

Conditions Precedent and Subsequent

In many circumstances of early-stage investment, there are things that investees have not considered that are necessary for an investor to invest. Particular to impact investing, there may be specialized conditions required to finalize the deal. For the most part, these can be overcome by creating conditions precedent and subsequent.

There are three critical components to a condition precedent or subsequent:

1. Establishing the necessary action required
2. Setting the event that the action is precedent or subsequent to
3. Creating the method for verifying that the condition is satisfied

Both parties should think about conditions precedent and subsequent carefully as they must be realistic to accomplish and verify.

Example Language:

> New Investor's signature to the Series A Preferred share's definitive documents is subject to the satisfaction of the following conditions:
> Written approval by Existing Shareholders to:
>
> - Authorize the number of equity shares required for the Series A Preferred investment round and for potential future conversion of the Series A Preferred shares into Common Stock.
> - Create the class of shares called the Series A Preferred share.
> - Waive any preemptive rights and issue shares to the New Investor.
> - Completion of a business, legal, accounting, and technical due diligence of the Company to the satisfaction of the New Investor.
> - All regulatory and legal approvals for the formation of a new holding company, as agreed upon between the Existing Investors and the New Investor.

Investor Viewpoint   The definitive documents will be introduced later, but they are basically the share subscription agreement (SSA) and the shareholder's agreement (SHA). These documents solidify the investment, but the investor should be guaranteed that the equity is there to be provided and that it is "clean." The term *clean* means that there is no contestations to the equity and that it can be distributed without worries of litigation. Additionally, the investor should be allowed time to complete all due diligences, particularly the legal and accounting ones, which may be initiated after the term sheet is signed.

Investee Viewpoint   The conditions precedent to definitive document signature presented above are fair requests by an investor. There can be circumstances when a condition precedent can become unfair though. For instance, if an investment round was predicated on finding a co-investor the new investor may require the co-investor prior to signature of the term sheet. However, if the new investor is abnormally selective, this could hold up the necessary investment for the company. The investee should put a time limit or a clause that states that approval should not be unreasonably withheld.

Another type of condition precedent is one prior to funding. These focus on actions that take place after signing the definitive documents, but before funds have been transferred and the investment round considered closed.

Example Language:

> New Investor's disbursement of the Series A New Investment is subject to the satisfaction of the following conditions:
>
> - The definitive documentation has been executed by all the parties.
> - The Articles of Incorporation have been amended per the new definitive documentation, in a form acceptable to the New Investor.

- Incorporate the social mission of the Company, as part of its business objectives, into the definitive documents and amended articles of incorporation.
- All required authorizations, approvals, and consents have been received.
- Closing certificates have been delivered.
- D&O insurance coverage to a level and with terms reasonably acceptable to the Director nominated by the New Investor.
- Current employees and consultants have entered into nondisclosure and proprietary rights assignment agreements, in forms acceptable to the New Investor.
- No material adverse changes with respect to the Company have occurred.

Investor Viewpoint   For the most part, the above requirements are basic to an investment in a company. The details of directors' and officers' liability insurance (D&O insurance) can cause issues as a new director wants to be covered against liability adequately, but an early-stage company needs to control costs. Material adverse change clauses can give investees concern, but an investor needs to be sure that nothing material has changed since due diligence was completed.

Incorporating the company's social mission commitment into the definitive documentation is a unique clause that stands out. An impact investor wants to make sure that the company remains focused on its social mission. The clause may be weak in this section, but can be solidified with more repercussions in other sections such as optional redemption.

Investee Viewpoint   The only points an investee should have with the above conditions precedent are that there are a few items that have the wording "acceptable to the New Investor." For items such as proprietary rights assignments, the language can become very detailed with legal jargon. This may require back and forth to agree on a final version that works with all parties.

The social mission clause may cause concern for an investee if it is too restrictive. What if, in future funding rounds the investee is trying to attract a more mainstream investor? Will the language in the definitive documentation from the current round detract from that investor investing?

Board Composition and Governance

The next critical section of a term sheet focuses on the board of directors, its composition, and governance. This may seem like a tedious detail, but critical decisions that can have significant impact on a firm are made at the board level.

Example Language:

1. The Board shall consist of three Directors with two Directors appointed by Existing Shareholders and one Director appointed by the New Investor.
2. Prior to a Board meeting, the Company shall send an agenda for the meeting that sets forth the items that will be discussed and voted on during the meeting. Quorum for a Board meeting shall be two Directors, provided that the New Investor's Director is present at the meeting. If the New Investor Director is not present at a properly noticed meeting and other quorum requirements are satisfied, the meeting shall be adjourned until 10 business days later. If the New Investment Director fails to attend the following meeting and the other quorum requirements are satisfied, the New Investor Director shall be deemed present at the meeting and shall be assumed to have approved items on the agenda for the meeting.
3. Board decisions shall be taken on a simple majority basis where a quorum is present, except for decisions requiring approval of the New Investor Director.

Investor Viewpoints   The number of directors is a topic that usually comes up. Normally, an odd number is preferred, with at least one director being an independent director. In the example, the company is still at an early stage where there is only a need for three directors.

The second part of the section is the more interesting aspect. Quorum requirements are necessary to ensure that meetings and decisions take place, but with sufficient participation. Earlier there were a number of decisions that the new investor required having approval over. These meetings have special quorum requirements where the new investor must be present and vote on those decisions.

In this example, the investor has an approval right, which requires management to seek approval from the new investor director. This is usually stronger than a veto right, where management can propose something and then the new investor director can veto. If the new investor director does not carefully follow agendas, something could be passed without his or her full understanding. An approval requires the specific approval of the new investor director, which would mean the director would have to be informed.

Investee Viewpoint   For board meetings, the investee wants to make sure that informed decisions can be made efficiently. Typically, smaller boards will have an odd number of directors to ensure voting is streamlined through simple majorities. To bring expertise, guidance, and connections, an investee may prefer an independent director who is a seasoned professional in the industry the company is operating within. Beyond direct operational strategy, the director can bring in valuable connections for future funding rounds and possible exit opportunities.

For the investee, a concern is that the new investor director will consistently miss meetings, thus delaying important decisions that have implications on the firm. To prevent this, there is language that defines a system for allowing decisions to be made if the new investor director is consistently absent. Specifically, the new investor director can miss a meeting, and any voting that requires the new investor director will have to be delayed. If the new investor director misses another meeting after this, properly noticed, then it is assumed the new investor director provided approval. Both investor and investee must be comfortable with quorum requirements.

Purchase, Sale, and Conversion Rights

A number of rights are negotiated surrounding the purchase, sale, and conversion of shares. Many of these rights are seen across early stage transactions and stem from the idea of preserving value of both the company and shareholding.

A risk that is always on an investor's mind is dilution, which can occur in many ways. One simple way that an investor can get diluted is when new investment rounds occur and new shares are issued. A protection that investors ask for to help mitigate this concern is *preemptive rights* on additional issues.

Example Language:

> The New Investor shall have the first right to subscribe to a pro-rata percentage of up to the entire new issue of shares or other securities, on the basis of his or her existing shareholding percentage in the Company.

Investor Viewpoint With this clause the investor preserves the right to purchase any new issuance of securities that the company may offer. The language states, "to a pro-rata percentage ... on the basis of ... existing shareholding." This allows the new investor to maintain his or her shareholding percentage even if a new issuance occurs. Keep in mind, though, that the valuation or the price per share of the new security is not set, so the investor will have to reassess the business and determine whether the price per share makes sense for further investment.

Investee Viewpoint The investee should be comfortable allowing an investor to have preemptive rights as long as the pricing or valuation is not set.

Founder/Management Restrictions

Alignment of interest is another concern of investors. If the founders or key management sell their equity stakes early in the investment period then there could be little incentive for them to keep working. Additionally, new management might take the company in a direction that the original investor did not intend. This is particularly important for impact investors, considering the original investment thesis incorporates the social mission of the business.

Example Language:

> While the New Investor maintains shareholding, the Founders will not transfer, encumber, dispose, or create any lien on any share or other securities in the Company.

Investor Viewpoint The wording should comprehensively prevent the investee from not maintaining a shareholding in the company. The investor invested with the idea that the founders were there to execute the business plan. To be properly incentivized and align interest the founders should maintain their shareholding.

Investee Viewpoint A valid counter to the statement above is that the investor might maintain shareholding for a long time. The investee may want to qualify the statement above with a time frame. For instance, the section could start with, "For a period of two years from the New Investor's Series A Preferred investment ... " This would provide management with comfort that the founders will be involved during a critical growth phrase. The investor may request that the founders maintain a certain minimum shareholding even after such a time period.

ANTI-DILUTION

If a future round of issuance is offered at a lower price than the investor paid for the prior round, then the investment can become diluted. There can be myriad reasons for lower valuations that lead to lower prices, but the most common is poor performance of the company. Anti-dilution clauses protect preference share investors by adjusting the conversion ratio of preference shares to common shares, to compensate for lower valuations. There are a number of established methods to calculate the conversion ratio adjustment, each one offering a different level of risk transfer between investor and investee.

The three primary types of anti-dilution methods include:

1. *Broad-based weighted average*: This method calculates a new conversion price[4] using all shares and options as part of the average.
2. *Narrow-based weighted average*: This method calculates a new conversion price using only the respective share class amounts as part of the average.
3. *Ratchet-based*: This method uses the down round price for the conversion prices.

To truly understand how these work, we will work through an Excel-based example of capitalization table shifts based on round conditions and different anti-dilution provisions. The Excel example AntiDultion.xlsx can be found on the book's website under the Chapter 5 folder.

Up Round

To set up a comparable basis, we will first look at an example where a company has gone through a Series B round of investment, the company has grown well and expects a higher valuation, and is now looking to close a Series C round. We can see that there is common stock, Series A Preferred stock, Series B Preferred stock, and options. The total number of shares for each type of stock is provided. We can also see the price per share for each of the preferred series, which has doubled from Series A to Series B. This allows us to calculate the "Paid In," which is how much money each preferred series actually put into the company. Finally, we can see under a conversion to common shares how many shares each class would have. In this situation the conversion ratio starts at 1:1, so the ownership for everyone, the "As if %," is directly calculated as each classes shares divided by total shares. Figure 5.1 summarizes this information.

If we move over the sheet to cell H5, we can see the start of a new section of calculations, where Series C has been added in. We assume that Series C has put in USD12 million, and the valuation for the company has once again doubled, so the share price is USD4 per share, and therefore Series C gets 3 million shares. The common conversion still takes place at a 1:1 ratio, and we see that the introduction of the Series C investment dilutes every share class. Figure 5.2 shows the data for this event.

---

[4]Note that the conversion price is not the same as the conversion ratio.

Series C - No Down Round & Convert to Common

	# of Shares	Price per Share	Paid In	Common Conversion	As if %
Common Stock	2,000,000			2,000,000	30.77%
Series A Preferred Stock	1,000,000	1.00	1,000,000	1,000,000	15.38%
Series B Preferred Stock	2,500,000	2.00	5,000,000	2,500,000	38.46%
Options	1,000,000			1,000,000	15.38%
Total	6,500,000			6,500,000	

FIGURE 5.1 In the first example, there is no down round and the Series B investor pays two times the valuation as the Series A investor. Converting to commons shares is done on a 1:1 basis.

Series C	# of Shares	Price per Share	Paid In	Common Conversion	
Common Stock	2,000,000			2,000,000	21.05%
Series A Preferred Stock	1,000,000	1.00	1,000,000	1,000,000	10.53%
Series B Preferred Stock	2,500,000	2.00	5,000,000	2,500,000	26.32%
Series C Preferred Stock	3,000,000	4.00	12,000,000	3,000,000	31.58%
Options	1,000,000			1,000,000	10.53%
Total	9,500,000			9,500,000	

FIGURE 5.2 We can see that the Series C investor gets .25 shares for every dollar invested in the no-down-round state.

Down Round, Broad-Based Weighted Average Anti-Dilution Rights

In the next example, which starts on row 13 of the Excel sheet, the starting point stays the same, but the subsequent Series C round takes place assuming a down round. The price per share is now USD.50, which is a quarter of the value of the prior round. This is a severe down round, but the severity is being used to really demonstrate the differences. We assume that the company has had to scale down its growth plans and only needs USD1.5 million. In such a case, the Series C investor would still get 3 million shares, but at a far lower cost. The conversion ratio for the Series C would still be 1:1.

The more interesting aspect, though, is that under a broad-based weighted average method, the conversion prices for the Series A and Series B preferred classes would increase above 1. The reason for this is the anti-dilution adjusted price drops after applying the broad-based weighted average method. The formula to calculate the adjusted price for a

Series C

	# of Shares	Price per Share	Paid In	Anti-Dilution Adj. Price	Conversion Ratio	Common Share Conversion	%
Common Stock	2,000,000					2,000,000	19.11%
Series A Preferred Stock	1,000,000	1.00	1,000,000	0.84	1.19	1,187,500	11.35%
Series B Preferred Stock	2,500,000	2.00	5,000,000	1.53	1.31	3,275,862	31.31%
Series C Preferred Stock	3,000,000	0.50	1,500,000	0.50	1.00	3,000,000	28.67%
Options	1,000,000					1,000,000	9.56%
Total	9,500,000					10,463,362	

FIGURE 5.3 In this example, the Series C investor invests during a down round. The Series A and B investors are protected by a broad-based weighted-average formula for conversion to common shares.

preferred series is:

Anti-Dilution Adjusted Price = Series Original Price Per Share ∗ (Total # of Shares Including As-If Converted Options + (New Round Investment Amount/Series Original Amount Invested))/(Total # of Shares Including As-If Converted Options + New Round Investment Shares)

We can then divide each series' original price per share by the adjusted price per share to get the conversion ratio. By multiplying the original preferred shares by the conversion ratio, we get the common shares. The percentage of converted common shares divided by the total common shares after all conversions is the ownership percentage. Figure 5.3 shows this calculation.

An interesting comparison is to look at the ownership percentages in example 1, compared to example 2. In the up round, the conversion ratio remained the same. However, in the down round scenario, the conversion ratios increased and the preferred share series increased their ownership percentages to compensate for the dilution given a down round. Keep in mind that the capital structure must total 100 percent. If the preferred series received more, it means that the other forms of equity were further diluted.

Down Round, Narrow-Based Weighted Average Anti-Dilution Rights

Another weighted average approach is to take a narrow-based weighted average calculation for adjusted price. This is very similar to the broad-based weighted average, but as the name implies, it uses a more limited scope to calculate the price. Instead of using all Total # of Shares including As-If Converted Options, the calculation uses the individual preferred Series #

Series C	# of Shares	Price per Share	Paid In	Anti-Dilution Adj. Price	Conversion Ratio	Common Share Conversion	
Common Stock	2,000,000					2,000,000	16.91%
Series A Preferred Stock	1,000,000	1.00	1,000,000	0.63	1.60	1,600,000	13.52%
Series B Preferred Stock	2,500,000	2.00	5,000,000	1.18	1.69	4,230,769	35.76%
Series C Preferred Stock	3,000,000	0.50	1,500,000	0.50	1.00	3,000,000	25.36%
Options	1,000,000					1,000,000	8.45%
Total	9,500,000					11,830,769	

FIGURE 5.4 A narrow-based weighted-average formula produces less dilution for investors with such a right.

of shares. Rewriting the formula would look like:

Anti-Dilution Adjusted Price = Series Original Price Per Share ∗ (Series

Original # of Shares + (New Round Investment Amount/Series Original

Amount Invested))/(Series # of Shares + New Round Investment Shares)

The effect of using this formula is that the adjusted price will be lower than if a broad-based average was used. A lower adjusted price means that the conversion ratio will be higher and therefore preferred series investors will have a greater ownership percentage than if they used a broad based average. This also means that the other share classes will experience a greater dilution. In Figure 5.4 we can see the calculations for comparison.

Down Round, Ratchet-Based Anti-Dilution Rights

Ratchet-based anti-dilution is the final type of anti-dilution rights to discuss and is rarely seen in modern term sheets. The reason it is hardly seen is that it is very investor-centric and effectively prevents any type of dilution due to a future down round. The method employed is to make the anti-dilution adjusted price equivalent to the price of the down round. When used in the conversion ratio, prior investors are made whole for the lower valuation by an issuance of shares to cover the difference. The calculation can be seen in Figure 5.5 and in the anti-dilution spreadsheet.

Down Round, No Anti-Dilution Rights

The final example to provide is if no anti-dilution rights existed. The case is clear that the old investors would take a significant dilution. This can be seen by using an example comparing example 1, without a down round,

Series C

	# of Shares	Price per Share	Paid In	Anti-Dilution Adj. Price	Conversion Ratio	Common Share Conversion	
Common Stock	2,000,000					2,000,000	11.11%
Series A Preferred Stock	1,000,000	1.00	1,000,000	0.50	2.00	2,000,000	11.11%
Series B Preferred Stock	2,500,000	2.00	5,000,000	0.50	4.00	10,000,000	55.56%
Series C Preferred Stock	3,000,000	0.50	1,500,000	0.50	1.00	3,000,000	16.67%
Options	1,000,000					1,000,000	5.56%
Total	9,500,000					18,000,000	

FIGURE 5.5   A ratchet-based anti-dilution method produces the best outcome for investors who paid high valuations; however, the mechanics could inhibit future investors.

Series C

	# of Shares	Price per Share	Paid In	Anti-Dilution Adj. Price	Conversion Ratio	Common Share Conversion	
Common Stock	2,000,000					2,000,000	21.05%
Series A Preferred Stock	1,000,000	1.00	1,000,000	1.00	1.00	1,000,000	10.53%
Series B Preferred Stock	2,500,000	2.00	5,000,000	2.00	1.00	2,500,000	26.32%
Series C Preferred Stock	3,000,000	0.50	1,500,000	0.50	1.00	3,000,000	31.58%
Options	1,000,000					1,000,000	10.53%
Total	9,500,000					9,500,000	

FIGURE 5.6   No anti-dilution protection clearly results in dilution after a down round and conversion to common shares.

to the current setup in example 5, down round with no anti-dilution. In example 1, we can see that the Series C investor paid USD12 million for 3 million shares. In example 5, we can see that the same investor only had to pay USD1.5 million for the same 3 million shares, since the valuation and thus per share price was much lower.

If we assume that the company needs the full USD12 million for the Series C round in a down round situation and there are no anti-dilution rights, then all other parties will be severely diluted. Change the number of shares in cell I45 from 3 million to 24 million. This will automatically change the invested amount to USD12 million. You can see the significant dilution that the other investors are forced to take in Figure 5.6.

Understanding the Dynamics of Anti-Dilution Rights

Anti-dilution can be complex since it could be both a consideration on the mind of an investor into a company that has shareholders with existing rights and also something the existing investor has to think about for future investment rounds. The easiest place to start is to look at ratchet-based anti-dilution, the most extreme anti-dilution right.

As shown in the examples and in the anti-dilution spreadsheet, ratchet-based anti-dilution provides a powerful protection against down rounds for an investor. What an investor has to realize, though, is that such a protection will be analyzed by future investors in the company and could very well be prohibitive to future investment rounds. For instance, in the example on the spreadsheet, if the Series C investor sees a ratchet-based anti-dilution right that the Series B investors have, the investor legitimately could be concerned that the investment would be worth less than expected. At investment, the Series C investor would have 3 million shares out of 9.5 million shares, affording that investor nearly 32 percent of the equity of the company. However, if the down round initiated the anti-dilution provisions, the Series A and B investors would get more common shares, thus increasing the investor's stake and also the total shares of the company. This course of events would cause the Series C investor to only hold 16.67 percent of the company, which is nearly a 50 percent loss in holding.

In a scenario involving weighted-average-based methods, the Series A and B investors would still be compensated, by more shares, but not as much as using a ratchet-based method. These methods are more of a middle ground for current investors and more commonly used, since future investors would not have as much risk as a ratchet-based method and current investors still maintain a protection.

As with the earlier term sheet sections, we will continue explaining topics, show example language, and provide viewpoints from an investor and investee.

Example Language:

> At any time, if the Company issues any shares or equivalent securities that are convertible into Preference Shares or Ordinary Shares at a price less than the price paid by the New Investor for the Series A Preferred shares, the Conversion Price used to calculate the Conversion Ratio for the Series A Preferred shares shall be reduced based on a broad based weighted average method.

Investor Viewpoint Anti-dilution rights are important to protect significant investors against future down rounds. The method utilized to calculate the protection, though, should take into consideration the possible need of future investors. Also keep in mind that while an investor may be compensated with additional shares, the company is still in a precarious position if a down round is taking place. The additional shares will only be useful if the company is able to turn things around and maintain or increase corporate value.

Investee Viewpoint An investee will likely agree to a reasonable anti-dilution provision. The investee must ensure that the terms are favorable enough though for future investment.

Right of First Refusal/Right of First Offer

Eventually, shares in a company will be sold to other parties. Both investors and investees worry about such shareholding shifts and negotiate rules around such sales. The first of these rules most encounter are the *right of first refusal* (ROFR) and/or the *right of first offer* (ROFO). The mechanisms are closely linked, so we should discuss both.

In respect to a ROFR, the seller of the shares seeks out purchasers for the shares, negotiates terms of the sale, and then must offer the same terms to the holder of the ROFR. The holder of the ROFR can then choose to purchase at those terms or waive the right. A ROFO is different in that the owner of the shares asks the holder of the ROFO to make an offer to purchase the shares. If the terms of the offer cannot be negotiated, then the seller can offer the shares to a separate party. However, most ROFOs are structured such that the seller cannot offer the shares at lesser terms (particularly in reference to price) than what the holder of the ROFO offered.

Example Language:

> If holders of Ordinary Shares of the Company intend to sell all or a portion of their shareholding, then the shareholder shall first offer the right to purchase such shares to the Company. If the Company chooses not to purchase the offered shares then the shares shall be offered to the New Investor. If the ROFO is waived, the seller cannot sell the shares to a third party for a price less than what was offered by the Company or New Investor. If the shares are not sold after a period of six months from the initial ROFO then the ROFO provisions reset. If holders of Series A Preferred shares intend to sell all or a portion of their shareholding, then the shareholder shall first offer the right to purchase such shares to the New Investor. If the ROFO is waived, the seller cannot sell the shares to a third party for a price less than what was offered by the New Investor. If the shares are not sold after a period of six months from the initial ROFO then the ROFO provisions reset.

Investor Viewpoint A ROFO and ROFR have different advantages and disadvantages to each party. In a ROFO, the investor has the ability to negotiate a price first with the seller. The seller can always try to force a high price; however, the critical language that an investor needs when securing a ROFO is that the seller cannot offer the shares to another party for a lesser price. This prevents the seller from avoiding selling the shares to the ROFO holder by demanding an exceedingly high price. A third party would probably not purchase the shares and months later the ROFO provision would reset.

A ROFR has the effect of limiting the number of potential purchasers and therefore reducing competitive negotiating on the terms. Many purchasers will be dissuaded from entering into negotiations if a ROFR is in place since purchasing privately held shares requires a thorough due diligence of the company. If the ROFR is executed then all of the work that a third party put into the due diligence and negotiations would be wasted.

The other critical item to notice is that there is a distinction between ordinary and preferred shares. In the example language the ordinary shares were first offered to the company and if the company did not exercise the ROFO then the new investor had the ability to purchase the shares. For the preferred shares, though, the new investor had the first ROFO. This is consistent with founders and management having the ability to maintain their own stakes in the company. If one of two founders wanted to sell shares, then the other founder has the right to purchase the shares. The total shares from a founder's point of view still remain in founder's hands. In the case of two Series A investors, if one wanted to sell shares, then the other Series A investor has the right to purchase the shares and maintain Series A ownership. This could be important for other shareholder rights that are predicated upon shareholding requirements.

Investee Viewpoint A ROFO and ROFR is a situation where the investee has similar concerns as the investor. They want fair terms in selling or acquiring shareholder shares. The main concern for investees should be focused on the sale of ordinary shares that their founding partners may have. Founders should have the ability to pick up other founder's shares. An investee should push back if an investor is trying to negotiate a ROFO or ROFR clause that allows them to have a first right on ordinary shares.

Tag-along Rights

When a shareholder has found a buyer of shares, the ability for other shareholders to join in that sale is another sale right that is typically negotiated. These *tag-along rights* allow a shareholder to sell the same percentage of shares that the other shareholders are selling.

Example Language:

> The New Investor shall have the right, but not the obligation, to sell to a third party a percentage of shares held by the New Investor that is proportional to shares being sold or transferred by Existing Shareholders. The terms of the sale shall be the same as the Existing Shareholders.

Investor Viewpoint If a strong sale opportunity exists, then an investor will want the ability to participate in it. A key clause seen in the example language, though, is that the tag-along rights are an option, not an obligation. Tag-along rights can inhibit the possibility of a sale, though, since an acquirer of the shares will have to purchase the proportional amount of shares from the holder of the tag-along rights.

Investee Viewpoint An investee will normally be more focused on who is purchasing the shares, rather than which investors are selling their shares. Overly restricting share sales causes friction amongst investors, but the investee should ensure the prior ROFR/ROFO rights are strongly worded since the entity ultimately invested in the company is the important focal point.

Drag-along Rights

While tag-along rights are focused on the ability of a shareholder to join in on a sale, *drag-along rights* can occur where a majority of investors want to sell, but a minority investor has not agreed. To prevent a hold up of the sale by a minority investor, drag along rights are often negotiated.

Example Language:

> On or after the Qualified Initial Public Offering (QIPO) Date or with the approval of the Board of Directors and the holder of a majority of the Series A Preferred shareholders, a majority of Existing Shareholders[5] who wish to transfer their shares to a third party shall have the right to require the remaining shareholders to join in the transfer, on the same terms as the requesting shareholders. The New Investor can only be required to transfer shares if the transaction yields the New Investor a net annualized return on investment of at least 25 percent on the initial capital invested by the New Investor.

Investor Viewpoint A group of investors who find a viable opportunity to exit their position should not be held up by a minority of investors. However, an investor has to be cognizant that the drag-along rights can apply to themselves. If the investors are getting dragged, they need to ensure that they will make an adequate return. We can see in the example language that there is a clause for the new investor that requires at least a 25 percent return.

---

[5] Usually worded with the phrase "on a fully-diluted basis," to ensure that the majority is fully achieved after all options are exercised.

Earlier investors most likely invested at a lower valuation than the Series A investor and could make a strong return at a lower sale price than the Series A investor would need. By ensuring the 25 percent return the investor prevents a situation where they are dragged at a low valuation, other investors make a strong return, but the Series A investor has a lower return.

Investee Viewpoint Drag-along rights are important to investees as well, since they too do not want a sale to be unnecessarily held up. Investee concern around a certain return percentage is minimal since they ultimately entered into the company with at-cost shares. Notice, though, in the example language that the drag-along rights are not initiated until after something termed the qualified initial public offering (QIPO) date. This means that the drag rights do not take effect until after that date. This allows time for the investment to grow without the worry about being dragged into sale too early. The QIPO clause, though, is also a signal that the preferred exit for parties is a QIPO and that selling the company is a secondary exit path.

Liquidation Preference

A liquidation preference is a right to priority over cash flow, the mechanics of which were discussed in Chapter 4. Earlier, we showed liquidation preference calculations and how the strategy of using one is designed to protect returns for investors. The concept is a core part of the transaction and should be expressed in the term sheet.

Example Language:

Upon liquidation, sale, merger, or acquisition of the Company, proceeds will be paid to the New Investor according to the following formula: The greater of (i) and (ii) below:

i. 200 percent of the amount paid by the New Investor for their Series A Preferred shares, plus any accrued, but unpaid dividends. If liquidation proceeds remain after payout, the remaining proceeds will be distributed pro rata to the Series A Preferred shareholders, assuming an as-if-converted basis, and to Ordinary Shareholders, until the New Investor received 300 percent of the amount paid by the New Investor for their Series A Preferred shares. If liquidation proceeds remain after such payout all remaining proceeds will be distributed to Ordinary shareholders.

ii. The amount due to the New Investor if the investor's Series A Preferred shares were converted to ordinary shares immediately prior to the realization of such liquidation.

Investor Viewpoint   The motivation for a liquidation preference is clear, but implementing one in writing can be opaque. In the previous example language, the first item that should be addressed is the definition of *liquidation*. While still at a term sheet level, the wording is such that if the company is sold, merged, or acquired the liquidation preference is initiated. Basically, a liquidity event causes the liquidation preference, which should be further refined in the final shareholder's agreement.

The next key item is that the liquidation preference is structured to ensure a maximum payout depending on two calculations. The first is the actual liquidation preference where the investor will receive 2x. Next, we can see that this is a partially participating preference where the investor receives a pro rata share of remaining funds, but is capped at a 3x return. After which, ordinary shareholders take the remaining funds.

The final part of the preference is the alternative payout, which is simply to convert to ordinary shares. This example language forms a very strong agreement for the investors, since they are protected in downside cases through (i) and in extreme upside cases they can benefit by (ii). Investors need to be careful, though, regarding how far they push the liquidation preference, since it creates a structure that can disincentivize management and other critical equity holders whose return priority resides below the liquidation preference.

Investee Viewpoint   The most important component for an investee is that the liquidation preference still allows for the investee to realize adequate return in a liquidity event to keep growing the business toward such event. The specifics of the language should detail exactly how much the preference pays and whether or not it is participating, participating with a cap, or nonparticipating. Overall, the balance of the liquidation preference in favor of the investor or investee is largely determined by the current risk profile of the company. Riskier companies with significant downside will be more susceptible to stronger liquidation preference terms.

Redemption/Buy Back/Put Options

Having the company buy back or redeem investors' shares is a measure of last resort. Investors are concerned that their investments will linger indefinitely with no method of returning cash. This is problematic for fund investors who must return money themselves to their own investors. Additionally, with an impact investment there can be concern of mission drift. An impact investor who has disclosed to the investee the requirements for investing in the company should feel secure that his or her investment funds are being used within the original social mission paradigm. In order to mitigate these concerns, a redemption, buy-back, or put-option clause can be negotiated.

Example Language:

> After the sixth anniversary of the closing of the Series A Preferred investment round, the New Investor has the option to require the Company to repurchase all of the shares held by the New Investor. The minimum redemption price must yield the New Investor an annualized net return on investment of at least 10 percent on the initial capital invested by the New Investor. In the event the redemption causes insolvency of the Company, the redemption amount shall be decreased to prevent such insolvency.

> At any time, assuming such right does not cause insolvency, the Company grants the New Investor the irrevocable option to require the Company to acquire or repurchase all of the New Investor's shares in the event of any material change in the nature and extent of the business and target market, especially any deviation from its intended social mission.

Investor Viewpoint   The first point that an investor should negotiate is when the redemption right kicks in. Usually, a fair amount of time should pass to allow other exit options to take place. This is usually five to six years, but it can be longer for impact investments given their elongated time frames. The second point is who actually buys back the shares and under what terms. The basic concern is that a company purposely delays a liquidation event or QIPO, buys back the shares at a low price, and then consummates the liquidation event or QIPO. Although unlikely, there are additional clauses that should be put in the shareholder's agreement that restrict actions after buy back. We can see in the example language that the price of the redemption is restricted by a minimum yield requirement for the investor.

The social mission section is investor focused, but for good reason. An impact investor's intent is to generate positive social return, which would be lost if the company switched strategies. While those shifts should be prevented, if they must be taken to preserve the viability of the company, the investor should have the right to exit.

Ultimately, though, a redemption clause is a fairly weak clause for an investor. If a company is in a situation where it is being forced to buy back shares it is unlikely that the company is doing very well. Usually a redemption is a last resort, which means that it was not an acquisition target by other companies and it was unable to float shares on a public stock market. Investors who rely on redemption clauses should remind themselves that the company needs funds in order to fulfill the redemption. Without the funds, the redemption clause is worthless.

Investee Viewpoint   An investee may disagree with a redemption clause, suggesting that the investor should be committed to the company. If, however, such a clause is required the investee should make sure that the redemption does not threaten the viability of the company. Any redemption requires cash and this could be problematic for a company that is unable to be acquired or have an initial public offering. There is language in the example that suggests the redemption should be scaled back if the company becomes insolvent due to the redemption. Additionally, the redemption can be tightened up by requiring a payout period, where the shares are redeemed in equal intervals over time. In regards to the social mission language the investee may want a stricter definition of the metric to initiate the redemption. As an example, in the case of Solero, the business and target market could be defined as a strategy to sell solar lamps to Indian households with monthly income lower than two monthly minimum wages (see Labor Bureau of India for official rates).

Exit Option—QIPO

Describing the preferred exit option of an IPO is a clause often seen in term sheets. These tend to be weaker clauses, since the possibility of a successful IPO is dependent on growth over time and the IPO market, which are factors beyond the immediate, direct control of most management and investors. There are important elements, though, to this clause that should be discussed.

Example Language:

> Within five years from the initial closing of the Series A Preferred investment round, commercially reasonable efforts toward an exit for investors through a Qualified IPO (QIPO) or share sale shall be made by the Company. The New Investor shall have standard registration rights in the case of a QIPO. At any time or in any manner the New Investor will not be considered a promoter of the Company for any current or future legal or regulatory purpose.

Investor Viewpoint   An investor wants to exit through IPO because it is often one of the more lucrative exit options. In order to do this, though, the investor may require certain parameters for an IPO, which is why the terminology "Qualified IPO" or "QIPO" is being used. The explanation of what constitutes a qualified IPO will be detailed later in the shareholder agreement. Usually, a qualified IPO will have certain exchange listing requirements in regard to exchange and minimum IPO amount.

Another issue that an investor should be aware of, for tax or regulatory reasons, is that they might want to avoid being deemed as a promoter. Depending on jurisdiction, promoters can incur lockup periods on stock after an IPO that extend beyond those of investors. Additionally, taxes may be different. Legal advice should be sought on this topic since the deal documents can have this clause, but local laws could supersede the agreement.

Finally, a clause that investors usually require is that the investors will have registration rights. Basically, the new investors want to be sure that they can fairly take part in the IPO.

Investee Viewpoint Investees also seek an IPO as they can realize the value of their equity. They must be careful, though, that the definition of *qualified* set out by investors is not too strict, preventing a viable and lucrative IPO.

Voting Rights

While board rights are important and the voting mechanisms were laid out carefully earlier, a number of issues arise that necessitate shareholder voting. For this reason, investors in preferred stock need to have clear definitions of their voting privileges.

Example Language:

> Series A Preferred shareholders will have an equal number of Ordinary shares as Preferred shares, upon conversion, when determining the number of votes for all matters presented to stockholders.

Investor Viewpoint Significant minority investors need to be able to guide important corporate matters and should therefore be able to participate in shareholder votes.

Investee Viewpoint As long as the conversion to ordinary shares is reasonable, the investees should understand that significant minority investors should be able to participate in shareholder votes.

Information Rights

Investors need to be able to know the status of the company at regular intervals. This information should provide enough detail to measure the company's performance versus projections, identify leading indicators of problems, and evaluate whether financial and social value is being added or lost.

Example Language:

> The New Investor shall receive corporate, financial, and social metric information and reports, related to the Company, on a quarterly basis and as detailed in the Definitive Documentation.

Investor Viewpoint While it might seem standard that companies should provide this type of information, without a clause requiring it management can become preoccupied with other matters and delay such reporting. For impact investing, this is particularly important since successful social impact is not as obvious as positive financial realizations. In Chapter 6, we will detail what metrics should be used to measure a company's financial and social success, but for now we need to understand that this information should be required by legal documents to be delivered to investors.

Investee Viewpoint Running a growing company is difficult with seemingly endless work in all aspects of the company. Adding a reporting requirement can be viewed as an unnecessary burden on the company. However, social entrepreneurs have to realize that if they want the backing of social impact investors and if they want to be able to define themselves as generating positive social impact, they will need to provide data to satisfy investors and support these claims. An investee should push back if the reporting requirements are overly burdensome and threaten the viability of a business plan. There is no point in reporting when the costs of generating the information bring down the value of the business, leading to a nonexistent entity with nothing to report.

Inspection Rights

Similar to reporting rights, an investor should be able to go onsite and inspect the business.

Example Language:

> The New Investor shall be allowed onsite inspection of the Company as detailed in the Definitive Documentation.

Investor Viewpoint While reading reports is an excellent way to understand how the company is performing, going onsite provides the deepest level of knowledge. An investor should be able to inspect all parts of the value chain with reasonable notice and cost considerations.

Investee Viewpoint   The investee should understand that the investor is part of the company and should be able to go onsite; however, time and cost constraints are reasonable bases for limiting the inspection ability of investors.

Representations and Warranties

One of the more important aspects of closing any business transaction, where there is a buyer and seller, is ensuring that the seller has properly and fairly depicted the item being sold to the buyer. Investing in a company is no different, where investors are buying shares in a company that investees are selling. Therefore, investees should be able to provide basic representations and warranties about themselves and the company that they have created. These representations and warranties will be finalized in the share subscription agreement (SSA) or stock purchase agreement (SPA).

Example Language:

> Management and the Company shall provide standard representations and warranties to the New Investors. Any disclosures to the representations and warranties shall be documented by written disclosure made to the New Investor.

Investor Viewpoint   Representations and warranties are very important to an investor, since they should be comfortable that the company they are investing in has been accurately portrayed. If there are any disclosures, such a written disclosure list should be delivered to the investor prior to the signing of any definitive documentation. Indemnification clauses should be in place that mitigate breaches of representations and warranties. We will discuss more on indemnifications later in this chapter.

Investee Viewpoint   An investee needs to be able to meet the demand of investors by properly representing the company. However, investees should be keen not to expose themselves to too much liability by providing unreasonable representations and warranties nor blanket indemnifications.

Confidentiality

Confidentiality of the term sheet and any negotiations surrounding it is a clause that has advantages and disadvantages for both investors and investees, depending on circumstances. At first glance, it might seem logical that the investor and investee should keep everything confidential. However, what if the investor finds a co-investor? Can the investor share details with the potential co-investor? Can the investee? Similarly, what if there are multiple, potential investors? If the investors wanted to collude they would have to share negotiation information. Perhaps the investee wants the investors to remain competitive to push up the valuation or get better terms. Confidentiality should generally start with the investor and investee and be modified as the investment circumstances change.

Example Language:

> The contents of this Term Sheet and all negotiations between all Parties surrounding the Series A Preferred shares investment will be kept confidential unless the prior written approval of the other Party is obtained, or unless disclosure is required by law or regulation. Disclosure to each Party's affiliates or employees will kept on a need-to-know basis.

Investor and Investee Viewpoint   As mentioned earlier, confidentiality can work or be against both parties and can be modified by written approval, but it is assumed as a starting point for finalizing an initial term sheet.

Exclusivity

An investor could be hesitant to engage in final due diligence unless the signing of the term sheet constitutes an exclusive engagement. The concern is that significant expenses and resources are expended during the final due diligence, which would be wasted if another party also had the opportunity and was chosen at the end.

Example Language:

> While the New Investor is completing due diligence and documentation, the Company and Existing Shareholders agree that for a 90-day period from the execution of this Term Sheet ("Exclusivity Period") they shall not directly or indirectly solicit, discuss, negotiate, or seek in any manner other forms of capital for the Company nor discuss or negotiate the sale, transfer, or encumbrance of shares in the Company.

Investor Viewpoint   An investor should have comfort that after signing the term sheet and engaging in legal and accounting due diligence that they are the only ones contemplating investment. One minor point is that not only should an investor have a clause that covers other potential investors, but one that prevents the investees or existing shareholders from selling the company after the term sheet is signed.

Investee Viewpoint The primary concern of an investee for this clause is the time period of exclusivity validity. After signing the term sheet, the investee has to be patient while the investor finalizes due diligence and the final documentation is negotiated. However, as time passes the situation is clearly worse for the investee as they require funding. The time period for the validity of the term sheet should be capped at a reasonable timeframe for the investor to conduct legal and accounting due diligence and to finalize definitive documentation. If the time frame requires modification, this can be done in writing with both parties' consent. However, if the investor is taking too long, the investee should have the right to engage other investors.

Expenses

Uniquely, the expense section of a term sheet often causes emotional negotiation, when in fact the amount of expenses typically pale in comparison to the investment size. That being said, if an investment negotiation and finalization fails between parties, there will be costs incurred that on a standalone basis are significant.

Example Language:

> The Company shall bear all issuance expenses related to the Series A Preferred shares and reimburse the New Investor up to a maximum of USD50,000 for legal and due diligence expenses.

Investor Viewpoint An investor should be reimbursed for normal due diligence and other costs related to the investment. The amount of costs should be relative to the amount being invested. A USD50 million investment should have a deeper due diligence and more extensive legal and accounting evaluation than a USD1 million investment.

Investee Viewpoint An investee should negotiate the cap on expenses. As mentioned in the investor viewpoint section, the cap should be relative to the investment amount. Additionally, the investee might want to negotiate a breakage fee since it, too, will have costs if the investment fails in the final stages.

Amendment

A more obvious clause in a term sheet, but basically the term sheet should not be amended without the mutual consent of both parties.

Example Language:

> The Term Sheet may be amended by Parties with mutual consent in writing.

Investor and Investee Viewpoint   The most common amendments will be in terms of confidentiality, if other parties enter into the transaction, and exclusivity, if the validity period needs to be extended.

Governing Law and Arbitration

Two aspects of the term sheet and the transaction in general are the chosen domicile for governing law and arbitration if there are disputes.

Example Language:

> The Term Sheet and the Definitive Documentation shall be governed by the laws of New York, United States of America. In the event of dispute between the Parties regarding this Term Sheet or the Definitive Documentation, the dispute will be arbitrated in accordance with the rules of the American Arbitration Association, in New York City.

Investor and Investee Viewpoint   Both parties should strive for governing law that is fair, consistent, and stable. Arbitration is often used as it is much less costly than having legal battles ensue during disputes. Finally, the arbitration location should be balanced for parties if there are significant differences in location. For instance, if a New York based investor is investing in an Indian company, both parties may decide on the United Kingdom as governing law and arbitration in London.

Legally Binding Clauses

An interesting part of a term sheet is that most of it is not legally binding. That being said, it is very poor convention to sign a term sheet and back out of the agreement later. In that event, and for other reasons, there are parts of the term sheet that are identified as legally binding.

Example Language:

> The terms in this Term Sheet are not legally binding between parties, except for the following clauses:
> - Confidentiality
> - Exclusivity

- Expenses
- Amendment
- Governing law and arbitration

Investor and Investee Viewpoint   The real documentation that finalizes the investment is the share subscription agreement, the shareholders agreement, and the final, modified articles of incorporation. However, each party should take comfort in confidentiality, exclusivity, expense reimbursement, prevention of amendment, and the location of governing law in case any of the legal clauses need to be disputed.

DEFINITIVE DOCUMENTATION: THE SUBSCRIPTION AGREEMENT

The term sheet is a more informal agreement that covers key terms of the investment. It can be boilerplate in nature or highly detailed, but the core idea is to establish an understanding between parties prior to expensive legal and accounting due diligences. Once the term sheet is signed, an investor's legal team begins to go through all of the company's existing documents, registrations, and legal statuses. At the same time, two important definitive documents are created: the subscription agreement and the shareholder agreement. The subscription agreement conveys the terms of the specific investment round and contains most of the representations and warranties relevant to the sale of the securities. Core sections of a subscription agreement include:

I. Party Identification and Definitions: This is very similar to the term sheet, but in more detail.
II. Subscription Details: Similar to the term sheet section, but in much more detail.
III. Conditions Precedent: Once again similar to the term sheet, but here exact conditions are detailed, the method of satisfying the completion are comprehensively laid out, and the acceptance by the investor is explained.
IV. Actions Pending Completion: This section is somewhat covered by the term sheet, but the core idea is that no material changes occur before the completion of the documentation and finalization of investment.
V. Completion Actions: The precise steps to finalizing the investment are listed. Typically, references are made to the capitalization table to ensure that the investment is executed and the resulting shareholding is as both parties expects.

VI. Representations and Warranties: As referenced in the term sheet, the exact representations and warranties are covered in the subscription agreement. The core representations and warranties include the following:

- *Organization and existence*: Basically, the company must be legally organized and exist in its stated domicile. Also, it should be free and clear of any pending litigation.
- *Power and authority*: The company should be able to enter into all agreements that are part of the investment round.
- *Legally binding*: The parties understand that these documents are legally binding, as opposed to much of the term sheet, which was not.
- *No conflict*: The investment round and the agreements contemplated for it should not conflict with any existing agreements that the company has, nor should it conflict with any laws or regulatory statutes.
- *Corporate particulars*: The company should be able to represent that the company's capitalization structure prior to investment is what was shown to the investor. Similarly, it should be able to represent that the company has the ability to issue the contemplated round of investment.

Additional representations and warranties are often included. The basis for these is that any information that has been submitted to the investor should be able to be represented transparently, truthfully, and in a way conducive to investment. Keep in mind that representations and warranties should only be historical in nature or as a matter of fact. For instance, an investee may be reluctant to state simply, "The business complies with the law." This is because there could be breaches the investee does not know about, which are actually in violation of the law. More likely, the investee would agree to a statement saying, "To the best of the investee's knowledge, the business has complied with all laws and regulations." These types of additional representations and warranties usually cover the following in detail:

- *Constitutional and corporate matters*: Similar to the first core representation and warranty, but in more detail on the specific organization of the company.
- *Compliance with law*: The company and all of the employees have complied and to their knowledge currently comply with the law.
- *Litigation*: There is no pending litigation.
- *Ethical business practices*: This is to make sure no bribery has taken place.

- *Assets/licenses*: The company owns all of the assets that it states it does, freely and clearly.
- *Employees*: The employees met and discussed are all part of the company and that there are no significant outstanding loans to them.
- *Contracts*: The investor's legal team has been provided all contracts.
- *Taxation*: The company is current on its taxes.

VII. Indemnification: When a representation is false or a warranty is breached, there is often some type of mitigation through indemnification. Indemnities are basically risk transfers. In the case of a private investment, there are usually two types of indemnities: general and specific.

A general indemnity covers breach of warranties and misrepresentations. Along with the indemnity language is a limitation on liability. An investee will be hesitant to sign away a blanket indemnity and bear all of the risk. For that reason, there are usually limits to the liabilities that can arise from an indemnity. The limits typically bound the duration of the validity of the indemnity and the amounts that can be paid out at any one time and in aggregated.

Occasionally, due diligence will find specific problems that can be mitigated with an indemnity. For instance, in one impact investment it was found that the investee had unknowingly violated a commercial statute in selling their product in a foreign country. There was risk that the governing body would penalize the company. Since this was done prior to the new investors funding round, the new investors did not want to bear any risk of loss that could arise from the violation. In this case, a specific indemnity was crafted to indemnify the new investors from any repercussions arising from the specific violation at hand.

DEFINITIVE DOCUMENTATION: THE SHAREHOLDERS' AGREEMENT

While the subscription agreement covers the specifics of the transaction, the shareholders' agreement covers the agreements and rights that endure for shareholders throughout the duration of investment. The main focus of the shareholders' agreement is on the following:

- *Board of director governance and matters*: This typically covers the authority of the board, director allocations and composition, removal and replacement provisions, and board meeting details, such as quorum and voting.

- *Shareholder meetings*: This covers all matters relating to shareholder meetings, such as voting and quorum.
- *Reserved matters*: Earlier in the term sheet section we detailed specific rights that the new investor would have, such as preventing debt of a certain amount. These reserved matters are listed in detail in the shareholders' agreement.
- *Operations and management*: This section covers the requirement for auditors, a budget, and other functions required to operate.
- *Information and inspection*: As mentioned in the term sheet, information and inspection rights are detailed in the shareholders' agreement.
- *Preference share rights*: A large part of the shareholders' agreement is all of the rights discussed in the term sheet, such as anti-dilution, tag-along, and drag-along rights.

Once the investment is executed, the shareholders' agreement usually becomes the basis for amending the articles of incorporation. This way, all of the rights that were hammered out are solidified in binding corporate documentation.

FINALIZING THE INVESTMENT

We have seen now the full investment process: sourcing, screening, pre–due diligence, full due diligence, valuation, structuring, term sheet creation, and final documentation. The process may seem daunting, given the details that arise and even more so for an impact investor since such a style of investing necessitates additional requirements and considerations. However, a rigorous approach to each of the steps is important in order to invest for the best possible financial and social outcome.

From an example point of view, we should assume that the Solero investment was completed at the valuation ending in Chapter 4 and under many of the terms from this chapter. Knowing the investment has been finalized will assist as we progress through the investment life cycle.

The next steps for most investors are to either take a passive approach by waiting to realize an exit or take an active approach, build value, and help guide an exit. Whether active or passive toward exit, an interim step that is almost always a requirement for any investor is monitoring the investment. Proper post-investment duties require knowing what to look for, how to analyze submitted data, and, most importantly, how to act if the investment is in trouble or as the investment nears exit.

CHAPTER 6

Post-Investment Monitoring, Management, and Value Building

Sourcing, structuring, and finalizing the investment may have seemed like an exhaustive amount of work; however, that process represents a fraction of the lifespan of most impact investments. Post-investment an investor can take on a spectrum of responsibilities and involvement. Passive investors may want to only receive reports showing the progress management is making, while more active investors may establish a significant presence amongst the board of directors.

Passive or active, financial and social data reporting is usually the first key topic after the closing of the investment. A passive impact investor will want to see the growth of the company and the social value achieved. An active investor has the same desire to understand the current state and recent achievements of the company, but is also looking for indicators of problems. Beyond initial capital, seasoned active investors have the ability to spot trouble before small issues turn into severe company crippling predicaments.

With a reliable and informative reporting system set up, an investor then knows where to target efforts. Additionally, the investor has to work with the company to see where the investor's skills and experience are most useful to building financial and social mission success. Impact investors usually have the unique experience to assist in maintaining and improving the social mission as the company scales up. Other investors may have operational experience in the specific industry, financial backgrounds and connections that can assist with the future financing of the company, or management backgrounds that help the company stay on track as it grows.

While all investors and management hope that growth is achieved according to plan, it is rare to find a company that does not encounter challenges along the way. Foreseeing, planning for, mitigating, and resolving social mission, financial, and operational problems are all actions that an active impact investor will have to undertake. In this chapter, we will explore three case studies of challenges post-investment and how they were resolved. Whether through mitigating challenging situations or assisting a successful company as it scales, social and financial value can be built that can enhance exit possibilities and have a positive effect on the company long beyond the close of investor's participation.

REPORTING AND MONITORING

Financial and social data reporting is the primary window an investor has on the invested company. It is critical, then, that the data itself are meaningful and presented in a timely, cogent manner. From a financial perspective, there are many established *financial and social data reporting metrics* that track the health of a company. The format is also standardized through financial statements that adhere to accounting standards such as GAAP and IFRS. From a nonfinancial perspective, the IRIS indicators referred to in this chapter come closest to the standardization and harmonization that GAAP or IFRS bring to accounting. Operating data on the company, though, are usually tailored, depending on the industry. For instance, in the case of Solero we would want to know when a new region has been entered, how many distributors have been hired, and how many have departed. In other industries, though, the operational metrics could be very different. Later in this chapter, we will explore a few different industries common to impact investing and the metrics that might need monitoring.

Social data collection is a unique and vital requirement for impact investing. Social missions can vary widely and therefore present a challenge in standardizing reporting requirements. One company's social mission, even in the same industry, might justify different metrics than another. For instance, in the case of Solero, we may want to collect data on the number of lanterns sold per household and try to translate that into a number of kerosene lanterns displaced. Another company selling solar products might be targeting commercial vendors and cell phone charging. They might report on the creation of jobs and reduced travel and time for villagers to charge phones.

A social entrepreneur reading this section is immediately thinking of the time and resources it will take to collect data, scrub it, and generate reports. By no means is the entrepreneur wrong in thinking such, as onerous reporting requirements can impede on a company's ability to focus on its core financial and social missions. A balance between meaningful, timely data and limited investee burden needs to be agreed upon.

Reporting Requirements

	Metric	Data Type	Frequency	Source	Lead Reporter	Comments
Financial	Gross Margin	0.00%	Monthly	Corporate HQ	CFO	
	EBITDA Margin	0.00%	Monthly	Corporate HQ	CFO	
	Warranty Returns	0.00%	Monthly	Manufacturing	CTO	
	Shipping Costs/Revenue	0.00%	Monthly	Corporate HQ	CFO	May want to split air vs. sea.
Operational						
	# of New Distributors	#,###.0	Monthly	Corporate HQ	CEO	
	# of Distributors Quit	#,###.0	Monthly	Corporate HQ	CEO	
	# of Distributors Fired	#,###.0	Monthly	Corporate HQ	CEO	
Social						
	# of Kerosene Lanterns Displaced	#,###.0	Monthly	Corporate HQ	Social Performance Manger	
	Equivalent Carbon Credits	#,###.0	Monthly	Corporate HQ	Social Performance Manger	

FIGURE 6.1 Agreeing on key reporting requirements can be eased by laying out the reporting requirements and related details.

Establishing Reporting Requirements

The first step an investor should take with a newly invested company is to create dialogue regarding proposed reporting requirements. A good way to do this is to use a spreadsheet to track the reporting requirements. Figure 6.1 shows an example of what this may look like.

In Figure 6.1 we see that there are three types of reporting data: financial, operational, and social. While some of this may be contained in financial reports, we should go through the six fields:

1. *Metric*: A general description of the metric should be presented. It is very important, though, to clarify exactly what is part of the definition of each of these items. For instance, for Gross Margin, does this include the warranty returns, or has this been deducted? For New Distributor count, does this include ones that have only been hired or ones that have been hired and made sales? For the carbon credits, exactly what type of carbon credits are being used?
2. *Data Type*: Surprisingly, what might seem so obvious can get lost in translation quickly. Gross margin might get reported as a dollar amount or the new hire metric might be shown as a growth percentage. Establish early on what the metric calculation should be.
3. *Frequency*: This is the critical field for entrepreneurs. Monthly data reporting should only be done on metrics that are easily calculated. Quarterly ones might be more of a reality, particularly with companies that operate in rural areas, where it may physically take time to aggregate data. Also keep in mind that low frequency items, such as annual data, may take time to finalize when the annual reporting requirement comes around. It may be worth reporting quarterly to prevent a rush of throwing resources at reporting at the last minute.

4. *Source*: It's important to determine where the data are coming from to make sure it is as accurate as possible. Also, determining the source of the data begins the responsibility focus and makes each area of the business aware of what they will be responsible for.
5. *Lead Reporter*: Related to the source of the data is the specific person responsible for reporting. If this is not done it is easy for an organization to say, "Oh, we thought the other person was responsible for that." Make it clear who is responsible for which metric.
6. *Comments*: While we can attempt to create as much order as possible, there are always nuances that must be described. Work through the data issues from the start to avoid costly errors later when the data are being used to make key decisions regarding the company.

COMMON REPORTING METRICS

The common reporting metrics are primarily financial. Social and operating metrics tend to be investment specific. For that reason, we will lay out common financial metrics that are tracked over time and how they may provide indications of corporate health. Subsequently we will look at social metrics in more detail, the challenges establishing social metrics, and suggested methods for implementation. Finally, a number of operational metrics will be provided that relate to common impact investing industries.

Financial Metrics

Sales growth (%): ((n **period sales** $-$ ($n - 1$) **period sales**)/($n - 1$) **period sales**), where n is the time frame. Usually year on year, or quarter on quarter sales are a very common performance measurement to understand the general growth of a company. Be careful to understand what qualifies as a "sale" in this measurement. Companies should follow GAAP or IFRS when recognizing revenue. Sales can be inflated by including orders that have not shipped. The term *net sales* is often used, which removes invalid sales such as returns, warranty use, or discounted sales. Additionally, one-off revenue such as asset sales should be removed, since the goal is to understand the corporate performance.

Gross margin (%): (**Gross revenue** $-$ **Cost of goods sold**) / (**Gross revenue**). The problem with looking at just revenue is that it could come at a very high cost. Companies can have significant sales if they offer a product that is at a low margin, but such a strategy is not sustainable in the long run. Early stage companies that manufacture products or offer services normally always have to increase their margins to sustainable levels.

Operating expenditure (%): (**Operating expenditures / Gross revenue**). Expense control should be a focus point on early-stage companies. While a company should not be too constrained, a careful eye needs to be focused on what it costs to operate the company. For many companies the primary operating expenditures are selling, general, and administrative (SG&A). Converse to margins, a lower operating expenditure ratio is desirable, but clearly not one that impedes corporate growth.

EBITDA margin (%): (**EBITDA / Gross revenue**). Many people look to the EBITDA margin as the ratio that defines corporate performance. The ratio takes into account sales, costs of goods sold, and operating expenditures. Since it is prior to interest, taxes, depreciation, and amortization, it is agnostic to capital structure and an indicator of corporate performance. Early-stage companies have volatility and often negative EBITDA margins until they grow and stabilize.

Net profit margin (%): (**Net income / Gross revenue**). While the capital structure is not relevant for the EBITDA margin, it cannot be ignored and the net profit margin addresses it. Ultimately, net income is the basis for any potential dividends or growth of equity value. Changes to the net profit margin can be difficult to track over time since a number of items can vary leading up to it. However, if all other indicators are in line up to the EBITDA margin and the net profit margin is out of line with the industry average, then we know something about the capital structure is causing the aberration.

Current ratio (#): (**Current assets / Current liabilities**). When liquidity dries up, companies become susceptible to insolvency very rapidly. For early-stage companies with limited cash and borrowing ability the liquidity position of the company is incredibly important to track. The current ratio does this by examining current assets over current liabilities, which is effectively a test on the working capital of the company. When this ratio dips below 1, it means that the company may have stress meeting its immediate debts. However, some businesses are able to operate with low current ratios, depending on inventory churn, which is what we will examine next.

Cash conversion cycle and components (#): (**DSO + DIO – DPO**). The cash conversion cycle was discussed in Chapter 3, since we were concerned by the speed at which Solero created cash flow. For many companies, particularly early-stage ones with liquidity concerns, the cash conversion cycle should be monitored each month. The three subcomponents, DSO, DIO, and DPO should be tracked separately in order to hone in on the source of cash flow problems.

Free cash flow ($/month): (**EBIT * (1 – Tax rate) + Noncash items – Capital expenditures – Working capital requirements**). The free cash flow calculation seen in Chapter 3 shows how much cash can be spun off from the company to calculate value. In early-stage companies though the FCF is normally negative and cash is being burnt. Investors in early-stage companies should always know the cash positions of their invested companies and how long the current cash will last until the companies turn to positive FCF, debt is issued, or the next round of equity funding takes place. Management and investors must be acutely aware of the time frame to acquire debt and equity funding and ensure that the cash burn estimation is in line with this time frame.

Interest and debt service coverage ratio (#): **(EBITDA or EBIT / Interest due)** and **(EBITDA or EBIT / Interest + Principal due)**. More of a concern for debt investors, the interest and debt service coverage ratios seek to test the ability of the company to service interest and debt.

Fixed-asset turnover ratio (#): **(Net sales / PPE)**. Asset-light models are more common with social enterprises, but investment does occur in businesses with capital-intensive plans. To track such a business' effective use of capital expenditures (which translates into PPE), fixed-asset turnover ratio should be used.

Operational Metrics

Measuring the success of a company is hard to do without understanding the operations itself. This extends beyond just financial metrics. The following are common areas of impact investing, with their relevant operational metrics:

Energy: For companies seeking to provide renewable energy solutions that are more grid-like, the following metrics are useful.

- *Price/Cost per kWh*: Customers, regardless of whether they are rural or urban, are savvy when it comes to pricing. An energy company using different technologies has to be aware of price per kWh with price-sensitive customers. Additionally, competing energy sources and their pricing must be tracked over time since utilization of a product or service that becomes more expensive than alternatives will witness a rapid drop in customer base.
- *Project ROI*: While a financial concept in nature, an energy company working on larger-scale solutions will be asked to project the return on investment for each project. The customer paying for the project will assess the ROI versus other possible solutions. For instance, a company providing a solar/wind hybrid solution to power rural telecom towers will have to demonstrate that its products and services produce a higher return on investment than utilizing the standard diesel power generation method. Investors in these types of companies should track project ROIs

and how they compare against competitors and across competing technologies.

Mobile money: In almost every country there are mobile money companies offering solutions for electronic, cashless payments. These metrics can help track the development of such companies.

- *Active subscribers*: The number of active subscribers is a metric that should be reported. Active can mean many different things, so it is important to understand how the company defines activity. Typically this would be a customer transacting a certain amount or certain number of transactions per month.
- *Revenue/Active subscribers*: How much revenue each active subscriber is generating is important to monitor. One has to be very careful how revenue is reported for mobile money companies. Actual revenue is fee generated, based on the transactions that the subscriber undertakes. Loading funds and transferring funds should not be counted toward revenue, even though in some accounting systems the flow of subscriber funds is lumped into a revenue category. Mobile money companies also generate revenue from "float" or interest off of unused funds that subscribers leave in the system. This should be netted out.
- *Cost of subscriber acquisition*: Mobile money companies must heavily market when they enter new areas. They must also pay fees to agents who sign up new users. All of these are costs required to acquire the subscriber. A mobile money company can quickly burn cash if their cost of acquiring subscribers is high.
- *Fee %*: The fees that are generated per category should be tracked over time. Fee compression is a concern amongst mobile money companies. If mobile money follows the telecom industry, the fees that they are able to charge may have to come down.

Healthcare: Hospital and clinic companies that service low-income populations are popular social enterprises. They have a range of specialized metrics.

- *Bed occupancy rate*: Similar to how hotels gauge their performance, the percentage of total beds that are being utilized is an important metric. For companies that provide tiered services, like the example company Mtoto Clinics, the utilization rates should be calculated for each service cohort.
- *Length of stay*: How long do patients stay in the clinic or hospital? Depending on price and cost structure, this can have an important effect on the long term performance of the company.

■ *Time to EBITDA positive*: For each clinic or hospital that the healthcare company creates, the length of time for that clinic or hospital to become EBITDA positive is important. If the time frame is too long, it could take significant time to scale the business to a point where an early-stage investor would realize a strong return. If the investor had to sell shares in a short time frame, the investor would be subject to implied valuations based on long-term projections, where other investors might not attribute the same value.

Housing: Housing projects and companies that target affordable housing have unique indicators.

■ *Project/Phase completion %*: Housing projects are normally done in phases, where the sale of the earlier phase can be used to finance the building of the next phase. Each phase normally follows an expected timeline. Any stresses to that timeline will reduce the IRR of the project.

■ *Conversion ratio*: Of the number of people that visited the housing project and had a touch point with a sales associate, how many chose to purchase? If the conversion ratio declines throughout phases, there should be an investigation as to the reasons why.

■ *Interest rates/Debt availability*: Housing projects rely on customers who often require mortgages to purchase properties. If interest rates and mortgage availability change drastically over time, there may be a drop off in customers. This could require mitigating actions such as seeking preferred lenders or lining up mortgage financing.

Distribution: Companies can be oriented in a variety of industries such as small-scale solar energy, energy-efficient products such as cook stoves, health products, or mobile money, but ultimately, if the company sells directly to customers, particularly in rural areas, then the company will be significantly beholden to distribution system forces. For that reason, there are a number of core metrics to track when a company has a significant distribution system.

■ *Active distributors*: Companies with teams of distributors like to report as many employees as possible. However, frequently there are distributors on the books of these companies who have not made a sale in months. A person analyzing the company should establish a cut-off for what constitutes an "active" distributor, such as making one sale in the last month.

■ *Distributor efficiency*: Similar to what was shown for Solero, distributor efficiency can be determined by breaking down the sales per distributor, per product, and also by the "seasoning" or time in role for the distributor.

- *Distributor churn*: The total number of distributors each month should be broken down into the components of current active distributors, new distributors, and departed distributors.
- *Distributor margin*: The amount that distributors make off each product is important because in many areas, it determines the incentive of the distributor to sell. In many rural markets, if a person walks into a store and asks the storeowner which solar lantern to purchase, typically the owner will push the product with the higher margin. Companies and investors must be acutely aware of how their product's distributor margins stack up against competing similar products and also other products that the distributor can sell in comparable volumes.

SOLERO'S EXAMPLE IMPACT REPORTING FRAMEWORK

While some of the operational metrics may be social mission related, we should expand on the social mission metrics. To do this we will focus back on Solero and examine a possible *quarterly impact reporting framework*, which is contained on the website under the Chapter 6 folder, in the Excel file Solero_Qtly_Rpt_Framework.xlsx. This contains the indicators we selected during the deal negotiation phase of the investment process and shortly after disbursement of the investment funds. The reporting framework lists the IRIS code of the indicator, the name of the indicator, the definition of the indicator, the indicator's reporting format, a baseline measurement for the indicator, and the indicator's calculations. The benefit of referencing to IRIS[1] indicators is that these are generally accepted performance indicators, selected and validated by a standard setting body. Figure 6.2 shows an overview of the quarterly impact reporting framework.

The quarterly reporting framework focuses on output indicators. Selecting adequate indicators may or may not be easy. Occasionally, many exclude important indicators or track data that is not relevant to the expected impact. Selecting indicators to track should be done in close consultation with the investee, in an iterative manner. In building the quarterly reporting framework, it is critical to check and agree on the source of the data, and obtain assurance from the investee on its quality, timeliness, and availability. It is also important to include all assumptions and calculations for any processed

---

[1]IRIS indicators are available in two languages (English and Spanish) at http://iris.thegiin.org/metrics.

Solero Quarterly Impact Reporting Framework									
IRIS code	Indicator name	Definition	Reporting format	Baseline 31.12.2014	Source & Calculations	3/31/2015	6/30/2015	9/30/2015	12/31/2015
OD5890	Reporting currency		Currency	INR	N/A	INR	INR	INR	INR
OI8869	Permanent Employees	Number of people employed by Solero at the end of the reporting period. This is the sum of all paid full-time and part-time employees. Does not include contract manufacturing nor distributors	Number of people	4	Company records	5	6	8	8
OI2444	Permanent Employees: Female	Number of females employed by Solero at the end of the reporting period. This is the sum of all paid full time and part time female employees.	Number of people	0	Company records	0	1	0	0
PI1263	Solar lamps/Units Sold Total cumulative since inception	Total number of solar lamps (all models) sold by Solero **since inception (cumulative)**	Number, based on Unit of Measure (PD1602) selection	1540	Calculations (sum)	7369	15375	26120	40315
PI1263	Solero lamps/Units Sold Total this quarter	Total number of solar lamps (3 models) sold during the reporting period.	Number, based on Unit of Measure (PD1602) selection	1540	Calculations (sum)	5829	8006	10745	14195

FIGURE 6.2 Solero's quarterly impact reporting framework details a number of indicators relevant to social mission monitoring and evaluation.

data and to identify one contact person at the investee's company that is in charge of collecting and submitting the data. The frequency of reporting should also be discussed to ensure that timelines are feasible and in sync with investors who must report data to shareholders.

Reduced misunderstandings and the ability to perform cross-portfolio aggregation and benchmarking are benefits of using a standardized system, like IRIS indicators. Without such standardization, data quality and data collection systems can be suboptimal. The number of people involved in consolidating data across corporate offices and remote locations adds to the error potential and possibility of misinterpretation. Reviewing each indicator's name, definition, and unit of measurement with counterparts helps reduce these errors and misunderstandings.

NOTES FROM THE FIELD

For one Indian investment, the investee was tasked with providing the number of people employed by the company. The investee added the number of employees in month 1, 2, and 3 to provide the number of employees at the end of the reporting quarter. Clearly, this was double and then triple counting. After a few iterations of calculations, we understood that a more exact definition indicating "Number of people employed by the organization at the end of the reporting period (non-cumulative)" was better than the original wording of "Total number of people employed by the organization during the reporting period."

Returning to the impact reporting framework table, there are two types of data in the table: raw or original data and processed data. Raw data are data actually collected by the company. Processed data are data resulting from calculations that may or may not involve assumptions such as the amount of greenhouse gas emissions sequestered. The quarterly impact reporting framework contains the original data points, derived information, assumptions, and calculations.

As an example, Solero reports the number of lamps sold. This indicator is tracked on the quarterly impact reporting framework per model and aggregated on a quarterly cumulative basis since inception. The number of beneficiaries, or end users, on the other hand, is not tracked directly, but results from a calculation. We assume, based on evidence collected through client surveys, that the three models of lamps have different numbers of average users. Solero actually produces four models, but the fourth model sells primarily in industrialized markets for campers and outdoor leisure, which does not correspond to the population that is being targeted for impact.

In the assumptions on the impact reporting framework, we indicate one average user for Solero Mini, two for Solero Standard, and four for Solero XL. This allows us to roughly estimate the number of users per quarter. Clearly, this is not a perfectly quantifiable system. One problem is that we fail to account for repeat customers or households with more than one product. The beneficiaries being counted may not be unique clients. Moreover, we are not able to identify the usage of the lamps. They could be used for income-generating purposes, children doing homework and studying after dusk, or the family simply playing cards. The different usages have different social impacts, which would preferably be known.

The quarterly impact reporting framework makes the following additional assumptions:

- Conversion rate GHG per lamp[2]: Calculated as the number of lamps multiplied by 0.092 tCO_2 (Total lamps sold × tonnes of CO_2 emission mitigated per lamp per year)
- Number of persons in household: Five members[3]
- Number of lamps per household: 1
- Average lifetime of lamp: 2 years

Ideally, an impact reporting framework should contain output and outcome targets. However, establishing outcome targets in terms of people

---

[2] AMS-III.AR, "Substituting Fuel Based Lighting with LED/CFL Lighting Systems Version 4.0," https://cdm.unfccc.int/methodologies/DB/41A0Q0QT5CUP3TMD57 GC6RZ4YRV28M.

[3] India Census 2011, www.censusindia.gov.in/.

reached, income or savings generated for target populations, or employee numbers (per gender or socio-economic segment) is challenging. To help provide context for these challenges and an example of how to work through them, the impact reporting framework in the Excel file lists example baseline and actual values for Solero in columns, E, G, H, I, and J.

Finally, we should think about how we interpret the data that are collected. The post investment monitoring for the first few quarters of Solero reveals:

- *No major change in the number of employees or number of distributors.* There is apparent difficulty in recruiting or retaining female employees and female distributors, which is not surprising given the rural, remote, off-grid sales locations. These regions commonly have 100 percent male salesforces, even when the majority of buyers may be female.
- *The solar products have different distributor margins that change over time.* In December 2014, the Mini had a distributor margin of 9.09 percent, the Standard 5.26 percent, and the XL 26.59 percent. The differences in margins could induce distributors to favor sales of the XL over the Mini and then over the Standard. Monitoring sales of each product helps assess if there is a need to incentivize the sales force differently from a social target point of view. Overall, the data on the margins and distributor earnings do not reflect a significant concern, though. The distributor earnings have increased slowly, but steadily.
- To complement this quarterly dashboard, we could conduct customer surveys and test some of our assumptions. Surveys can be done physically by recruiting interviewers in the field, through focus groups, or through mobile phone interaction. This would allow us to vet key data points such as:
  a. Household size
  b. Number of lamps purchased in the last six months or one year
  c. Actual use of lamps and disposal of batteries
  d. Satisfaction with quality, pricing, and payment
  e. Satisfaction with sales and after sales service
  f. Perception of benefits including savings in kerosene and kerosene lamps
  g. New desired product features

POST-INVESTMENT CASE STUDIES

To provide a more relatable perspective to the post-investment management process, we will work our way through three case studies. These case studies will touch briefly on the investment rationale, but more importantly cover relevant and realistic issues that investors might encounter post-investment. Note that while these case studies have their origins in actual events, the details have been modified for explanatory purposes.

Natural Gas in East Asia

At first glance, the idea of supplying natural gas in an East Asian country may not seem like a social enterprise, but the original mission of this company is to provide gas-powered refrigeration units to the Ministry of Health, in order to preserve vaccines in rural areas. The investment thesis showed high social value, with the ability to meet the demands of rural vaccine refrigeration and to also sell gas for cooking that created jobs and provided improved alternatives to charcoal stoves. Financially, the company would make a margin off the gas sale and could also expand to other sectors such as the commercial and retail markets for its products.

Operationally, the company was set to achieve these social and financial goals by importing natural gas from a separate company, purchasing it in bulk at the seaport, filling a variety of sized cylinders, depending on customer type, and then distributing the cylinders across primarily rural areas of the country. The largest cylinders support industrial applications such as the vaccine refrigeration power and also kitchens in large institutions such as hospitals. Commercially, medium-sized cylinders were sold to restaurants and hotels for cooking purposes. Small retail versions were also sold for home use in cooking and occasionally to power lighting equipment.

The original investment took into account the capital-intensive nature of the business and a heavily regulated environment. In particular, in the country of business, gas prices were subject to regulated margins by the government. A prominent local with global fame was extremely interested in the success of this company and provided some mitigation to these sovereign risk concerns. Additionally, the investment was structured in phases, where specific conditions had to be met to get the other phases' funds.

The conditions were tied to revenue targets, but a unique condition was that an experienced natural gas company CEO had to be hired. Both were achieved early post-investment, but the first hint of a problem came when EBITDA margins had declined rapidly. Upon an onsite surveillance trip, it became clear that the new CEO had hired a substantial amount of local staff, beyond the original business plan expectation. Exacerbating the situation was localized price inflation that caused violent riots in the capital of the country. The government responded by maintaining strict margin control on all consumer facing products; natural gas being one of these.

Faced with limited margins and costs spiraling out of control, the investors conducted a thorough on-the-ground assessment. Four interesting findings came to light:

1. *The CEO was very highly paid versus the other staff and largely found to be ineffective.* While he had a respected name in the industry, he lacked the operational and financial experience to manage a medium-sized enterprise. The second in command, the regional director, was seen as doing much of the operational work and held the respect of employees.
2. *During financial forecast discussions, the CFO constantly relied on his accountant for answering basic questions on the corporate finances.* It became clear that the CFO was overpaid for his work and the accountant was able to provide all of the analysis required.
3. *The main office was located in the capital of the country with a high rent cost and a number of office employees that the CEO had hired.* Originally the logic in the corporate headquarters being located in the capital was because imports originated there, but all of the filling stations and sales were located in rural regions.
4. *The day's sales outstanding metric was consistently increasing.* When this metric was reviewed during the on-the-ground assessment, it became clear that a large number of key accounts were severely delayed in paying their gas bills. Adding to the complexity of this problem was that the government ministries, including the Health Ministry, were the main delinquent accounts.

In this investment, the board of directors had significant involvement and powers to direct management in the company. After a series of board meetings, the following actions were taken:

1. *The CEO was laid off with an amicable severance package negotiated.* The regional director was temporarily promoted to a CEO level. This still seemed risky, as he was relatively inexperienced at running the whole company, so performance targets were created for him to hit in order to receive higher pay.
2. *The CFO was similarly laid off.* The accountant was provided an increase in pay to take over responsibilities.
3. *The capital city office was closed with much of the additional staff that the CEO had hired, laid off.* Corporate headquarters were moved to a regional office located in the center of the rural geography that the company covered. A small presence remained in the capital city to manage gas importation.
4. *Collection efforts were intensified.* Future gas supply stopped for non-paying customers.

5. *The prominent local contact was contacted frequently.* Discussions concerned the margin constraints to see what relief could be achieved through that channel.
6. *Reporting was shifted from monthly to weekly.* A cash ledger was used to account for all transactions.

Readers may be surprised at the severity of these actions, but should recognize that the company was burning cash quickly. None of the actions were done callously, but after careful consideration and weighing all options. For a commercial enterprise like this to remain in business, especially with regulated margins, costs had to be controlled. Additionally, nonpaying customers could not continue to be serviced.

One of the predicaments that highlights a real challenge in impact investing was the accounts receivable problem. In any traditional company, a customer who does not pay does not receive a product or service. In this situation, though, the customer who was not paying was the primary social mission client: the Ministry of Health. How do investors explain to people that they cut off gas supply to the Ministry of Health that was using the gas to power refrigeration units for vaccines?

This situation is precisely where fully commercial impact investing tests the question of trade-offs between impact and return. There are a spectrum of answers, but the argument that will be made here ties back to the discourse on the cost of capital. A fully commercial impact investor must avoid any trade-offs for social impact. In this situation, the business value would be diminished by nonpaying clients that would filter down to the investor's return. If the investors have a commercial-based cost of capital, they cannot allow their investments to be managed in an incapacitated manner. A charitable impact investor who runs on a very low to nonexistent cost of capital could tolerate a certain amount of value deterioration.

Ultimately, though, if the business viability is threatened, the sources of the stress must be eliminated. How can such a moral quandary of not providing gas to the Health Ministry exist if allowing the problem to perpetuate means that the business becomes insolvent and ceases to operate? The repercussions of this course of action would result in the original supply loss problem, plus loss of service to all other customers, loss of employment at the company and at ancillary companies, reduction in taxes paid to the state, and so on.

After these actions were taken, the company slowly began to see the effects. Within a year, sales were at peak levels. Nearly two years later, the company was having strong growth and beginning to have months that were EBITDA positive. This allowed the company to build cash to reinvest in additional cylinders and help with expansion.

With the company stabilized, the investors were now able to work on more value-added tasks. The first task was developing a natural connection that the investor saw between another company that he was invested in and the natural gas company. Recall that the natural gas company sold lighting powered by natural gas to rural, nonelectrified villages. The investor noticed that these lights were not very popular sales. When he asked why this was the case, he learned that the lights were almost too bright and emitted an intense heat. The other company that the investor had invested in was a company similar to Solero, which sold solar lanterns. With a distribution system in place and employees already frequenting rural villages on a regular cycle, it made sense to connect the two entities so that lanterns could be sold through the natural gas company's distribution system.

The second value-added task was thinking about a potential *exit*. The local and regional stock markets were very small and illiquid, making IPO a remote possibility. Without an IPO, an acquisition or secondary share sale are the next options. Keep in mind that this exact reason is why a large illiquidity discount, as discussed in Chapters 3 and 4, should be applied when investing in companies like this. During an acquisition or share sale, the next investor will most likely take such illiquidity into account.

To help foment an exit, the investor began engaging in conversations with a large local company that sold natural gas cylinder tools and accessories. The company saw the natural gas company's distribution network and customer base as a possible enhancement to its own business. At the same time, talks started with another local investment fund for a possible secondary share sale.

There are myriad lessons to learn from this impact investment. The first is to make sure a rigorous investment process was applied in the first place. Here, the margins were always a concern, but sovereign involvement made the risk unquantifiable. Having the support of a prominent local can be critical when dealing with sovereigns. It would have been even better if that local were a co-investor, as it would solidify alignment of interests.

The use of monitoring as an early warning sign was clear in this investment. When operating expenditure percentages and DSO calculations went out of line, it became clear there were problems with the operational structure. The metrics initiated an on-the-ground assessment that led to major corporate changes, which in the end greatly benefited the company. It is important to notice here that the metrics themselves were not the answer, but valuable insofar as providing an early warning signal to the investor. The real value was added by the investor understanding the problems and initiating actions to overcome them.

Cafés in South America

Similar to natural gas, a café seems like an unlikely social enterprise. Some unique ones do exist, and one such business is a small chain of cafés in South America that employs former sexual abuse victims. The company is assisted by a nonprofit entity that provides counseling and support to the disadvantaged employees. After counseling, the beneficiaries are employed by the company in various roles in the back of the café, away from customers so that they can build skills without the pressure of customer contact. Eventually, the beneficiaries graduate up to working with customers in a service-oriented role at the café.

At the time the investment was made the company was at a very early stage and had two operational cafés. The cafés target expatriates living in the area, providing Western-style drinks, ambience, and service. The founders were foreigners who had moved to Latin America many years ago and started the business, growing it from a single café to the small chain of four cafés it had now become.

The challenges were clear from the due diligence. Scaling the business was critical to profitability, but where and how to scale were not fully worked out. The first challenge that emerged was accurate financial reporting. About a year after the investment, the financial statements had inconsistencies, making it difficult to reconcile the cash position of the company. Quickly, it became clear that the cash position was lower than expected, and more debt or equity funding would be needed in a matter of six months.

One of the reasons the capital raise was necessary was that the company was burning more cash than expected. The cash burn was due to higher-than-anticipated costs opening new cafés and one particularly unprofitable outlet. As the reasons to the problems were dug into, it became clear that the foreign owners were incurring more costs than local owners would. Rents were being raised in excess of local market standards and when contested the landlords threatened legal action and business disruption. Additionally, it was challenging to maintain staff, thereby incurring customer dissatisfaction with poorly trained employees.

As the investors looked into the staffing problem more, an issue unique to this social enterprise arose. One reason the staff was turning over rapidly was that many of the staff, including the workers who were former victims of abuse, would get trained at the company, gain a few months of experience, and then get jobs at higher-paying brand-name foreign hotels and restaurants.

Also, tensions mounted between the "normal staff" and those from severely disadvantaged groups. The former failed to understand the protective attention offered by some managers toward these staff, which at times were perceived as less efficient. Café managers, too, were less understanding of the demanding nature of their special staff, in spite of having been sensitized to their condition. Managers and colleagues perceived the "special staff" as undermining their capacity to profitably run the cafes.

As the problems began to mount, the founders became increasingly frustrated and motivation began to wane. One particular issue was that the core private investment group only held small stakes in the company of less than 10 percent each. The main owners were the founders and the nonprofit that provided the counseling and support services. The founders believed that the private investors had given up on the business, providing very little guidance and assistance. The investors though had other investments that were much larger, with the exception of this investment. Dedicating significant amounts of time to the investment did not make sense vis-à-vis the other larger investments.

Although a small part of the investors' total portfolio, they did uphold proper corporate governance and through the board of directors, gathered to discuss the need for more transparent information, the imminent liquidity issue, cost problems, and scaling in general. Overall, they decided that another investment round was necessary, worked out a plan to cut costs, including shuttering the unprofitable café, and asked management to provide refreshed scaling plans.

Liquidity was the most immediate need of the directives the board decided on, but the first to run into trouble. Not all of the investors were willing to participate in the proposed funding round. Two of the three investors had agreed to fund the company, but the third was reticent about putting more money into the company. Given the circumstances, two of the three investors laid out a highly punitive term sheet if the third investor chose not to fund the next round. The term sheet included a 3x liquidation preference for the latest round, which would greatly diminish the nonparticipating investor's returns, as detailed in Chapter 4. Faced with such a term sheet, the third investor chose to participate and helped create a more balanced investment structure.

The next issue to tackle was cost control. A cost-cutting plan was put into action by closing the unprofitable unit and moving a café to a new location with more business friendly landlords. The staffing challenge, though, actually uncovered more problems when it was looked at in detail. Very low numbers of graduates were matriculating through the nonprofit support program to work at the cafés. A much smaller percentage of the staff was being cultivated through this program than originally expected. This was problematic, as the impact case for investing in this company was built on the premise that the model trained and integrated severely disadvantaged people into the workforce. The mission statement of the company indicated this commitment. The board of directors decided to discuss this misalignment between the stated mission and the actual outreach. After several meetings, the board decided to modify the company's mission statement to reflect the reality. The company and the investors risked being accused of mission drift or mission dilution; however, the new mission adequately reflected attainable social goals.

Finally, the realization of many of the problems was delayed due to poor reporting. The board required more frequent and transparent reporting. To respond to this, the company revamped its operational projection model and began sending out more organized financial and operational statements.

At the end of the day, all of the investors remained committed to the investment, successful additional rounds were completed, and the business started entering into discussions with a competing café chain for potential acquisition. There were a number of core lessons learned from these experiences:

- *Reporting must be timely and transparent.* Similar to the first case study, this one picked up on problems through the reports and metrics that were being sent over. It's imperative to have information and inspection rights in an investment.
- *A subtle, but substantial problem in this transaction was a poor alignment of interest.* The investors simply did not have enough "skin in the game" to offer the full support that they would on a larger investment. This should either be established earlier on, where the investors would be characterized as passive investors or the limits of their activity should have been disclosed. The lack of active investors led to demotivated founders and management, who felt they were left alone without guidance. Investment size and fund-based investors, such as in this company, will be discussed more in Chapter 7.
- *The investors and management were not afraid to retrench.* Closing the unprofitable café was a challenging decision, since it was a very tangible failure. The investors hopefully took potential failed cafés into account when they did their analysis, very similar to when we looked at Mtoto Clinics and the estimation that a certain number of clinics would not work. Ultimately, though, the decision to shutter a café was the right one, as it led to a stronger company that was more attractive for acquisition.
- *Finally, the fortitude of management should be identified as a strong characteristic of the investment.* Investors should look for this in their potential investments. Having founders and management who are invested in the business for the long haul is a huge advantage. Rather than pack up and return to their home countries when times were tough, the founders stuck through a disheartening scale back and pushed forward.

Biogas Energy in Indonesia

The third and final case study is a more traditional social enterprise, a company that produces electricity for small, rural villages using a biogasification generator. The process of biogasification is to take biomass, such as dried-up crop remnants, and utilize high-temperature gasification or anaerobic digestion to convert the biomass to energy. The company itself started out by producing the biogas generators through a proprietary design and piloted the system in small villages that were off the main electricity grid in Indonesia.

The business model involved setting up a biogas generator in a village, which is powerful enough to provide energy to one, possibly two villages. Wires are run through the village using bamboo poling to connect households. Customers pay simplified monthly bills, calculated by the number of bulbs/equipment connected to the grid in their households. The plan was to scale up from just a few generators in villages to hundreds, possibly thousands.

The original investors were composed of an impact investing fund that is funded primarily by charitable donations and a private, for-profit-oriented impact investor. At first, the company executed on its plan by developing nearly 20 generators in different villages. Quickly, though, the company realized a series of challenges:

1. *Servicing the generators was a significant task, as it required specialized mechanics and engineers.* Properly trained service specialists were in short supply and required a number of training hours to adequately prepare.
2. *Running mini-utilities at each of the villages was a time-consuming task.* Employees had to be managed to calculate billing, collections required extensive tracking, wiring was constantly in need of maintenance, and ensuring a steady supply chain of biomass was always a concern.
3. *Building the generators and setting up the villages was more capital intensive than anticipated.* The profits from charging customers was slow to come in after setting up. Essentially, a large amount of money had to be fronted for a low, but steady stream of income. Additionally, to create more trained employees the company set up a training division that required more funds than expected.

Investors noticed these problems as margins were far under expectation and cash burn was high. The private investor was experienced with businesses that seemed too capital intensive and slow to realize profits. She suggested franchising the business by selling the generators to local businessmen who would then run the utility and earn profits through operations.

The company would provide the sale of all necessary equipment and offer specialized service technicians to maintain and repair the generators.

The company found success in this business model and began to scale up even more. It sold generators throughout Indonesia and was now powering nearly 100 previously unelectrified villages. During this time, the success was heavily promoted by the charitable investment fund investor, with increasing donations being one of the goals. As the investment progressed, the margins still remained thin and the company tried to raise its prices. The product became expensive for many local businessmen that historically were using government grants to subsidize the pricing.

During this time the company needed to raise more capital and the founders engaged with the investors for the next equity round. Since both investors knew the company well and saw its growth and potential, the preference was for both existing investors to complete the investment round. The founders had seen the popularity of their investment through the huge media that had been generated, felt that they had the potential to massively scale, and set a very high valuation target.

When met with the founders' requested valuation, both investors pushed back. This caused the founders to take a strategy of pressing each individual investor separately, trying to break up cohesion among the investors. As the investor's reassessed the company's value, they both came up far short of the founders' valuation target, citing the pricing pressure and recent, limited growth. The founders began to consider taking the round outside of the two existing investors since the investors' right of first refusal meant that a third party could agree and then the current investors would either have to match the terms or pass and allow the third party to invest.

The charity-backed investment fund investor complicated the process further by receiving nontraditional investment feedback directly from the CEO of the investment fund. The CEO knew the media attention the investment received and told the investment manager that they wanted to be able to still say they were invested in the company, even if it was at a higher cost. The private investor's position was weakened by this turn of events, as it was getting pressured into agreeing to a valuation higher than expected.

Ultimately, the middle ground that was achieved was a convertible round that provided the high end of the valuation if targets were met and floored at a level that both investors were comfortable with.

The post-investment analysis for this example revealed a number of key learnings:

1. *As mentioned in Chapter 2 during sourcing strategies, make sure to understand the type of company that is being invested in.* Here the company is capital intensive as opposed to asset light. Fortunately the

investor had experience in such companies and could mimic an asset light version by creating a franchisee system.

2. *Don't be afraid to suggest and carry through with changes to the business model.* Many investment funds try "playbooks" where they slightly tweak the business model until they get it right. It appears one of the investors was doing this when it suggested switching to the franchisee model.

3. *Similar to Case Study 1 in this section, unique challenges occur in impact investing, often caused by the variety of investors' entity types and interests.* In this example, one of the investors was not fully commercial, but a charity-backed investment fund that invested in for-profit entities. Returning to the thoughts on entities and their cost of equity in Chapter 3, we can see the issue becoming a real problem during investment-round negotiations.

   The charity-backed investment fund could afford to invest at a higher valuation since it only had to generate returns that ideally covered expenses. Also, the public exposure generated by the specific investment provided an opportunity to generate donations. Effectively, any positive rate of return would help validate the charity's unique model and, along the way, the investee story provided an excellent advertisement for donation. The private investor, though, had a normal cost of equity, tied to the capital asset pricing model. This required a much higher return than the other investor and meant that agreeing to a high valuation would make it difficult to achieve the required return.

In Chapter 8, we will discuss the different entities and their investment strategies. For now, we need to recognize that some of the differences that set impact investing apart from traditional investing can propagate into challenges that will need to be overcome. In this instance, a convertible structure was the solution that both parties agreed to, but in other circumstances it might not work as well.

METHODS OF EXIT

Now that we understand reporting, monitoring, and situations where value was built or protected, we move on to various forms of selling off the investment to realize financial return.

Secondary Share Sale

Selling a noncontrolling interest of shares to another party is one of the more common forms of exit for early stage investors. Typically, the company has grown in value and the per-share price negotiated allows the seller to profit.

A buyer purchasing a noncontrolling interest of shares will do so for a number of reasons. First, they may understand that the seller may be a fund and has a specific holding period requiring the seller to exit the position. The buyer believes there is value in the company and that the investment will continue to grow, even if they are paying a price beyond what the seller paid. Alternatively, the buyer may believe that there is value they can add to the business, which will increase the value far beyond the purchase price. Just as the original investor followed the investment process outlined in this book, the new buyer will do a very similar analysis to understand the value of the company, incorporating their own assumptions along the way.

Prior to looking for buyers, though, an investor thinking about selling shares to another party should consider the following:

- *Confidential information*: Most likely, there are numerous confidentiality clauses that must be signed. What information can the investor send to a prospective buyer without getting permission from the company or other investors?
- *Verifying documentation*: The investor selling the shares should check the existing signed shareholder agreement. The investor should be aware of whether a ROFR or ROFO exists, whether tag-along rights must be followed, whether investors are restricted from sale due to a time period obligation, or whether the purchaser is a competitor that is prohibited from purchasing shares due to clauses in the documentation.
- *Notification*: If the opportunity arises or if the investor is seeking out a share sale, the investor should announce this to the company and existing investors. If a ROFO exists, then there should be proper notification to the parties who have the rights. If a ROFR exists, then the potential buyer of the shares will want to know about it immediately.

Who the party is that is purchasing the shares can be a consideration that is unique to impact investing. For a noncontrolling interest, this is not always a relevant concern, but regardless, the new buyer may not be aligned with the social mission of the company. If this is the case, there could be discontent and problems during shareholder and board of director votes that determine the strategy, operations, and direction of the business.

Once a buyer is engaged in purchasing the shares, a due-diligence process ensues, similar to the investor's original purchase. The buyer will most likely want to perform a full operational, onsite due diligence, and then have the buyer's legal teams go through the existing shareholder agreements to understand all rights and clauses. The seller should do basic due diligence on the buyer and work with a legal team to create a suitable purchase agreement and representations and warranties. Finally, the seller needs to work with an accounting team to consider the tax implications of the sale.

Acquisition

As opposed to selling a noncontrolling interest, an acquisition involves a buyer purchasing enough shares to take control of the company. The value proposition is a bit different in such a scenario. When a company wants to acquire another company, it is usually for a strategic reason and the acquiring company believes synergies exist between the two companies. The strategic reason and the synergies hold value to the acquirer.

A company selling to a strategic buyer needs to be able to understand the strategy and synergies, since the current value of the company plus the synergies is the maximum that the buyer would be willing to pay. The following example shows this calculation, which can also be found in the Chapter 6 folder on the website as the file named Acquisition_Example.xlsm.:

1. In this example, we will examine two companies. One is the acquirer, while the other is the target firm. In order to understand the maximum that that buyer would be willing to pay, we first need to understand the value of the companies on their own. Valuing the companies should be done using an extensive method, as detailed in Chapter 3, but for the purposes of this example we will use a condensed version that starts with assumptions that allow us to quickly calculate free cash flow to equity and the cost of equity, as shown in Figure 6.3.
2. Once we know the free cash flow and the cost of equity, we can establish basic valuations for the two entities, pre-acquisition. We can also establish the valuation of the combined entity before any synergies have been realized. These are shown in the "PV" column for each entity and the combined entities, and demonstrated in Figure 6.4.
3. Once we know the value of the combined entity, we then need to think about what synergies are possible. In this example there are three possible synergies: increased short term growth, increased long term growth, and reduced operating expenditures. In the Excel example a scenario selector, shown in Figure 6.5, has been created that allows a user to toggle through various synergy scenarios.
4. The next step is to calculate the combined entities value, after incorporating the synergy value. In the shown example, captured in Figure 6.6, we are only utilizing the growth synergy.
5. With the post-synergy valuation complete, we can calculate three important items: the first is the gains from synergy, which is the difference between the post-synergy and pre-synergy valuations, the second is the maximum that the acquirer would bid for the company, which is the value of the target company now plus the synergy gains, and the third is the premium over the current valuation that the acquirer would be willing to pay. Figure 6.7 shows the synergy gains from the worksheet.

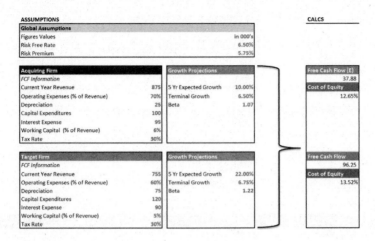

FIGURE 6.3 The cash flow and valuation assumptions for both companies.

Year	1	2	3	4	5	PV
Acquiror FCFE	41.66	45.83	50.41	55.45	61.00	
Acquiror TV					1,055.88	
Total	41.66	45.83	50.41	55.45	1,116.88	758.39
Target FCFE	117.43	143.26	174.78	213.23	260.14	
Target TV					4,104.97	
Total	117.43	143.26	174.78	213.23	4,365.11	2,778.49
Pre-Synergy FCFE	159.09	189.09	225.19	268.68	321.14	
Pre-Synergy TV					5,160.85	
Total	159.09	189.09	225.19	268.68	5,481.99	3,537.52

FIGURE 6.4 Calculating the FCFEs and terminal values allows us to calculate the acquirer's, target's, and combined entities' value.

Once the valuation and synergies are understood, the next step is to figure out how the acquisition company will actually pay for the target company. This can be done in all cash or in many situations for larger entities, using a stock swap. A stock swap is relatively easy to calculate and is done in a separate example in Excel, saved as StockSwap_Example.xlsx, available in the Chapter 6 folder on the website. The basics of a stock swap involve these steps:

1. Calculate the per-share value for each entity.
   Acquiror: 8.22
   Target: 21.71

Scenario Selector	
Growth Synergy	
New ST Growth	
	20.00%
New TV Growth	
	7.00%
New OpEx	
	50.00%

FIGURE 6.5 Various synergies create value.

Year	1	2	3	4	5	PV
Post-Synergy FCFE	160.95	193.14	231.77	278.13	333.75	
Post-Synergy TV					5,641.56	
Total	160.95	193.14	231.77	278.13	5,975.31	3,816.44
Scenario Data						
Growth Synergy FCFE	160.95	193.14	231.77	278.13	333.75	
Growth Synergy TV					5,641.56	
Cost Synergy FCFE	367.08	435.39	516.43	612.54	726.54	
Cost Synergy TV					11,697.24	
Growth & Cost Synergy FCFE	371.37	445.65	534.78	641.73	770.08	
Growth & Cost Synergy TV					13,017.00	

FIGURE 6.6 The post-synergy FCFE and terminal value is higher since it utilizes different short- and long-term growth rates.

Synergy Gains	278.92
Maximum Bid	3,057.41
Premium (%)	10.04%

FIGURE 6.7 The results of the analysis are the synergy gains, the maximum bid, and premium over the original value.

2. Understand the negotiated terms of the offer; typically a combination of cash and a stock swap ratio. The stock swap ratio is the number of shares that the acquirer is willing to exchange for a target company's share.

   In the example, we assume that the acquirer offers USD19 and .65 shares of stock for every target company share.

3. Determine if the proposition is above or below the estimated valuations. If it is above, the acquirer should not exceed the potential synergy gains.

In the example, the acquirer is offering USD24.35 per share (.65 * 8.22 acquirer equity share price + USD19 in cash). The target company is currently valued at USD21.71 per equity share, meaning that the acquirer is offering a USD2.63 premium for each share. This premium should capture the concept that there could be synergies between the two companies.

IPOs

One of the most desired methods of exits for investors is to use an IPO. Investors in early-stage companies technically sell their shares as a secondary offering after or during a primary offering. The key difference between a primary and secondary offering is that in a primary offering, new shares are created and sold. The more shares that are sold, the more dilution that can take place for existing shareholders. Normally, though, early-stage investors come in at a low per-share price that allows them to generate significant profits when selling at or after the IPO price.

The main concern for an investor is that the IPO is significant enough to generate a strong return. Although some stock exchanges have requirements on the size of entities that are listing, some do not, and companies can technically list with a very low share price and market capitalization. This is why we saw the term *qualified initial public offering* in Chapter 5, where the IPO must be of a certain size to be considered an IPO for investors holding preference shares. Investors also need to consider that an IPO incurs significant costs with investment banks and other entities. This needs to be factored into the analysis on what level of IPO is considered qualified.

Specific to impact investing, a successful IPO can provide proof that investing in companies serving low-income populations is a profitable business. However, an IPO's effect on the end client may be positive, negative, or neutral. The transparency requirements faced by publicly listed companies should have, in principle, positive effects. Yet, a profit maximization strategy that most public companies pursue may also lead an institution to deviate from the target population. It is important to balance financial and social returns carefully, during holding period and at exit. It is also critical to monitor closely the effects of different profit-maximizing strategies on end-customers.[4] It is important to operate efficiently and balance long-term social and financial return that recognizes the interests of clients, retail providers, and investors.

For many impact investments that are coming out of emerging markets, the desired exchange is the other concern for investors. The major exchanges

---

[4]The two most quoted IPOs in the impact investing field took place in microfinance, one in Mexico, Compartamos (2007), and the second SKS in India (2010).

around the world have very liquid markets, but are composed of different sets of investors. Companies want a public investor base that understands their company and value. Additionally, foreign currency exchange complexity can be encountered when shares are traded in different currencies than what the original investor used for the early rounds.

Liquidating Structures

The final exit that we will look at are liquidating structures. These are investment vehicles that are set up to automatically liquidate and pay investors out. Usually, such investment vehicles are created as special purpose vehicles (SPVs) for project-type investments such as housing.

Using a low-income housing project as an example, investors would invest in an SPV that is specifically created for the project. Equity and debt funds would be pooled and mimic the capital structure of a company. The critical difference, though, is that the SPV is set up specifically for the purpose of building and selling off the housing. Therefore, funds are used to create the housing, staff the sales team, and sell off the properties. As sales occur money is transmitted through the SPV and distributed according to a very specific set of instructions that are written into the shareholder agreement, known as a priority of payment or *waterfall*. Investors receive money over time as the project sells off and ultimately until the last house is sold. At that point, the SPV is dissolved and investors have generated their return.

Using an SPV structure is an excellent way to ensure liquidity in a project-based investment, but the language of the shareholder agreement needs to anticipate many different scenarios. It is often difficult to change the SPV agreements partway through an investment. Therefore, getting the language right from the start is critical to the successful use of an SPV liquidating structure.

THE END OF THE INVESTMENT PROCESS

From sourcing, screening, valuing, structuring, documenting, finalizing, monitoring, and finally, exiting, we have seen the full process for an impact investment. While much of this process is standard to any investment approach, we have understood along the way the differences that can occur when investing in social enterprises. The perspective we have taken throughout this process has been from a single, generic impact investor. In actuality, many of the impact investors active in the market are not single individuals, but private equity funds. The next chapter examines how these funds are set up, function, and operate within the world of impact investing.

CHAPTER 7

Impact Investing Funds

As social entrepreneurship and investing with a strong social purpose gain popularity, many nonprofessional investors and non–impact funds want to direct their money toward such investments. Those interested can be as diverse as high-net-worth individuals who want to devote part of their wealth to social impact, retail investors who want to see an allocation of their money in similar assets, or even government bodies looking to generate positive social return with their funding. As this book has shown thus far, making just one of these investments on a professional level can be a meticulous ordeal requiring a rigorous investment process. This may work if the investor wants to place a few million dollars, but the amount of interest in impact investing and the capital available far exceeds an individual's investing capability.

To address this gap in the market, funds have been created over the years that specialize in channeling investor money into direct-impact investments. Many of the entities that have emerged though are unique in the investing world as their funding sources and investment theses stray significantly from a traditional investment fund. We have touched on some of these particular challenges in the context of the individual investor, such as how an investor's cost of equity can filter through varying levels of valuation comfort, but the issues intensify on a fund level.

Understanding these difficulties is best done with a solid base in how a traditional private equity fund operates and the economics involved in creating and successfully managing one. Once we understand the traditional setup, we can then examine the additional complexities that a social mission mandate adds to the organization.

PRIVATE EQUITY OR VENTURE CAPITAL?

Prior to delving into how funds are set up, it's best to cover a few semantics. Frequently, the terms *private equity* and *venture capital* are thrown around synonymously. The key differentiator between these two terms is the stage of the business. Even though a venture capital investment is technically a private equity investment,[1] the stage of a venture capital investment is usually very early. Typically, friends and family put in start-up money and then an angel investor or a venture capital fund may provide additional capital or a more formal Series A round. These investments can range from a few hundred thousand dollars to a few million.

Private equity investments target more developed companies that are seeking rounds of capital beyond Series A, even up to a bridge round to IPO. The investments range in the tens of millions of dollars. Investment funds are generally set up to do either venture or private equity since the strategies and the post-investment requirements can be markedly different. In this chapter, unless specifically noted, we will use the term *private equity fund* to mean both early stage venture capital and more seasoned private equity investments.

THE BASIC CONSTRUCT OF A PRIVATE EQUITY FUND

The simple idea of a private equity fund is that a group of professional investors can utilize significant amounts of capital, beyond their own, to make direct private equity investments. In most cases, the people providing the capital—*the funders*, or the more technical nomenclature, *limited partners*—invest money into a fund manager, *the general partner*, which, in turn, invests the money directly into businesses. The characteristics of the fund managers and the fund's investment thesis are normally dictated by the requirements of the people providing the funding. These funders, in most cases, are different entities than the investor[2] and negotiate with the investor on investment criteria and expectations.

In order to operate, the fund manager is allowed to use part of the investment funds as a *management fee*. This fee is normally about 2 percent, but can vary depending on prior fund performance, investment thesis, and overall negotiation with the limited partner. Beyond the management fee, the fund manager is incentivized to make good investments in order to earn excess returns, known as *carry*. Specifically, a hurdle rate is established between limited and general partners, whereby if the fund manager generates

---

[1]Theoretically, a venture capital investment can be debt, but that distinction will be covered in Chapter 8.
[2]Technically, an investor and a funder can be the same person, which takes place frequently in the venture capital and private equity markets. It has also taken place in the impact investing industry.

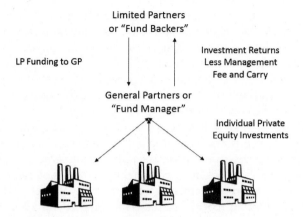

FIGURE 7.1 A basic overview of a private equity fund.

returns above the hurdle rate, the fund manager shares in those returns. The percentage of sharing is typically about 20 percent, but also can vary from fund to fund. With the 2 percent management fee and the 20 percent carry above a hurdle, the term "2 and 20" is often used to describe a standard fee arrangement. Figure 7.1 illustrates this setup.

The day-to-day operation of a private equity fund has many similarities to the responsibilities that an individual investor may have. Once a private equity fund receives committed funds and draws down funding, the "IRR clock" starts ticking. This means that the money must be put to work as soon as possible. Normally, a chief investment officer (CIO) is well versed in the fund's strategy and utilizes methods in the section on sourcing to generate investment leads. Similarly, any investment manager will also be working on lead generation. The screening process begins once business plans flow in, with the CIO having the ultimate screening authority.

For each individual investment, the investment process follows similarly to Chapters 2 to 6 of this book. However, there are a few distinctions that a larger entity may allow. One such exception is an investment committee. In some funds, an investment committee is established to ultimately decide if an investment should be made. The CIO and investment managers build a case for the investment following the investment process described and then present that case to the investment committee. Depending on fund governance, the investment is voted on and either made or rejected.

Another difference are responsibilities pre- and post-investment. Sourcing, structuring, and closing investments is a different process than building value in an investment to exit. Some larger entities have professionals that focus on investment generation, while others focus on value building and exit.

Regardless of specifics of responsibilities, the day-to-day activities are bound together by an alignment of interest. Investment managers normally have *carried interest* in investments. This can be structured in many ways, but the overall idea is that if the fund returns over a hurdle rate, then carry is generated for the fund. Of this carry, investment managers who are making, managing, and exiting investments earn their share of the carry.

With all of the similarities, there are some key roles in a private equity fund that differ from an individual investor. One of the primary differences is reporting. Limited partners who may have provided significant funding treat their investments in the private equity fund just as a direct investor views his or her investment in a company. Reporting requirements are typically part of the limited partner agreement, with quarterly reports often a standard. Generating reports can take time and resources from multiple parties at the fund.

Another key difference is the treasury operations or internal finance of the fund. An individual investor has a much more limited world of expenses and can manage a handful of investments. A fund, though, that is making multiple investments and utilizing tens or hundreds of millions of dollars can have a complex financial situation. In many funds, there is a finance manager or CFO role to guide the management of the existing fund and plan for future funds.

THE ECONOMICS OF A PRIVATE EQUITY FUND

The concept of a private equity fund is very attractive for investment professionals. They tend to think about their investing experience and magnify that by the ability to make many more investments in sizes larger than they normally would, using a fund paradigm. And this thought is not too far off base, as we will see when we dig into the economics of a fund; the performance of the underlying assets is critical. However, the full economics of a fund can be elusive, unless properly laid out. In order to help understand fund economics, a fully functional private equity fund model has been provided in the Chapter 7 folder on the website named PE_Fund_Model.xlsm. Prior to using it to explain the nuances of fund economics, we will go through a basic overview of how the model works.

Private Equity Fund Model Overview

Open the private equity fund model named PE_Fund_Model.xlsm from the website under the Chapter 7 folder. Readers who utilized the individual investment model provided will notice that the Control sheet is very similar, where assumptions are laid out going down the rows and various scenarios

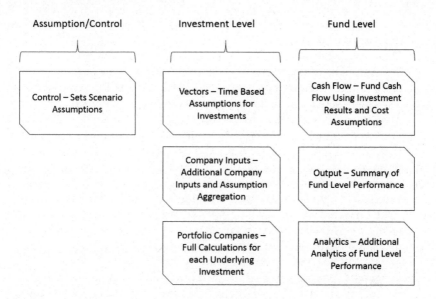

Assumption/Control   Investment Level   Fund Level

Control – Sets Scenario Assumptions

Vectors – Time Based Assumptions for Investments

Cash Flow – Fund Cash Flow Using Investment Results and Cost Assumptions

Company Inputs – Additional Company Inputs and Assumption Aggregation

Output – Summary of Fund Level Performance

Portfolio Companies – Full Calculations for each Underlying Investment

Analytics – Additional Analytics of Fund Level Performance

FIGURE 7.2 The private equity model is organized by creating scenarios around investment-level performance and integrating expenses to get fund-level expectations.

across the columns. The scenario that is active can be switched by changing the number in cell C4. Figure 7.2 depicts an overview of the private equity fund model.

Control Sheet: As mentioned earlier, the Control sheet allows a user to toggle through assumptions to build scenarios. Going down the Control sheet, the primary assumptions include:

- *Initiation Date*: This is when the fund is started. Dates are very important, since return calculations are time dependent.
- *Committed Capital*: When a fund is first started, it might not have all of its investors. Usually, an anchor investor seeds the fund and "dry commitments" then become actual commitments. Over time, a fund can ramp up commitments as others see who has made investments in the fund. It's important to model the commitments, since a fund is ultimately constrained by the amount of committed capital.
- *Commitment Period End Date*: An interesting dynamic of funds is that the management fee can change depending on the base it is multiplied by. When funds first start out, the management fee is calculated off of committed capital. At some point in the life of the fund, the base for the management fee is changed to cost basis. This makes sense, since as

investments are exited there is less work managing the investments and the cost basis goes down.

- *Drawn Capital*: A very important assumption is how the fund draws down from its commitments. One of the key roles of the finance manager or CFO is to optimize this process. If one draws all of the commitments immediately, then the IRR for that drawdown begins immediately. If the fund manager is unable to utilize and place all of the funds, then there is drag on the returns, since the time value of money continues to erode the IRR. However, a worse situation exists where the fund manager does not draw enough money and there is not enough funds to cover expenses. Be careful with this assumption, as some of the formula have custom values, while others reference the capital required to make investments.

- *Asset Origination Dates*: These dates dictate when the underlying investments are assumed to have been made. The time it takes to make investments is a factor, since the longer it takes to place investments, the more money will be spent on operational expenses.

- *Portfolio Composition*: Each of the underlying assets can be a different type of investment. This is largely tied to the private equity fund's investment thesis. In the example model, the fund is assumed to invest in social enterprises that are a mix of asset-light and capital-intensive businesses. In reality, the investment thesis of a fund can be very specific as fund investors are looking for fund managers with unique investment ideas and experience that can generate returns in excess of the benchmark.

- *Assumptions by Asset Class*: Each of the types of investments can have different profiles. For simplicity sake we have kept it to two asset classes. The performance expectations of the underlying investments is one of the most influential variables in the model.

- *Expenses*: A fund has a number of expenses from the salary of employees to due diligence expenses to tax and audit expenses. These can be based on a number of different factors such as the number of investments. Within this last section are the fees and fund mechanics such as hurdle rates.

Vectors Sheet: The Vectors sheet lays out monthly assumptions for the underlying investments. In the example model we have projected the growth rate, the gross margin, and the EBITDA margin for each style of investment. Theoretically we could have unique assumptions for each investment.

Company Inputs: This sheet aggregates all of the inputs from the Control sheet and lays them out where each row represents a company's assumptions. The information here allows us to create a fully functioning corporate projection including income statement, balance sheet, and cash flow statement information.

Portfolio Companies: The culmination of the Control, Vectors, and Company Inputs sheet is a series of calculations for each underlying company. This section can be thought of as a condensed version of the investment model reviewed in Chapter 3, for each underlying investment. The income statement, balance sheet, and cash flow statement are projected out for each period. Return assumptions are integrated, which allow us to make assumptions about investment, corporate performance, and eventual exit.

Cash Flow: Once the investment cash flows are known and expense assumptions are established, the complete fund cash flows can be aggregated and calculated on this sheet. This sheet has two very important aspects to be aware of. The top part focuses on keeping a cash balance with all of the sources and uses of cash. Liquidity is paramount in the economic analysis, as expenses must be met by committed capital or exit returns. The second important part is toward the bottom, where the total IRR calculations are created.

Output: To help summarize and visualize data, the Output sheet puts key items in an easily readable format.

Analytics: More detailed analysis is done on this sheet. In particular, rows 28 to 41 are important because they calculate the fund's use of money for expenses. Most limited partnership agreements distinguish between fund expenses and management fee expenses. Here, we try to separate the two out to make sure the management fee is not exceeded, making the economics untenable.

How Traditional Funds Are Measured for Success

Before we look at key considerations in fund economics, we should jump ahead a bit to understand what a standard investor expects a fund to accomplish. Just like traditional underlying investments, a fund is expected to return funds to investors. Often, a "J curve" is referred to since a fund has a finite inception point of investment, a period of funds deployment, and then a period of harvesting the returns of the investments. In the example model on the Output Summary sheet, we can see that the starting base case has a typical J curve chart showing, as replicated in Figure 7.3.

Thinking about each phase of the J curve reveals the dynamics of a fund and how shifts in those underlying aspects affect performance. The first step of the J curve is the downward slope, where the fund managers draw down funds from investors. This can be thought of as negative cash flow because in an IRR calculation, this is money going out to make investments. The second phase is the period of investment where fund managers are placing

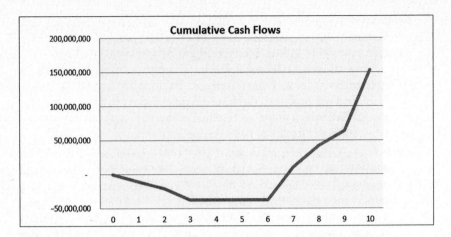

FIGURE 7.3 A fund has a period of draw down, investment, and then return.

the investor funds into companies. There may be a few upticks in the curve from early exits or dividends, but mainly the curve here will be flat. The third and final phase of the J curve is the return component where investments are being exited. For a fund to break even without consideration to the time value of money, it needs to get the J curve back up to the 0 point on the *x*-axis of the chart. Anything beyond that is return.

The J curve chart also shows us the two types of metrics that investors look at to measure the financial success of the fund: IRR and money multiple. We know IRR from our individual company investment analysis. It works just the same in this situation. If phase one occurs very quickly and the investment money is quickly drawn down, then the other phases need to occur rapidly as well. Otherwise, the IRR will be diminished. If it takes a long time to place money in companies during phase two and that part of the curve is drawn out, then the IRR will be diminished. Finally, if exits are longer than expected and phase three has a lower slope, then the IRR will be diminished. The opposite occurs as well. In an ideal situation, a fund draws down funding, places it quickly in investment, and then exits in a rapid manner.

While having a compressed J curve will help the IRR, the steepness of the third phase is what matters. We could have a very quick investment cycle with a positive IRR, but the amount of funds being returned may not be significant. Investors care about the absolute amount of money being returned, which can be expressed by the money multiple. The money multiple is simply the total amount of money that is returned divided by the total amount of money invested. In some cases, it may be worth letting an investment take more time until exit if the money multiple is high.

TABLE 7.1 Fees and Management Carry Reduce the Gross Asset Returns

Description	IRR %
Asset Returns	28.81%
Fund IRR Net of Fees	23.71%
Investor IRR Net of Fees and Management Carry	21.55%

We can see that fund dynamics mimic those of investing in a standard company. However, fund investing differs in that fund investors pay fees and normally share in the returns with the fund managers. These costs can be significant and must be deducted from the gross returns in order to express a more realistic net IRR and money multiple.[3] Looking at the Output Summary sheet again, we can see the transition in IRRs from the example model's base case. See Table 7.1.

Ultimately, the measurement of a fund's success is how it performs against a benchmark. A benchmark is a similar or group of similar assets. For instance, the S&P 500 is an index of 500 firms with high market capitalization that are listed on the NYSE and NASDAQ. The return of an investment strategy could be compared to the S&P 500's performance for the same time frame. Ideally, an investment strategy exceeds the benchmark; otherwise, an investor would have been better off simply investing in the benchmark. For private equity, there are a number of firms that create their own benchmarks based on private market performance, such as Cambridge Associates. We will examine benchmarks in more detail, later in this chapter.

KEY CONSIDERATIONS IN FUND ECONOMICS

With a general understanding of how funds are set up, operate, and the economics behind them, we should move into a more detailed look at key items. The primary ones include expected asset performance, exit timing, fund placement timing, resource allocation, and operational expense management. For each of these, there is a preset scenario in the fund model. We will toggle through each scenario to see the differences in assumptions and the effects they have on the fund. For this section, it is recommended to have the fund model open and ready to use.

---

[3]Taxes and any foreign exchange costs are a final calculation that investors will have to take into account when finalizing their own IRR numbers.

Expected Asset Performance

The performance of the assets that a fund invests in are the primary determinant of a fund's performance. This is why two thirds of this book has been focused on how to establish and manage a rigorous investment process. We can see this effect by looking at scenario 2 in the example fund model. Open the fund model to the Control sheet and enter the number 2 in cell C4 to switch to this scenario. Scenario 2 is identical to scenario 1 except for the following differences, with their respective effects:

- *Differences*: Reduced EBITDA growth rates for both asset-light and capital-intensive investments (cell H491 and H507 on the Control sheet).
- *Effects*: Investment returns reduced for asset-light investments to 14.57 percent and capital-intensive investments to 10.95 percent. The expected fund IRR net of fees, but gross of carry is 9.16 percent and 8.87 percent after management carry. These effects can be seen on the Output sheet of the fund model.

If the growth rates of the underlying invested companies are impaired, the fund returns can be heavily impacted. When starting a fund, the projections of the underlying assets should be analyzed in detail. Varying levels of analysis can be done, with some as simple as entering in expected rates of return or, as the example model does, fully laying out the economics of the future investments.

Exit Timing

Related to asset performance is a delay in the expected exit of investments. Exits can be delayed beyond normal time frames for a variety of reasons: longer time frame to increased margins and profitability, unexpected setbacks and strategy shifts, or opportunistic reasons. In most cases, the delay is caused by negative events and can lead to a lower fund IRR. Switch the scenario to 3 in the Control sheet of the example model and observe the following differences and effects:

- *Differences*: Exit years for both types of investments are pushed back by two years (cell I495 and I511 on the Control sheet). Additionally, EBITDA growth rates are slightly reduced (cell I491 and I407 on the Control sheet).
- *Effects*: Total asset performance is reduced to 23.86 percent, the fund IRR net of fees, gross of carry is 20.25 percent, and net of management carry is 15.85 percent. These are visible on the Output sheet.

While this may seem like a reasonable outcome, the situation is actually worse than it appears. Look at cell N4 on the Control sheet. This cell tracks the amount of unfunded fees that should have been paid. We can trace the root of this problem by going to the Cash Flow sheet and looking at the fees that are due and paid. In March 2022, the delay of the asset exits causes a shortfall in cash to meet fund, management, and operational expenses. In this situation, management needs to plan for potentially delayed exits; otherwise, there can be a liquidity crisis.

When examining exit dates, one has to be cognizant of the reasons for the delay. If the EBITDA growth rate is very high, delaying the exit can produce increased returns. This can actually be a reason for delaying exit, but in many circumstances a negative situation has occurred that requires reducing other asset-related assumptions.

Fund Placement Timing

Delays placing investor money into investments materialize into economic loss from higher total management fees over an extended fund life. The economic impact is dependent on how long the delay is in place and whether time can be made up by accelerated exits.

Due diligence expenses on investments that do not get made are another economic loss associated with longer placement times. While searching for investments that fit a fund's criteria, investment managers are most likely entering into due diligence for a handful of deals. A number of these investments may not get completed, but do incur travel, legal, and overall resource allocation costs. Scenario 4 in the example model shows the effects of a slow fund placement rate.

- *Differences*: The time to place each investment has been extended by six months (cells J382:J391 on the Control sheet). Additionally, the number of due diligences required for each completed investment has been increased from two to six (cell J837 on the Control sheet).
- *Effects*: The fund IRR both net of fees, gross of carry and net of carry is reduced slightly. However, the asset IRRs remain the same since none of the economics of them have changed in this scenario.

We can see that delay in investing has an effect on fund economics, but it seems relatively slight for a six-month delay. Try changing the delay so it is one or two years.[4] When this is done, there are situations where fees may go unpaid and there is a liquidity issue.

---

[4]Be aware that in the example model the asset placement dates must take place in sequential order for each asset. Thus, asset 1 must be originated before asset 2, and so on.

Resource Allocation

When a fund management team receives funding, the team must be very careful with each hire. The team is limited to the management fee that is generated each period. The general thought, then, is that *resource allocation* should follow along with the number of assets being managed. Many organizations are set up in a pyramid structure where a small number of investment managers are assisted by junior associates and analysts.

One particular problem is if a fund makes more investments than its strategy can handle. An example of this is if a growth-oriented fund raises USD30 million and starts testing the waters by placing small USD500,000 investments. Soon there will be a large number of investments to monitor and grow. If that same fund gets additional funding and decides to make larger investments, it will now have to contend with monitoring and building value in the larger investments and leave the smaller ones less managed. The issue with this is that the resource allocation strategy should be clear from the start. Either the fund manager knows that he or she will make many small investments and allow a number of them to go bad or will make a select few larger ones and manage them carefully. Mixing the allocation can cause internal confusion with the fund and external frustration with investees when they are unable to get the attention they need.

We can see the effect of resource allocation by switching the example model to Scenario 5.

- *Differences*: The number of deals that an investment manager and analyst are able to cover has been reduced (cells K824:825 on the Control sheet).
- *Effects*: With fewer deals per investment manager and analyst, the number of required personnel increases. This costs significant amounts of cash and stresses the fund to the point where it cannot meet its obligations, demonstrated by a large unpaid fee amount seen in cell N4 on the Control sheet.[5]

Keep in mind that the number of professionals a fund requires to manage its assets does not have to be a perfectly linear function. As funds grow in size, they begin to realize economies of scale benefits that a smaller firm

---

[5] Be careful when analyzing cost increases, as they may not flow through to the IRR calculation, depending on setup. In the example model, if a cost is unpaid it is tracked for the user; however, it does not generate a negative cash flow, which would account for the shortfall in the IRR. Putting in this type of functionality is a preference, depending on how a person wants to analyze stressed scenarios.

does not. Using a simple example, imagine a fund that has USD30 million of assets under management with a 2 percent management fee. Assuming the general partner did not capitalize any of the fund, there would be USD600,000 per year to operate the fund. Salaries alone would take up most of this money. While new funds will have to promise carry for senior investment managers, the base salaries in developed markets would only allow for a single senior manager and one to two junior staff. These three will have to do everything from sourcing, screening, structuring, closing, monitoring, building exit value, reporting, and internal finance functions.

Now if we think about a USD300 million fund with USD6 million per year, there are many more possibilities for hiring specialized staff. Senior investment managers can cover a number of deals with lower-salary junior workers working on numerous investments each. Specialized roles such as a finance manager can be hired that cover reporting and internal finance duties. Constraints encountered in smaller funds are alleviated, allowing each professional to focus more intensely on his or her tasks at hand.

Operational Expenses

While salaries tend to be the highest expense in a fund, other expenses can eat away at a funds returns. A common area where cost overruns tend to surface are on due diligence costs and unreimbursed closing costs. Recall in Chapter 5, when we discussed the term sheet, there was a section for expense reimbursement. However, a cap on the reimbursement had been negotiated. In many cases, the legal and accounting expenses can exceed these caps and the fund has to pick up the remaining costs. Scenario 6 shows such a situation.

- *Differences*: Three expense assumptions have been increased: the amount of unreimbursed costs per investment closed, the cost of completing an onsite due diligence that is not reimbursed (particularly in cases of noninvestment), and the cost of ongoing surveillance (cells L822, L838, and L839 on the Control sheet, respectively).
- *Effects*: Once again, we look to cell N4, where unfunded fees are tracked. We can see that there is a shortfall, which would impact the fund returns.

THE DIFFERENCES BETWEEN TRADITIONAL FUNDS AND IMPACT INVESTING FUNDS

One of the common problems echoed in the impact investing industry is that it is difficult to source and find quality investments. If we look at traditional private equity funds, investment managers sift through hundreds of proposals a year, review a number of business plans, conduct due diligences, and end up investing in only a handful of investments. Now imagine this exact same process, but add a social mission criteria. The additional criteria limits the world of possible investments.

A limited investment pool translates into longer times to deploying funds and making investments. As long as there is the expectation that the investments will take longer than average to make and that costs may be higher than normal, then such a model works. However, *impact investing funds* that market their fund with traditional timelines may struggle to keep up with such timing, incur higher costs than anticipated, and return a lower IRR than expected.

Some impact investing funds adapt to the problem of delayed time frames by altering their social missions or criteria. Funds that start out with a very strict social criteria could encounter investment placement difficulties as their fund size grows. In order to compensate for this, they must either become very creative in their sourcing strategies, delay the investment process, or loosen their financial or social criteria. The first option can be achieved by employing unique strategies, such as finding traditional investments that do not realize their social impacts. The second option of delay is not preferential as we have seen, where time costs money and returns. The last two options of loosening financial and social criteria can be very problematic and contentious.

Loosening financial criteria means making investments in companies that will either bear higher risk of failure or lower return expectations. Funds may be ill-prepared for the circumstances if they reduce the rigor of their investment process. For instance, imagine a fund that historically has never invested in venture stage companies, but instead focused on growth stage. If it is having trouble placing money and chooses to invest in venture stage companies, it may not have the ability to handle the strategy and scaling of the individual investments or, from a fund-level view, manage the volatility of its portfolio correctly.

Social criteria reductions can be very problematic for investors who placed money with the fund for a specific social reason. If the fund is having trouble placing money and it relaxes its social criteria, it could alienate these investors. Also, the further an impact investing fund loosens its social criteria, the more traditional it becomes and the more focus falls on pure financial performance.

Compounding the issue of timing and placing funds are longer-than-average exit time frames for impact investments. A majority of impact investments are in businesses that operate with real assets, as opposed to tech-oriented investments, in foreign markets. These businesses take time to scale, to reach EBITDA breakeven, and to become profitable. The markets that social entrepreneurs tend to operate in are economically and politically challenging. All of these factors lead to delayed exit timings. Similar to deployment timing, as long as the expectation upfront is that the exit time frames could be longer and returns diminished due to it, there is not a problem. However, if unrealistic exit time frames are presented and missed, then the fund will produce lower than expected returns.

Impact investing cost inflation also incurs in other areas of fund economics. Impact investing funds adhering to a social mission criteria have to contend with a higher ratio of unsuccessful due diligences than a traditional fund. When a good investment is found that has a strong financial and strategic outlook, but does not fit into the social mission, then it must be passed on. As we saw earlier in this chapter, failed due diligences cost money and can add up when done a number of times by multiple investment managers.

Another area where impact investing funds differ from traditional funds is resources. Impact investing funds are selling an investment strategy that is predicated on providing a positive social return. In order to demonstrate such a return, a substantial amount of data must be collected, scrubbed, organized, and reported. Such tasks require additional resources, including specialized ones such as a social performance manager who is experienced in properly collecting and analyzing social mission related data.

Impact-Based Compensation Structures

In traditional private equity funds, the compensation of the fund manager is linked to maximization of profit alone. Since private equity impact investors seek to deliver both financial and social/environmental returns, it appears logical that the compensation of the fund manager should be linked to achieving both financial and social/environmental returns. Yet, this is easier said than done. While there is significant consensus today on what constitutes an acceptable financial return depending on benchmark and there is agreement on how it is measured, there is less consensus on what constitutes a desirable social target.

Two elements constitute the fund manager's compensation: a management fee and the carried interest. While we have discussed management

TABLE 7.2 Social Target–linked Compensation Can Help Promote the Social Mission

15%	+5%	+10%	= 30%
Base carry for achieving financial hurdle	If target 1 is reached	If target 2 is reached	Final GP carry

fee and carried interest, an impact private equity fund could link the fund manager's compensation to the achievement of social targets.[6] This means that once the fund manager is entitled to the standard carried interest (above a hurdle rate of around 8%[7]) it becomes eligible to earn a social portion of the carried interest according to its impact performance. Suppose the impact objective is established in terms of percentage of low-income customers reached by portfolio companies. The fund could base the impact component of the carried interest on this quantitative metric. Two targets could be specified:

- Target 1: Minimum of 30 percent of portfolio outreach is low income.
- Target 2: Minimum of 50 percent of portfolio outreach is low income.

If we suppose the base carry for achieving the financial hurdle is set at 15 percent, we could imagine reaching target 1 adds a further 5 percent and reaching target 2 another 10 percent. The final fund manager carried interest would be 20 percent if target 1 is met, or 30 percent if the fund manager reaches target 2 (and 15 percent if neither is met).

Linking carried interest to social impact targets is a way to protect the fund's mission. If the fund manager's compensation is linked to serving a low-income population, the fund manager will use his or her leverage in the company to ensure that the company does not drift from serving this population.

In the case of Solero, the model above could tie the fund manager's interest to Solero selling at least 50 percent to low-income populations. If the company decides to focus its marketing and sales strategy to target U.S. and European recreational enthusiasts, these targets would not be met. In the same way, the company will know from the outset that its new investor has an incentive to target the low-income user. This impact-based incentive structure adds transparency of expectations and contributes to clarifying investor-investee alignment of goals.

Another impact metric could be a third-party impact assessment. As an example, a fund manager who is rated every year by the Global Impact Investing Rating System (GIIRS) will obtain an annual overall score (based on ESG and impact performance of the fund manager and its investees). This score could be used as the threshold to determine the portion of carry based on impact.

---

[6]For examples see GIIN brief http://www.thegiin.org/cgi-bin/iowa/resources/research/332.html.
[7]This is a negotiated figure between the general partners and limited partners.

What appears evident is the need to define the fund impact goals and impact targets. The targets to reach should be clear and verifiable, and they should be aligned to the overall objective of the fund. A third-party validation of achievement of targets adds the necessary credibility to the compensation scheme (GIIRS, NRSRO rating company, or one of the Big Four auditors are some options).

Additionally, the investment managers may receive an annual bonus linked to annual performance targets determined in advance with their managers. Traditionally, these performance targets are financial and operational targets. Some examples of financial targets for investment manager bonuses include:

- USD5 million or above in new equity investments sourced and successfully closed by year end.
- USD100 million in loans disbursed (into a debt financing institution) by year end.

Establishing nonfinancial targets is less common, and here again, there is less agreement on what targets reflect higher impact.

Examples of annual social targets include:

- Portfolio company completes third-party social rating or impact assessment.
- Portfolio company is internally assessed using social performance scorecard.
- Investment manager collects nonfinancial data on time and verifies quality, conducts trend analysis, and provides feedback to investee.
- Investment manager supports investee company in a specific initiative with high social impact, such as:
  - Develop a product targeting a chronically underserved community.
  - Facilitate obtaining a technical assistance grant (support in reaching out to grant giver, helping draft proposal, supporting implementation or evaluation).
  - Offer support in improving ESG practices (better client protection practices, for instance).

Relevant to these discussions, and worth examining for their social innovation, are social impact bonds as developed initially in the United Kingdom and now in the United States and Australia. Social impact bonds are a form of contract where the investor is paid for improved social outcomes if these are met.

BENCHMARKING

Many of the differences between traditional fund investing and impact fund investing noted earlier in this chapter alluded to the potential for diminished returns. Traditional or impact oriented, it is difficult to discuss returns without context, which is why *benchmarking* is necessary. Private equity fund returns are measured for success against benchmark returns. Benchmarks can be established in multiple ways, from the point of view of the performance of very similar private investments, narrowly focused public indices such as electronically traded funds (ETFs), or widely focused indices such as the S&P 500.

One of the key aspects to benchmarking is comparability. Understanding the underlying asset composition of each benchmark is very important, since varying asset blends have differing risk and return profiles. It would be entirely invalid to compare the performance of a North American domestic debt fund against an emerging market equity fund. Asset type and geographical focus should be aligned.

Similarly, time frames are also important when constructing benchmark data. It is deceptive to state that a fund is outperforming a benchmark, if the time frames are markedly different. Return information generated from short or specifically cut time frames can be volatile versus long term averages. For private equity benchmarks, time also comes into play regarding when the comparable funds were started. These funds are often aggregated into "vintages" by year in order to increase the comparability of performance. To help understand benchmarks, we will examine the return data in Table 7.3.

Table 7.3 shows returns for private and public market indices, measured using various time frames. Depending on the time frame, we can see that returns can vary significantly for some indices. For instance, looking at the MSCI Emerging Markets index the returns were as low as the year to date (January 1, 2013 to September 30, 2013) at –4.1 percent to a high of 13.2 percent for a 10-year time frame.

Additionally, we should understand how the private market data are constructed. As mentioned earlier, the private market data are usually created from vintages. What is challenging about looking at historical private fund vintages is that we have to know how much of the fund has been exited. It would be incorrect to examine a 2013 vintage where there could be very little exit information. For this reason, certain vintages are usually selected that have representative data. Also, the vintages can be weighted to produce the final aggregate return figure.

From a financial perspective, it would make sense for an impact investor to look to the 5- to 10-year returns. Based on the previous data they would expect at least a 7.6 percent return if they were considering an international

TABLE 7.3 Global Ex-U.S. Developed and Emerging Markets Private Equity and Venture Capital Indices

For the Periods Ending September 30, 2013	Quarter	Year to Date	Year 1	Year 3	Year 5	Year 10	Year 15	Year 20
Ex-US Developed Markets PE and VC	6.7	9.1	14.4	11.8	6.8	14.4	13.5	13.8
Emerging Markets PE and VC	3.7	5.9	9.5	8.1	9.5	11.8	8.3	7.7
Public Market Indices								
MSCI EAFE	11.6	16.1	23.8	8.5	6.4	8	5.5	5.4
MSCI Emerging Markets	5.9	−4.1	1.3	0	7.6	13.2	12.3	7.1
S&P 500	5.2	19.8	19.3	16.3	10	7.6	5.3	8.8

Sources: Cambridge Associates LLC, MSCI Inc., Standard & Poor's, and Thomson Reuters Datastream. MSCI data provided "as is" without any express or implied warranties. Data specifically from: www.cambridgeassociates.com/news/articles/private-equity-investments-in-ex-u-s-developed-and-emerging-markets-posted-solid-q3-returns-and-improved-significantly-over-their-q2-performance/.
Returns (%) in U.S. dollars, periods ending September 30, 2013.

strategy and investing in a public strategy such as the MSCI Emerging Market index. However, it does seem there is a premium for the risk of private investments, with return expectations above 9.5 percent for private, international PE and VC investments.

While we can isolate the financial performance, we should keep in mind that impact investments also provide a social return. Benchmarks could be set up with cohorts constructed around GIIRs ratings. Financial returns could be aggregated and calculated for each type of GIIRs rating over time. Then, funds that have a certain mix of GIIRs rated assets could be compared to such a benchmark.

Benchmarking for both financial and social return is important because it demonstrates the value proposition of investing in a specific fund. Investors look for the *alpha,* or returns in excess of the benchmark, to assess the relative performance of fund managers and to establish preferences for investing. Establishing both a financial and social benchmark is important for impact investing since some investors may have preferences toward the social mission, while others will want to see balance, and others lean toward more traditional financial return with some aspect of impact.

A final point on benchmarking, regardless of financial or social, is consistency. Once a fund chooses benchmarks it must be very careful on changing these frequently. Investors will become suspicious of frequent benchmark changes, since it could be perceived that the fund managers are trying to fit the benchmark to demonstrate the highest possible returns. A consistent, comparable benchmark provides investors with a look at the fund manager's financial and social investment expertise.

CONCLUDING THOUGHTS ON IMPACT INVESTING FUNDS

Impact investing funds are an excellent means to channel large pools of money into direct investments that have a high degree of social impact. Market participants have responded to the demand by forming a number of impact investing oriented funds, but there is a considerable range of financial and social orientations. The challenges enumerated in this chapter apply to these funds to varying degrees and unfortunately many first-time fund managers do not identify these issues themselves. Fund managers must be transparent about the risks and the realities that their investors are taking when investing in their funds, particularly in relation to investment deployment, exit time frames, expected returns, and social criteria. Investors in these funds must be clear about their financial and social return preferences and ensure that the fund(s) they have chosen are aligned.

CHAPTER 8

Investment Alternatives, Challenges, and Outlook

At the end of 2010, J.P. Morgan issued a report titled "Impact Investments: An Emerging Asset Class," which suggested impact investing was evolving in such a way that it should be defined as a new asset class. The report proposed that the way for impact investing to grow was to define itself as an asset class; otherwise, if impact investors sought "… to assign their investments to traditional asset classes such as equity, debt and cash … this would lead to a fragmentation of impact investing skills and constrain the industry's potential growth."[1] Such a proposition seems tenuous, given the diversity of expertise required to professionally invest funds using different mediums. The development of impact investing over the years has supported a non–asset class approach, with a variety of products available ranging from equity to debt to even receivables financing.

Although the methods of investing for social impact is developing on the right track, there are still critical issues to address. Disparate costs of equity from nontraditional funding sources have led to unsustainable businesses being perceived as commercially viable. The excitement over investing into such enterprises and anticipating traditional returns sets up the possibility of falling significantly short of expectations. Additionally, the dearth of high impact, commercially viable investments will lead impact investment funds to alter criteria from their marketed levels. Investors with unmet expectations and potential investors who learn about their experiences will ultimately pull away from deploying future capital into the sector. Establishing the correct investment and social mission expectations and fulfilling them through sound, rigorous practices can overcome these challenges and allow the impact investing industry to grow.

---

[1]Nick O'Donohoe, Christina Leijonhufvud, and Yasemin Saltuk, "Impact Investments: An Emerging Asset Class," *Global Research* (November 29, 2010), 9.

While impact investing has gained traction, with more investors and entrepreneurs understanding that profit and positive social change are not opposing forces, the depth of the market will be constrained by the limits of proper capital allocation. If the challenges of mismatched expectations between investors and investments are hammered out, what remains will be the natural market evolution where commercial and noncommercial capital is properly placed. For commercial impact investing, an argument can be made that the forefront of this evolution is very local investment vehicles, which adhere to strict impact investing processes, but also have the ability to invest in traditional investments. These entities break down the classical thought of emerging market investing from the confines of developed market financial hubs and the requirement that all investments must be impact oriented.

INVESTMENT ALTERNATIVES

Prior to looking at one strong alternative to current impact investing strategy, it is worth examining the range of alternatives that are in the market. The bulk of this book has been a guide to investing in equity of social entrepreneurships. The last few years has seen a wave of new types of investors that offer debt, specialized financing, guarantees, and charity/grants that are deployed as investment. Each of these types of financings require different skill sets to deploy the proper investment process. We will briefly take a look at what the major alternatives to investing equity in impact investments are and the considerations for such investment.

Debt

Not only have wealthy angel investors provided debt financing, but debt funds have been created that focus on impact investments. *Debt* has traditionally been less common for early-stage entities since it usually requires one of two things that are in scarce supply for such companies: collateral and/or cash flow.

Debt issuers offer capital at lower rates of return than equity because they are due a fixed, consistent return and have priority over assets and cash flow. A debt investor looks at getting repaid and takes comfort in the cash flow coverage the company maintains over the required debt payments. These metrics are often expressed as interest coverage ratios (ICRs) or debt service coverage ratios (DSCRs).[2] When investing debt, the investor looks at

---

[2] A standard ICR is calculated as EBITDA or EBIT / Interest due. A standard DSCR is calculated as EBITDA or EBIT / (Interest due + Principal due).

the historical cash flow levels and the expected cash flow under varying stress scenarios, and determines the appropriate leverage to offer. The interest and principal payments due to the debt investor normally take priority over any equity investor, including preferred equity.

A debt issuer will also ask for certain covenants to protect the debt issuer's position. A covenant is either positive or negative, meaning that it is a requirement or restriction of the company. For instance, a common covenant is a tangible net worth or a borrowing base test. In such tests, if the value of the company decreases below a certain threshold or, in a worse case, below the book value of the debt, then repayment changes may be required. A common change would be a rapid amortization of the debt where all excess cash is used to pay down the principal of the debt as soon as possible.

Covenants can also be used to enforce social missions. A debt funder can establish responsible social covenants in loan agreements and define the results of a breach. For instance, an investor in a microfinance institution may define in the loan agreement the limits of what is considered responsible lending. The investor can also establish the reporting requirements that will allow them to monitor progress in achieving these targets. In 2012, a group of social investors in microfinance developed a set of *Lender's Guidelines for Setting Covenants in Support of Responsible Finance.*[3] The guidelines aim to be conducive to responsible financing by establishing three financial ratios (capital adequacy ratio, return on assets (ROA), and open currency position). These ratios are indicators of the sustainability of the institution and its effect on end clients. The guidelines establish thresholds beyond which the institution is in breach of the loan agreement. Also included are reporting requirements of *social undertakings*, measured by social metrics using a third-party validated standard (such as SPI4).

Lenders in other sectors such as healthcare, education, or housing will use other standards and benchmarks when integrating social undertakings and covenants in their loan agreements. Lenders requiring the borrower to undergo a social rating or conduct a full third-party assessment on its social performance (such as a GIIRS rating for instance) can also be envisioned.

In addition to priority over cash flow and protective covenants, debt investors seek collateral in case their debt payments are missed. Collateralizing debt can be very general, to the extent of the entire company, or very specific, to the extent of specific assets. Debt holders analyze the value of the collateral during stress situations and try to size their debt amounts such that

---

[3]The guidelines have been integrated in the Principles for Investors in Inclusive Finance. Social Performance Task Force, social investor working groups, *Lenders' Guidelines for Setting Covenants in Support of Responsible Finance.*

in a worst case scenario, where the collateral must be seized and liquidated, the funds from liquidation pay off the outstanding debt.

For early-stage companies, debt can be hard to get at reasonable terms since collateral is scarce and cash flows are often negative. One exception to this is the venture debt market, which has gained traction in developed markets, such as the United States. Venture debt is another form of venture capital, but instead of an equity investment into a venture stage company, debt is provided. The interest rates on venture debt are usually reflective of the risk of an early stage company.[4] However, there are a few key characteristics of venture debt that make it a worthwhile proposition for experienced investors.

The first key to venture debt is warrants, which are often a requirement for venture debt investors. Warrants are issued by a company and allow the holder to purchase shares in the company for a set price. Venture debt investors negotiate a certain level of warrant coverage in case there are liquidity events in the company. If the company is acquired or goes public, the warrants are converted and the warrant holder becomes a shareholder, which is able to enjoy in the upside of the liquidity event. Warrants can enhance venture debt returns to the level of low equity returns, but with the consistent coupons they often have lower volatility in returns than pure equity.

Another important element to venture debt is pairing with a private equity investor. Rarely would a venture debt investor provide a round of funding without a well-known private equity investor. This allows the venture debt investor a reduction in due diligence costs if they trust the private equity investor's investment process. Additionally, the venture debt investor can analyze the cash burn rate and size of their investment amount such that the equity funding plus company cash flow is enough to service the debt.

Additionally, a venture debt investor usually requires to be paid off if another round of equity occurs. This allows the venture debt investor to either reinvest or leave with the interest earned plus the warrants from the initial round. If they choose to reinvest they can then do a full credit assessment at that point in the businesses lifecycle.

The final characteristic of venture debt is collateral. While many early-stage companies have very little collateral, certain tech and biotech companies can have extremely valuable intellectual property (IP). Venture debt investors can negotiate claims to IP for a failure to meet interest and/or principal payments.

---

[4]This can vary, depending on the prevailing spreads and benchmarks, but is typically in the teens.

Outside of the United States, venture debt is not very common. In fact, lending to small to medium-sized enterprises is a challenge for companies in emerging markets. Local banks typically charge very high interest rates and may require stringent personal guarantees from the business founders. These harsh terms have significantly limited the debt markets for small- to medium-sized companies in many areas that social entrepreneurships are trying to flourish.

NOTES FROM THE FIELD

Debt will always be challenging for early-stage companies to secure, and during my investment sourcing I came across numerous business plans that had economics based on debt-related costs of capital. While there are some changes occurring with online lenders reducing underwriting costs and supplying loans to small businesses, the interest rates or embedded costs are extremely high and such loans are only taking place in developed markets. Investors need to be aware of business plans that assume unlikely forms of financing.

For developing markets and social entrepreneurs I've come across unrealistic expectations in terms of debt. One small scale solar lantern company operating mainly in Africa told me that they were not considering equity investments and offered an investment into a debt vehicle. They suggested that they would securitize the payment streams coming off of their lighting products. In theory the idea is not crazy, since as a securitization professional I have encountered entities securitizing virtually any consistent stream of payments. However, given their size, stage, countries of operation, limited time of operation, and lack of any real collateral, the prospect of a securitization was far beyond a reality. Regardless, the company's fund-raising strategy was based on obtaining debt, which wasted valuable time to raise required equity and invest in scaling the company.

Receivables Financing / Factoring

Receivables financing or *factoring* is a specialized form of lending that has seen some traction with impact investing. In this type of financing the receivables that a company generates from selling its product are sold to an investor at a discount. The company continues to service the receivables, but directs the funds to the investor. There are unique risks related to this:

- *Default risk*: A typical debt investor can claim against the company for failure to pay interest and debt. Under a receivables purchase or factoring agreement, an investor normally does not have recourse to the company. Therefore, he or she relies on his or her assessment of the credit risk of the main parties paying the receivables. If those companies default on their receivables, more than expected, then the investor will lose his or her return and possibly his or her principal invested.

- *Commingling risk*: When funds are transmitted from the entities owing the receivables, they are usually paid to the company that originated the receivables. Effectively, the company acts as a servicer. Under this agreement, there could be a concern that the funds are commingled with other funds of the company and if the company is encountering liquidity issues it could use the funds owed to the investor. This would defy the purpose of specific receivables financing and is usually mitigated through trustees and lock-box arrangements.

- *Servicer default risk*: An advantage of receivables financing is that the default risk is borne by the entities owing the receivable and not the company. However, the company often acts as the servicer, collecting the receivables. If the company goes out of business, then the investor would either have to service the debts himself or herself or hire another specialized receivables servicer. This risk can be mitigated by having a backup servicer on standby.

One of the distinct advantages to receivables financing or factoring is the short-term nature of the exposure. If the political or economic environment is changing a receivables financing can quickly be wound down in a matter of months, as compared to standard debt, which can be outstanding for long periods of time.

Credit Guarantees

Another form of impact investing that is employed by larger entities such as the International Finance Corporation or even the social impact arm of large banks, are *credit guarantees*. A credit guarantee works by a local bank providing financing to an entity and the guarantor ensuring the timely payment of debt service. If the company fails to pay the local bank the guarantor pays the local bank the owed funds. Usually, the guarantor requires a fee in order to offer the guarantee.

This type of financing helps local projects get debt funding, since local banks can be very prohibitive in lending to small, unknown companies.

It also tends to get used by project financings where there is solid collateral behind the loans, such as housing, port, airport, bridge, or toll-road projects.

NOTES FROM THE FIELD

Credit guarantees are valuable forms of financing that were used in a South Asian housing project I was involved in. The project was a mixed low- to middle-income development being completed by a local developer. In order to finance parts of the phases, debt financing in local currency was required. Given the volatile currency and political risk of the country where the project was taking place, it was unlikely to find foreign debt. Local banks were hesitant to provide financing; however, a large investment bank that has a social finance group was interested in providing a credit guarantee. For a below-market fee, the social finance group would guarantee the debt payments to the local bank. The local bank easily recognized the name of the entity providing the guarantee and agreed to lend money at a standard rate with the guarantee in place. Overall, the financing cost with the local funds and the guarantee cost was far under the cost of raising more equity.

Grants

Grant funding social entrepreneurships can be viewed as a form of impact investing, but one with no cost of capital and no return expectation. *Grants* are effectively donations of money to a company that do not have to be repaid. They can be general grants, available for use however the company sees fit, or restricted grants that must be utilized for a specific purpose. Grant funding may also require additional reporting requirements from the grantee to the grantor.

Grantors can establish tranched disbursements that are released only if and when evidence of fulfillment of social targets is received and validated by the donor. A strong example of this performance-based funding is the Global Fund to Fight AIDS, Tuberculosis and Malaria. Through competitive calls for proposals, the Global Fund finances interventions to fight these diseases. A performance framework is established with the grantee in which clearly defined, time-bound annual indicators are established. Progress in achieving these targets is examined by auditing companies in the recipient country and information is then crossed with the grant recipient's own performance accounts. If the Global Fund Secretariat is comfortable with the grant's performance, it authorizes further disbursements.

Grants can also come from a number of other sources, ranging from governments to private corporations. For instance, in India, the Ministry of New and Renewable Energy (MNRE) has offered grants for products and services that provide clean, efficient energy. Large corporations often give grants for public relations purposes or to stay involved in developments in their sectors. As a related example in energy, large oil companies provide funding for solar or renewable energy businesses.

There are two main challenges with grant funding for investors: business sustainability and revenue inflation. The first of the two, business sustainability, is derived from the fact that grant funding is not a permanent source of capital. The decision process behind grant funding is not based on market dynamics such as supply and demand. Government election cycles can rapidly change the funding that supports programs and corporate strategies can shift depending on urgency. Grant funding can stop abruptly. Therefore, while grant funding can provide catalytic capital to nurture the growth of an industry, analyses need to be completed on the viability of the business without the grant funding.

Additionally, during negotiations over valuation, grant funding should be removed as a source of income. Particularly if a relative valuation approach is being used, it would be fallacious to include grant funding in the base figure that gets applied to a multiple. The multiple is used to grow the base figure into a perpetuity state. Assuming that a company will receive grant funding in perpetuity is an extremely aggressive assumption.

The one deviation from this line of thought is when grant funding affects the balance sheet. Meaning, if the grant funding is to be used to create a specific, tangible asset, should it count as value? Take, for instance, a technology company providing a grant of funds for a new SMS-based data system that tracks user data for a company. The answer as to whether this should be valued depends on if there are restrictions for equity holders. If the grant-funded asset is restricted in any way—say, in our example, if the company is sold or liquidated and the SMS-based system must be returned—the value is unchanged. However, if the asset is unrestricted, then it should be counted toward value.

Indirect effects should also be understood. In the example above, an SMS-based data system may provide valuable user data that can be monetized. If the company was monetizing this data, it was counted as revenue, and now the grantor is taking back the system due to a sale of the company, the stream of income could be impaired. Such impairment should be taken into account during the valuation.

NOTES FROM THE FIELD

A small clash erupted during a secondary round of investment for a company. On one end was the representative from a large energy company who provided grant funding to the invested company. He was adamant that the grant funding his company was providing to the company should be included in the valuation as corporate value. On the other end was myself, performing a valuation for the secondary round, who believed that the grant funding should not be included.

I argued that the grant funding was temporal, noncontracted, and could stop in any given year. His argument was that as a professional grant funder, he knew that businesses like the one we were discussing would always receive grant funding from his organization and that it was truly like a flow. Investors are free to choose how they value companies, but a noncontracted flow of funds that is entirely dependent on another entity's decision-making process does not contribute to long-term value.

IMPACT INVESTING CHALLENGES

Many differences between traditional and impact investing have been cited throughout the book. A number of those differences are not problematic, but require specialized thought and analysis. A few of them, though, have the potential to develop into problems, particularly the possibility of *valuation bubbles*, *scalability*, and *suitability*.

How Valuation Bubbles Can Be Created

As we can see from the various investing alternatives, impact investing has the ability to mobilize funds from various sources, some very nontraditional compared to standard investing, and place them in mostly traditional methods such as equity and debt. At the same time, one of impact investing's most unique qualities is also its most pressing challenge. A disconnect has emerged between multiple investors with varying capital costs, channeling funds in traditional methods to companies, which establishes a false sense of sustainability and value.

Impact investors vary widely from purely philanthropic organizations deploying money with no expectation of return to fully commercial funds seeking traditional equity-style returns. Investors not seeking to maximize financial return is not a new concept. Pseudo-governmental organizations such as the International Finance Corporation (IFC) have existed for decades and openly state that they, " ... will back projects for catalytic or impact reasons as long as the business model can at least cover our cost of capital. The expected return on these funds may make them less relevant for an Institutional investor."[5] This works for entities like the IFC, which have well-established, known missions and answer only to their constituent countries.

Modern impact investing has seen a swell of participants establishing investment vehicles that invest side by side with charities, governmental entities, and other "below market cost of capital" organizations. Such investment works if expectations are clear and interests properly aligned. Unfortunately, the root sources of funding often have expectations set by investment funds that overextend their return levels and timelines. Additionally, conflicts of interests easily occur between these incongruent investors.

An excellent example of this occurring is a real-world example of a social enterprise that has a range of investors, including a charity providing grants, pseudo-government equity investment, a charity equity investor, a private social investing group utilizing excess funds from its larger, traditional business, and a fully commercial private impact investor. At first glance, interests seem aligned since all participants want the company to succeed. However, each participant has a different level of success that is necessary. The charity providing grants wants to show that the grant money has a positive effect. The equity investors want the value of equity to increase, but the charity may only need to break even on the investment, the pseudo-government investor may want to earn a small return to cover costs, and the fully commercial investor will want a market-based equity style return, commensurate with the risk.

Further intensifying the issues is the fact that the company's product is currently only commercially viable due to local government subsidies. In this example, we now have a company that is well funded by multiple market participants with varying interests and ultimately selling a product that is subsidy-dependent. As scaling issues develop and future investment rounds are required, the company was still able to obtain a high valuation, as some investors with low capital costs wanted to be able to convey their support of the social mission.

---

[5]David Wilton, "A Frontier Markets Case Study: What Are the Risks in Frontier Markets Private Equity and How Do You Mitigate Them?" Presentation at Super Return Conference, June 25–28, 2012, Geneva, Switzerland.

The more interesting issue develops as to whether or not the fully commercial impact investor chose to invest at a high valuation. First, as we have seen from discussions on liquidation preferences and other investment structures, there are many punitive options that investors can deploy if one investor from an investor group chooses not to join in a follow-on investment. An investor who chooses to opt out has to be prepared to be heavily diluted and expect diminished returns. Second, the fully commercial impact investor has to consider what the alternative investment options are with the funds that they have available to deploy. Does he or she want to seek out an entirely different investment or pay a premium to stay with a company that he or she knows well? As we have seen, depending on social criteria, the potential world of impact investments can be limited. Placing the money with a company he or she knows well might be a better option, as seeking out a new company can have a long time frame.

Unfortunately, investment rounds such as this set precedents. If other comparable companies are able to ascertain the details of the investment,[6] they can use the transaction as a comparable point for negotiating their own valuation, even though the valuation of the social enterprise might be inflated and the real value much lower. Extending such an example to multiple companies, the possibility of valuation bubbles are created. The key is to identify and label investments that are not done based on market-based valuations as pseudo-charitable donations and ones that are truly based on market-based valuations as investments. Conveying these differences can help prevent industrywide valuation bubbles.

An Issue of Scale

In the previous example, while underlying motivations may have differed, all parties wanted to remain invested in the company because of the lack of alternative companies that offer the possibility of commercial success with high, positive social impact. The lack of quality investments that also fit into a social criteria mean investors are faced with one of three decisions: invest in companies that are not financially suitable, invest in companies that do not fit into the current social criteria, or do nothing and invest less.

The first option, to invest in companies that are not financially suitable, works if the investor's cost of capital is aligned with expectations. Effectively, this type of investment subsidizes the underperformance through a

---

[6] While most of these investments are private, the general terms of the investment are often released in press releases.

below-market cost of capital. Commercial impact investors do not have this option, since the underperformance would translate to lower returns.

The second option, to loosen social criteria, works conversely. Commercial impact investors may try this since they need to first source investments that are financially sound. Organizations with lower costs of capital are most likely operating off of funds that have been contributed either through charity or by governments for specific social returns. If those social returns are diminished, then the funding for investment could be reduced or revoked.

The last option is to ensure that the investable amount is proportionate to the potential investments that can be made. Unfortunately, if a fund draws down funding that they cannot place, the IRR clock begins to tick, and doing nothing is actually punitive to returns. The natural suggestion to this issue is to make sure impact investing funds are sized correctly or establish a criteria and investment thesis that allows for both impact and traditional investments. Flexibility to invest in traditional investments would allow the fund to scale properly, which is particularly important, since as we have seen in Chapter 7, small-sized funds struggle to afford resources to follow a proper investment process. Overall, scalability is challenging for purely commercial impact investors.

Suitability

A recent trend noticeable at impact investing conferences is discussions on how to open up investments to retail investors. Some industry participants want to go as far as offering impact investments as an option for an allocation of a person's retirement plan, such as a 401(k) in the United States. The major concern here, of course, is suitability.

The range of knowledge for a retail investor can vary widely. Some recognize large names and choose them because of the brand recognition, while others perform detailed financial analyses that mimic professionals. Many retail investors trust their savings and retirement to financial advisers who then allocate their money. For both retail investors and their financial advisers, a core challenge is understanding what underlies certain investments.

A large blue chip stock is very clear, as a lot of public information is usually available and numerous analyses are often available. However, as we can see from this book, assessing the value of private equity investments is difficult. Now layer in private equity investments in emerging markets. And finally, layer in private equity investments in emerging markets that have a social benefit. Understanding the risks in this type of investing can be very demanding for a retail investor, or even a financial adviser who is not used to these assets.

If this is the case, why are there private investors currently investing in impact investments or private equity in general? The answer is that most of those investors have significant wealth and can afford to allocate a portion of that wealth to this style of investment. Many retail investors have much lower levels of wealth and should be very careful on how they allocate their savings and retirement.

IMPACT INVESTING OUTLOOK

The challenges of impact investing are clear and have been discussed in great detail throughout this book. Along the way, we have offered solutions to these problems and methods of mitigating risk through a rigorous impact investment process. However, as the impact investing industry matures, the challenges and solutions evolve.

Geographic-related risks are among the first issues that emerge in many of the chapters. We have seen that most impact investments are done in emerging markets, many with volatile currencies, heightened sovereign risks, and difficulty sourcing the best entrepreneurs. While hedging and sourcing strategies can assist, the simpler answer is to have local-based investment funds making the investments in local currency. These funds are closer to the investments to source, they monitor and help build value, the professionals establishing and working in them will have more connections to influential figures in the country, and the direct currency risks can be avoided.

Foreign currency exchange risk is still a challenge since the local investment fund must get funding in some way and usually an international investor provides such capital. Additionally, local talent can be hard to find and the investment fund size can be limited, given the specificity of a social impact mandate. We have seen how resource and allocation issues can be a significant problem in Chapter 7. However, an interesting alternative that helps alleviate these risks are local funds that make both non–impact- and impact-related investments. A large fund that has a majority of its investments in non–impact-related investments, but also has targeted a percentage of impact-related investments is much better positioned to handle problems. Resources are shared among the investment managers, allowing for economies of scale. Investors can assess and negotiate the percentage of impact versus traditional investments they would like exposure to. While the fund may not have the allure of a pure impact investing entity, its chances of providing repeatable return and social benefit can be higher.

The other noticeable issue has been liquidity problems with equity investments. Many equity investors struggle to exit their investments. Some are turning to debt as the alternative, with mission-based debt funds becoming increasingly popular. These have similar challenges as the equity investing funds and are probably done better locally as well. The challenge here, though, is whether the debt investors are fully commercial and seeking to maintain proper risk-based debt pricing or are from entities that can lend at below market rates of debt.

There does seem to be a strong argument for local debt funds in many emerging market countries, given the existing banking systems and the lack of reasonably priced debt. Many local banks in emerging markets have very onerous lending terms. Funds can undercut these rates and still make healthy returns if a proper investment process is followed. Unique structures such as warrants or cash flow royalties can be layered into the investments to boost the returns so they are commensurate with risk.

Impact investing is still in a nascent phase and going through its growing pains. Entities on every level, from individuals to foundations to fully commercial investors, will experience both benefits and detriments to making impact investments. Overall, though, when equipped with the right knowledge and skill, the investments will be done properly and professionally, and the social and financial returns will make it all worthwhile.

About the Companion Website

Readers will find professional-level investment material on this book's website: www.wiley.com/go/impactinvestment (password: allman15).

They are organized by chapter, as described below:

CHAPTER 2

Sourcing and Screening Folder

Country Ranking.xlsm: A spreadsheet designed to rank countries for potential investment sourcing, based on user-defined attributes and data sets. A default data set customized toward impact investing has been uploaded and analyzed for examples in the text.

FX_IRR.xlsx: To demonstrate the effects of direct and indirect foreign exchange risk, a spreadsheet has been provided that shows the calculations.

Corporate Teasers Folder

MtotoClinics.pdf, PagaPago.pdf, Solero.pdf: Toward the end of Chapter 2, we take a look at three hypothetical, potential companies for investment. The corporate teasers are provided.

CHAPTER 3

Solero_Distributor_Log.xlsm: Distributor-level information is provided for the Solero analysis.

Solero_Distributor_Log_Analysis.xlsm: A complete analysis of the Solero distributor level information.

Solero_FS_2012.xlsx, Solero_FS_2013.xlsx, Solero_FS_2014.xlsx: To assist with the Solero analysis, prior years' financial statements are provided.

Solero_Tech_Specs.pdf: Additional detail on Solero's products.

Solero_Model.xlsm: Making an investment decision, impact or traditional, requires an in-depth understanding of how a company's operations and finances work and interact together. Building a comprehensive model can be a daunting task for some investors, depending on their career backgrounds. The corporate model provided in this book is highly developed and delves into the detail expected of a professional investor. It is used frequently through Chapters 3, 4, and 5, and it is strongly encouraged to have it downloaded and open for reference while going through those chapters.

Readers should not be concerned by the corporate model's level of complexity, as there is no requirement to build the model from scratch. The purpose of the model is for readers to understand how a company works numerically, be able to understand how valuations are done, and see the effects on value given changes to assumptions. For readers interested in learning more on corporate modeling and the mechanics behind designing and building one, *Corporate Valuation Modeling: A Step-by-Step Guide*, by this book's primary author is an excellent resource.

Solero_Impact_Map.xlsx: Part of the desktop due diligence is the start of the social impact analysis. This is done by building an impact map, which is saved here.

Solero GIIRS B Corp Impact Assessment.

CHAPTER 4

ConvertibleBond.xlsx: To assist with explaining convertible debt structures, an example of both a simple convertible bond and convertible debt investment are provided.

LiqPrefs.xlsx: Liquidation preferences are very important to understand when crafting investment structures. Variations on liquidation preferences are demonstrated in this file.

CHAPTER 5

AntiDilution.xlsx: While Chapter 5 heavily focuses on legal concepts, understanding anti-dilution provisions requires detailed calculations.

CHAPTER 6

Acquisition_Example.xlsm: As investments move toward exit, one possible option is an acquisition. This sheet shows how to calculate synergy value.

Solero_Qtly_Rpt_Framework.xlsx: Monitoring an impact investment requires a thorough reporting framework. This is completed for the example company, Solero.

StockSwap_Example.xlsm: Acquisition or corporate sales can be done by a mixture of cash and stock. A calculated example of a stock swap is provided.

CHAPTER 7

PE_Fund_Model.xlsm: Investment fund economics are difficult to fully grasp without examples. The Investment Fund Model takes a detailed look at investing in multiple corporate investments within an investment fund structure. Aspects of investment funds such as committed capital, management fees, resource allocation, investment placement, and exit timing are just some of the core concepts that can be analyzed. This model is used frequently in Chapter 7.

About the Authors

Keith Allman is a Director in Deutsche Bank's Structured Credit group, working on esoteric asset-backed securities. Previously, he was a Senior Investment Manager with Bamboo Finance, a commercial impact investment firm managing a unique portfolio of direct venture and private equity investments around the world. He was responsible for generating new deal flow and providing board representation on the following portfolio companies: VidaGas, Immersion, Greenlight Planet, and Vienova.

He currently engages in impact-related work as a Director on the board for Relief International, where he started out volunteering in the Middle East. Earlier, he was a Director at Pearl Street Capital Group, where he focused on private equity fund of funds and venture debt funds. He also founded Enstruct, which services clients worldwide in capital markets and equity valuation, distressed valuation, and quantitative-based training.

His analytical expertise originated at Citigroup, where he modeled structured products for its conduits and eventually emerging-market transactions for its Principal Finance group. He has published four books on quantitative finance–related topics, including: *Modeling Structured Finance Cash Flows, Reverse Engineering Deals on Wall Street, Corporate Valuation Modeling,* and *Financial Simulation Modeling.* He holds bachelor degrees from UCLA and a master's degree from Columbia University.

Ximena Escobar de Nogales is the Head of Social Performance and Impact Management at Bamboo Finance, a private equity firm investing in business models that benefit low-income communities. She is responsible for safeguarding the funds' impact and ESG (environmental, social, and governance) criteria; screening pipeline companies against the criteria; defining impact frameworks with investees; collecting data; and reporting progress to investors and the public.

Ximena actively participates in industry initiatives such as the microfinance Social Performance Task Force, the Global Impact Investing Rating System, and the Principles for Responsible Investment. She is a certified SA8000 auditor (social accountability) and trained in GRI and SROI (Global Reporting Initiative, and Social Return on Investment, respectively). Prior to joining Bamboo Finance, she worked at The Global Fund to Fight AIDS, Tuberculosis and Malaria.

Ximena has also advised several large firms in corporate social responsibility and sustainability issues. She is a member of the Social Performance Committee of Apoyo Integral (El Salvador) and a member of the executive committee of the Swiss Capacity Building Facility. She holds an MBA from the University of Geneva, an MA in International Relations from the Graduate Institute of International and Development Studies (Geneva), and an MA in Economics from the Universidad de los Andes (Bogotá, Colombia).

Accounting differences, 111
Accounts payable, 86, 87, 151
Accounts receivable, 85, 86, 87, 88, 151, 221
Acquisitions, 230–233
Active distributors, 69–70, 214
Active investors, 207
Active subscribers, 213
Activities, 28, 121
Acumen Fund, 5
Alignment of interest, 130
Alpha, 253
Amendment, of term sheet, 201–202
Analysis. *See* Investment analysis
Analytics sheet, 241
Andhra Pradesh microfinance crisis, 141
Annual impact assessment, 125
Annual Operating Plan, 122
Anti-dilution rights, 36–37, 170, 183–189
    broad-based weighted average, 184, 185–186
    down round, 185–188
    dynamics of, 188–189
    narrow-based weighted average, 184, 186–187
    no anti-dilution rights, 187–188
    ratchet-based, 184, 187
    up round, 184–185
Approval rights, 176
Arbitration, 202
Asset-light development, 52, 53, 56
Asset performance, 244
Attribution, 124–125
Attrition assumptions, 78–79
Auditors, 174, 175

Balance sheet, 75, 83–85, 89–91
    organization and functionality of, 93–95
Bamboo Finance, 5, 26
Base case, 117–118, 128
Basis risk, 20

Bed occupancy rate, in healthcare sector, 213
Benchmarking, 252–254
Beta, 101, 102–103
Big Society Capital, 122
B Impact Assessment (BIA), 125–127
Biogas energy case study, 226–228
Board of directors:
    composition and governance of, 180–182, 205
    meetings of, 131–132
    protective clauses for, 175–177
    rights, 172
    seat on, 36
    size of, 174, 175
Bottom-up analysis, 64–72, 96
Bribery, 204
Broad-based weighted average anti-dilution rights, 184, 185–186
Business cycle, 19–21
Business plans, 177, 178
Business strategy, 31, 130
Buy-back clause, 194–196

Cafés case study, 223–225
Capital:
    allocation, 256
    cost of, 99–101
    expenditures, 83–85, 94, 97, 178
    intensity, 32
    investments, 177
    structure, 106–107, 109
    weighted average cost of, 105
    working, 85–89, 94, 97
Capital advisors, 25
Capital asset pricing model (CAPM), 100–101, 104
Capital gains tax, 107
Carrier interest, 238, 250
Carry, 236–237
Cash, 85, 94

Cash conversion cycle, 87–89, 150–151, 211
Cash flow:
  discounting process, 105–107
  negative, 107
  private equity funds and, 241
  projections, 75
Cash flow from financing (CFF), 95
Cash flow from investment (CFI), 95
Cash flow from operations (CFO), 95
Cash flow statement, 95
Causality, 124
CDC Group, 5
CFF. *See* Cash flow from financing (CFF)
CFI. *See* Cash flow from investment (CFI)
CFO. *See* Cash flow from operations (CFO)
Charitable organizations, 5
Chief investment officer (CIO), 237
Class A preference shares, 91
Class B preference shares, 91
"Clean" equity, 179
Client protection, 143–144
Collateralized debt, 257–258
Colombia, 39–40, 42
Commercial impact investing, 256
Commingling risk, 260
Common equity, 91
Company:
  bylaws, 173
  inputs, 240
  sale of, 173, 174
  size, 103
  stage, 32
Company-controlled distributors, 49
Company-controlled value chain, 49
Company founders, 34–35, 130, 183
Comparable company analysis, 95, 108–110
Competitive advantage, 31, 33, 41, 48–50, 139
Competitive risks, 57
Conditions precedent and subsequent, 178–180
Conferences, 25
Confidentiality, 199–200, 229
Confidentiality agreements, 63
Contingency plans, 133–134, 135, 137, 138, 140
Contract enforcement, 14
Control premium, 104
Control sheet, 239–240

Conversion ratio, 162, 214
Convertible bonds, 162
Convertible debt structures, 161–165, 170
Corporate costs, 82
Corporate governance, 131–132
Corporate management risks, 150–151
Corporate operations, 140–141
Corporate structure, 169
Cost inflation, 75–76, 81–82
Cost of capital, 99–101
Cost of debt, 100, 104–105
Cost of equity, 99, 100, 103–104, 255
Cost of goods sold (COGs), 80, 87, 94
Cost of subscriber acquisition, 213
Costs, 66–67
  fixed, 81, 82
  increased, 147–148
  operating, 81–83
  variable, 81–82
Counterfactual, 125
Country economic analysis, 19–24
Country risk, 19, 47–48, 54–55, 103
Covenants, 257
Credit guarantees, 260–261
Currency exchange risk, 21–24, 47–48, 54–55, 59, 152, 158, 267
Current assets, 85
Current ratio, 211
Customer protection, 143–144
Customers, 143–145
Customer's needs, 134

Damodaran, Aswath, 103
Data aggregation, 16
Data sets, for geographic analysis, 13–15
Data weighting, 16
Days inventory outstanding (DIO), 87, 88, 89
Days payable outstanding (DPO), 87, 88, 89
Days sales outstanding (DSO), 87–88, 89
DBL Investors, 5
Deal breakers, 41
Debt, 4, 89–91, 94, 173, 175, 256–259, 267–268
  availability, 214
  convertible debt structures, 161–165
  cost of, 100, 104–105
Debt service coverage ratios (DSCRs), 256
Default risk, 260

Deployment methods, 31
Depreciation, 83–85, 94
Desktop due diligence, 64–65, 119, 128
Developed markets, 3, 18, 19, 80, 81
Dilution, 182, 183–189
Directors' and officers' liability insurance
    (D&O insurance), 180
Discounted cash flow (DCF) valuation, 73,
    95–98
Discounting process, 105–107
Disruptions, 133, 135, 136–137, 138, 140
Distribution, 137–138, 214–215
Distribution methods, 49–50
Distribution system risks, 148–150
Distributor log, 66, 68–72
Distributor margin, 80
Distributors:
  active, 69–70, 214
  attrition, 78–79, 149
  churn, 215
  efficiency of, 78, 214–215
  hiring, 149
  inactive, 69
  margin, 215
  new, 77–78
  productivity, 149–150, 158
  revenue from, 80
Dist Sys sheet, 77–78
Dividends, 92, 173–174, 175
Documentation, 8
  incorporation, 173, 174
  shareholders' agreement, 205–206
  subscription agreement, 203–205
  term sheet, 8, 167–203
  verifying, 229
Doing Business project, 13
Down round, 185–188
Downside case, 157–161
Drag-along rights, 36, 131, 192–193
Due diligence, 7, 29, 36, 43, 129–153
  board of directors and, 131–132
  corporate governance and, 131–132
  desktop, 64–65, 119–128
  existing investor meetings, 131
  by independent consultants, 146
  management meetings and, 129, 130
  operational and business, 129–130
  operational impact and, 125
  scenario stress levels and, 158
  secondary share sales and, 229
  stakeholder analysis, 142–145

  utilizing information collected during,
    146–153
  value chain and, 132–141

East Asia, natural gas in, 219–222
East London Bond, 15
EBIT (earnings before interest and taxes),
    96
EBITDA (earnings before interest, taxes,
    depreciation, and amortization), 44,
    52, 56, 82–83, 84, 85, 111–114,
    115–118, 211, 214
EBT (earnings before taxes), 90
Economic analysis, country, 19–24
Electricity, 45–47
Emerging markets, 3
Employees, 145
Employee stock option program (ESOP),
    169–170, 171, 177
Employment churn, 56
Employment generation, 121
Encumbrances, 173
End users, 143–145
Energy sector, 212–213, 226–228
Enhancer companies, 33–34
Enterprise resource planning (ERP), 139
Enterprise value (EV)/EBITDA, 111, 114,
    115
Enterprise value (EV)/Last twelve month's
    (LTM) revenue, 111
Enterprise Works/VITA, 5
Environmental and social (E&S) practices,
    135–136
Environmental audits, 136
Environmental goals, 120
Equity, 94
  "clean," 179
  common, 91
  cost of, 99, 100, 103–104, 255
Equity percentage, 116
Equity value, 114, 116
ESG (environmental, social and
    governance), 29
Evidence-based investments, 4
Exclusivity, 200–201
Exiting investments, 8, 61, 228–234
  acquisitions and, 230–233
  IPOs and, 233–234
  liquidating structures and, 234
  private equity funds and, 244–245
  secondary share sales, 228–229

Exit multiples, 98
Exit option, 196–197
Expenses:
  operational, of private equity funds, 247
  shipping, 79, 148
  tax, 92
  on term sheet, 201

Factoring, 259–260
Fees, 62, 213, 236, 243
Financial information, 56, 64–65
Financial metrics, 210–212
Financial returns, 12
Financials, 35
Financial statements, 208
  balance sheet, 75, 83–85, 89–91,
    93–95
  cash flow statement, 95
  of early-stag social enterprises, 94
  historical, 94
  income statement, 75–81, 84, 90–95
Financing needs, 36
Fixed-asset turnover ratio, 212
Fixed costs, 81, 82
Fixed interest rates, 20
Floating interest rates, 20
Foreign exchange (forex) risk, 21–24
Foreign exchange curve, 76–77
Foreign exchange devaluation, 158
Foreign exchange risk, 47–48, 54–55, 59,
    152, 158, 267
Foreign ownership, 37
Forward multiples, 111
Founders, 34–35, 130, 183
Free cash flow, 96–98, 211–212
Free cash flow to equity (FCFE), 96, 97–98,
    106, 107–108
Free cash flow to the firm (FCFF), 96,
    97–98, 99, 106, 107–108, 117
Fund manager's compensation, 249–251
Future equity value, 116
Future margin stress, 44

GAAP, 208
General partner, in private equity fund, 236
Geographic analysis, 13–19
  controlling the analysis, 16–17
  data aggregation and weighting, 16
  data sets, 13–15
  results, 17–19

Geographic expansion, 77
Geographic-related risks, 267
Global Fund to Fight HIV, Malaria and
    Tuberculosis, 261–262
Global Impact Investing Network (GIIN),
    3, 26
Global Impact Investing Rating System
    (GIIRS), 124–126, 250, 251, 253
Globals, 74–75
Governance, 29, 131–132
Governing law, 202
Government-funded investors, 5
Grants, 261–263
GrayGhost Ventures, 5
Gross margin, 80, 210
Gross PP&E (property, plant, and
    equipment), 84
Growth rate, 109
  long-term, 99, 117
Gyapa project, 97

Healthcare, 37, 52–57, 213–214
Historical financial statements, 94
"Home run" conundrum, 154
Household solar energy, 37, 45–52
Housing sector, 214
Human Development Index (HDI),
    14, 15
Hurdle rate, 236–237

Ibbotson Associates, 103
IFRS, 208
Illiquidity discount, 107, 152–153
Impact, 123–124
Impactbase, 26
Impact Business Model (IBM)
    Rating, 127
Impact investing:
  alternatives to, 256–263
  as asset class, 255
  challenges, 255–256, 263–267
  commercial, 256
  compensation structures, 249–251
  conferences, 25
  definition of, 3–4
  evolution of, 9
  finding balance in, 2
  growth of, 1
  introduction to, 1–10
  outlook for, 267–268

Impact investing funds, 235–254
  benchmarking, 252–254
  vs. traditional funds, 247–251
Impact investors, 4–5
Impact map, 27–30, 119–125, 128
Impact Operations Rating, 127
Impact Reporting and Investment Standards
    (IRIS) indicators, 119, 216
Impact reporting framework, 215–218
Inactive distributors, 69
Income statement, 75–81, 84, 90–91
  finalizing, 92–93
  organization and functionality of, 93–95
Incorporation documents, 173, 174
Indemnification, 205
Independent consultants, 146
India, 41, 45, 47–48, 262
Indonesia, biogas energy in, 226–228
Industry, 109
Inflation, 75–76, 81–82
Information availability, 175
Information exchange, 61–65
  desktop due diligence, 64–65
  nondisclosure agreements and, 63
Information rights, 197–198
Initial public offering (IPO), 170, 196–197,
    222, 233–234, 236
Innovative companies, 33
Inputs, 28, 122
Inputs sheet, 72–76, 84
Insolvency, 14–15
Inspection rights, 198–199
Intangibles, 85
Intellectual property, 177, 258
Interest, 94
Interest and debt service coverage ratio, 212
Interest coverage ratios (ICRs), 256
Interest rates, 214, 258
  on convertible bonds, 162
  fixed, 20
  floating, 20
  risk-free, 100, 101
Internal rate of return (IRR), 116–117,
    160–161, 237, 242–243
International Finance Corporation (IFC), 5,
    264
Inventory, 85–86, 87
Inventory turnover, 88–89
Investment
  alternatives, 256–263
  capital, 177

evidence-based, 4
exiting, 8, 61, 228–234
moving forward with, 57–59
stage and size of, 44
Investment analysis, 7, 61–127
  balance sheet and, 75, 83–85, 89–91,
    93–95
  bottom-up analysis, 64–72, 96
  capital expenditures and depreciation, 84
  cash flow statement and, 95
  comparable company analysis, 108–110
  desktop due diligence, 64–65, 117–126
  drag-along rights and, 192–193
  exit options and, 196–197
  information exchange and, 61–65
  long-term funding and, 89–91
  pricing analysis, 66–67
  projection model, 72–95
  top-down analysis, 64–65
  using income statement, 75–81, 92–95
  volume analysis, 67–72
  working capital and, 85–89
Investment cost, 116
Investment process, 5–8
  agreeing on terms, 165
  analysis and valuation, 7, 61–127
  building value to exit, 8
  continuing, 128
  due diligence, 7, 129–153
  end of, 234
  exiting investment, 8, 61, 228–234
  finalization, 206
  investment structuring, 7–8, 161–165
  moving forward in, 57–59
  sourcing and screening, 6–7, 11–59
  term sheet and documentation, 8,
    167–206
Investment structuring, 7–8, 161–165
Investors:
  active, 207
  anti-dilution rights, 183–189
  existing investor meetings, 131
  impact, 4–5
  information rights, 197–198
  inspection rights, 198–199
  minority, 171–172, 175–176, 177
  passive, 207
  protections for, 14
  redemption/buy back/put options,
    194–196
  right of first offer, 190–191

Investors: (*Continued*)
  rights of first refusal, 190–191
  tag-along rights, 191–192
  understanding other, 36
  voting rights, 197

J curve, 241–242

Kenya, 54–55
Key man risk, 133, 134

Labor audits, 136
Last twelve month's (LTM) revenue,
  111–113
Lead reporter, 210
Legal documents. *See* Documentation
Legality risk, 37
Legally binding clauses, 202–203
Length of stay, 213
Leverage changes, 111
Liabilities, 86
Limited partners, in private equity fund,
  236, 238
Liquidating structures, 234
Liquidation preferences, 36–37, 153–157,
  161, 175, 193–194
Liquidity crisis, 62
Liquidity risk, 152–153, 267–268
Literacy, 39, 45
Local capital asset pricing model (LCAPM),
  101
Long-term funding, 89–91
Long-term liability, 91
Long-term weighted average cost of capital
  (long-term WACC), 99, 116
LT Capital sheet, 89–91

Maintenance capital expenditures, 84–85
Management fees, 62, 236, 243
Management meetings, 129, 130
Manufacturing, 136–137, 139
Margin risk, 52
Margins, 109
Market-based risks, 151–153
Market capitalization, 109
Market rate, 162
Market risk premium, 101–102
Market share expansion risk, 51
Market size, 31–32
Maternal mortality, 15

Mergers, 173
Metrics, 208–215
  financial, 210–212
  operational, 212–215
  social mission, 215–218
Microfinance, 4, 9
Microfinance institutions (MFIs), 4, 9, 141
Micro solar energy, 45–52
Minority rights, 171–172, 175–176, 177
Mission locks, 118–119
Mission statement, 27, 118–119
Ministry of New and Renewable Energy
  (MNRE), 262
Mobile money, 37, 38–45, 213
Model clients, 144
Monetization, 32–33
Money multiple, 116–118
Monitoring and evaluation (M&E)
  capacity, 29, 30
Mozambique, 35
M-PESA, 39
Multiples, valuation, 111–117

Narrow-based weighted average
  anti-dilution rights, 184, 186–187
Nationally recognized statistical rating
  organizations (NRSROs), 100
Natural gas case study, 219–222
NDAs. *See* Nondisclosure agreements
Negative cash flows, 107
Net loss carry forward, 92
Net PP&E (property, plant, and
  equipment), 84
Net profit margin, 211
Nigeria, 41
Non-cash deductions, 97
Nondisclosure agreements (NDAs), 63
Nonrecurring items, 111
Norfund, 5

Obsolescence, 34, 51–52
One-off expenses, 148
Operating data, 56, 64–65, 208
Operating expenditures (Opex), 81–83,
  211
Operating margins, 64
Operational expenses, of private equity
  funds, 247
Operational impact, 125, 126
Operational metrics, 212–215

Outcomes, 29, 122–123
Outcomes Matrix, 122
Output, 29, 123, 241
Output indicators, 215–216
Ownership structure, 169

Passive investors, 207
Passive sourcing, 12–13
Peer groups, 108–111
Perpetuity calculation, 98–99
Pico-solar energy, 45–52
Piggyback distribution, 50
Place of domicile, 169, 204
Portfolio companies, 241
Post-investment, 207–234
  case studies, 218–228
  challenges, 207–208, 218–228
  methods of exit, 228–234
  reporting and monitoring, 208–218
Poverty Action Lab, 125
Powers of attorney, 177, 178
Pre-due diligence phase, 61–65, 128
Preemptive rights, 182
Preference shares, 91, 206
Preferred shares, 170
Present value, 106
Price/cost per kWh, 212
Pricing, 81–82
Pricing analysis, 66–67
Private equity funds, 8, 235–254
  basic construct of, 236–238
  benchmarking, 252–254
  compensation structures, 249–251
  economics of, 238–243
  expected asset performance and, 244
  fund placement timing, 245
  impact investing vs. traditional, 247–251
  internal finance of, 238
  key considerations, 243–247
  model overview, 238–241
  operational expenses, 247
  reporting requirements, 238
  resource allocation, 246–247
  success measures, 241–243
  vs. venture capital, 235–236
Prod Curves sheet, 76, 77, 80
Prod Detail sheet, 78–80
Product economics, 75–76
Product failures, 133
Productivity, 149–150, 158

Product stockouts, 139
Profitability, 52
Projection model, 72–95
  balance sheet, 75, 83–85, 89–91, 93–95
  capital expenditures and depreciation, 84
  Dist Sys sheet, 77–78
  exit timing, 244–245
  Globals, 74–75
  income statement, 75–81, 92–95
  Inputs sheet, 72–76, 84
  long-term funding, 89–91
  operating expenditures, 81–83
  Prod Curves sheet, 76, 77
  Prod Detail sheet, 78–80
  Vectors sheet, 72–73, 77
Project/phase completion %, 214
Project ROI, 212–213
Proposed Security Type, 170
Protective clauses for shareholders,
  171–175
Put options, 8, 194–196

Qualified initial public offering (QIPO),
  171, 192, 196–197, 233

Randomized controlled trials (RCTs), 125
Ratchet-based anti-dilution rights, 184, 187
Receivables financing, 259–260
Redemption clause, 194–196
Regional costs, 81
Regional deployment, 31
Regulatory risk, 35, 42, 57
Relative valuation, 73, 108–111
Relief International, 5
Reporting, post-investment, 208–218
  establishing requirements for, 209–210
  example impact reporting framework,
    215–218
  formats, 208
  frequency, 209
  metrics, 208–215
Reporting rights, 197–198
Representations, 199, 204–205
Research and design process, 132–134
Reserved matters, 206
Resource allocation, private equity funds
  and, 246–247
Retained earnings, 91, 94
Return analysis, 113–114, 117–118
Return on investment (ROI), 212–213

Revenue, 87
Revenue/active subscribers, 213
Right of first offer (ROFO), 190–191, 229
Right of first refusal (ROFR), 190–191, 229
Risk:
  basis, 20
  commingling, 260
  competitive, 57
  corporate management, 150–151
  country, 19, 47–48, 54–55, 103
  default, 260
  distribution system, 148–150
  foreign exchange, 21–24, 47–48, 54–55,
    59, 152, 158, 267
  geographic-related, 267
  key man, 133, 134
  legality, 37
  liquidity, 152–153, 267–268
  margin, 52
  market-based, 151–153
  market risk premium, 101–102
  market share expansion, 51
  mitigation, 127, 267
  obsolescence, 34, 43–44, 51–52
  regulatory, 35, 42, 57
  servicer default, 260
  systematic, 101
  technology, 34, 43–44, 51
Risk-free rate of interest, 100, 101
ROFO. *See* Right of first offer (ROFO)
ROFR. *See* Right of first refusal (ROFR)
ROI. *See* Return on investment (ROI)
Roles, 130
Rural distributors, 50
Rwanda, 18

Sales growth, 210
Sales performance curve, 70, 76
Scalability, 31–32, 57, 265–266
Scenario selector system, 16–17
Scenario stress levels, 158
Screening investments, 6–7, 11–12
  applied to potential investments, 37–57
  business strategy and operations, 30–35
  current investment round, 36–37
  process for, 26–37
  with social impact map, 27–30
Screening questions, 26
Secondary share sales, 228–229
Sector, 109

Senior management, 130, 145, 177, 178,
  183
Servicer default risk, 260
Shareholder meetings, 206
Shareholders:
  protective clauses for, 171–175
  rights of, 171–175
  voting by, 197
Shareholder's agreement (SHA), 179,
  205–206
Shares:
  creation of new, 173, 174
  dilution of, 182, 183–189
  preference, 91, 206
  purchase, sale, and conversion rights, 182
  sale of existing, 173, 175
  secondary sales, 228–229
Share subscription agreement (SSA), 179,
  199
Shipping expenses, 79, 148
Short-term assets, 85
Singapore, 18
SMART (Specific, Measurable, Achievable,
  Realistic, and Time scaled) targets, 122
Social data:
  collection, 208
  reporting metrics, 208
Social enterprises, 3–4
Social goals, 28, 119–120
Social impact, 4
  of mobile money, 42–43
  sourcing for, 25–26
Social impact bonds, 251
Social impact mapping, 27–30, 119–127
  activities, 122
  impact, 123–124
  inputs, 120–121
  mission statement, 119–120
  outcomes, 122–123
  output, 122
  social/environmental goals, 119–120
  third-party impact evaluation tool,
    125–126
Social impact validation and analysis,
  142–145
Social mission, 12, 179–180, 207, 208
Social mission integrity, 134–138, 141
Social mission metrics, 215–218
Social return on investment (SROI),
  142–145
Solar energy, 37, 45–52

Solar product distribution, 49–50
Soros Economic Development Fund, 5
Sourcing investments, 6–7, 11–26
   applied to potential investments, 39–40,
      47–48, 54–55
   country economic analysis, 19–24
   geographic analysis, 13–19
   for impact, 25–26
   methods for, 25
   passive, 12–13
   strategy for, 12–13
South America, cafés in, 223–225
Special purpose vehicles (SPVs), 234
Staff incentive structures, 140–141
Stakeholder analysis, 142–145
Standardization, 54
Stock prices, 162
Stock swaps, 231–233
Strategy, 31, 130
Sub-industry, 109
Subscription agreement, 203–205
Suitability, 266–267
Suppliers, 134–136
Supply chain disruptions, 135
SWOT (strengths, weaknesses,
      opportunities, and threats) analysis,
      57–59
Systematic risk, 101

Tag-along rights, 131, 191–192
Taxable income, 92
Taxes, 37, 79, 92–93, 96, 107
Technical specification sheet, 66
Technology risk, 34, 43–44, 51
Terminal value, 98–99, 104
Terms, agreeing on, 165
Term sheet, 8, 167–203
   amendment of, 201–202
   anti-dilution rights, 183–189
   board composition and governance,
      180–182
   conditions precedent and subsequent,
      178–180
   confidentiality, 199–200
   definitions, 168–170
   drag-along rights, 192–193
   exclusivity, 200–201
   exit option, 196–197
   expenses, 201
   founder/management restrictions, 183
   governing law and arbitration, 202
   information rights, 197–198
   inspection rights, 198–199
   legally binding clauses, 202–203
   liquidation preferences, 193–194
   overview of, 168
   protective clauses for boards of directors,
      175–177
   protective clauses for shareholders,
      171–175
   purchase, sale, and conversion rights, 182
   redemption/buy back/put options,
      194–196
   representations and warranties, 199
   right of first refusal/right of first offer,
      190–191
   tag-along rights, 191–192
   transaction details, 170–171
   voting rights, 197
Theory of change, 27
Third-party distribution, 49
Third-party impact evaluation, 124–126,
      250–251
Tiered pricing systems, for healthcare, 53
Time to EBITDA positive, 214
Time value of money, 61, 99–100
Toniic, 26
Top-down analysis, 64–65
Total credit sales, 87
Transaction details, in term sheet,
      170–171
Transaction multiples, 112
Transparency, 62, 174, 175

United Nations Development Programme
      (UNDP), 15
Up round, 184–185

Valuation, 7, 61
   base case and, 157–161
   beta, 101, 102–103
   bubbles, 263–265
   company size and, 103
   comparable company methodology, 95,
      108–111
   control premium and, 104
   cost of capital and, 99–101
   cost of debt and, 100, 104–105
   country risk and, 103
   debt and, 89–91

Valuation, (*Continued*)
  discounted cash flow, 73, 95–98
  discounting process, 105–107
  FCFF vs. FCFE, 107–108
  internal rate of return, 116–117
  money multiple, 114–115
  multiples, 111–117
  relative, 73, 108–111
  terminal value, 98–99, 104
  triangulating a value, 115–117
  valuation caps, 161–165
  weighted average cost of capital and, 105
  working capital and, 85–89
Value-building phase, 8
Value chain, 33, 49, 50–51, 58, 132–141
Value creation, 33, 56
Variable costs, 81–82
Vectors sheet, 72–73, 77, 240
Venture capital, 235–236, 258
Venture debt, 258–259

Veto rights, 176
Viability, 133, 135–138, 140
Vietnam, 41
Volatility, 102
Volume analysis, 67–72
Voting rights, 197

Warranties, 199, 204–205
Warrants, 91
Warranty expense, 151
Warranty utilization, 52
Waterfall, 234
Weighted average cost of capital (WACC), 105
Weighted average life (WAL), 100
Working capital, 85–89, 94, 97
  timing and the cash conversion cycle, 87–89
World Bank, 13
World Bank Group, 5